PRAISE FOR *INSIDE OUT*, BY MARK TEWKSBURY

"To reach the pinnacle of Olympic Swimming takes incredible dedication, resilience and courage that few possess. To reach your true self takes these attributes and a great deal more courage so, therefore, even fewer arrive at this point in their lives. Mark Tewksbury is one of these courageous people who achieve so much and through pain, suffering, daring and pure fight, become who they truly are, inside and out."

Duncan Armstrong O.A.M., Australian Olympic Swimming Legend

"It took talent, honesty, courage and guts for Mark Tewksbury to take on the world and become an Olympic champion. It took the combination of the same qualities to write this book."

Richard W. Pound, International Olympic Committee, Chairman of the World Anti-Doping Agency

"A fascinating inside look at the life of one of Canada's most outstanding sports figures. What it was like to be teased in high school though he was already an outstanding athlete. What it was like to explode into Olympic stardom with a gold-medal upset in swimming, to come out as a gay man amid post-Olympic celebrity, to become an advocate for athletes in the cutthroat, behind-the-scenes politics of sports. Mark Tewksbury has given us the unusual in an Olympic sports memoir—richly textured and deeply moving."

Patricia Nell Warren, author of The Front Runner

"Mark's story is not just about being a gay man in the world of sport. It's a story about a human being that is true to himself no matter what! By sharing it he inspires all of us to do the same."

Johan Kenkhuis, Olympic swimming bronze (2000) and silver (2004) medallist, The Netherlands

"Mark's story is motivation for all who seek great achievement and will face obstacles along the path to that success. Straight talk indeed—and a fascinating peek inside the world of Olympic politics."

Neil G. Giuliano, President, Gay and Lesbian Alliance Against Defamation (GLAAD), and Mayor of Tempe, Arizona, USA, 1994–2004

"Mark Tewksbury traces his journey from shame and fear to pride and courage as a gay man. His story is especially inspiring because he is one of only a handful of world-class gay male athletes who have publicly embraced their gay identity. Along the way, Mark shares his perspectives on the developing international LGBT sports movement and a vision for how sport can change the world for all of us regardless of our sexuality, gender or athletic ability."

Pat Griffin, Author, Strong Women, Deep Closets: Lesbians and Homophobia in Sport *and Director of It Takes A Team! Education Campaign for LGBT Issues in Sport*

"Mark Tewksbury's story of hurt, outrage and frustration, as a man who happens to be gay, is also a story of strength, boldness and human rights. A must-read for parents, educators, athletes and anyone who cares deeply about creating a safe harbor for all kids."

Barbara Coloroso, Educator and Author, Just Because It's Not Wrong Doesn't Make It Right: From Toddlers to Teens, Teaching Kids to Think and Act Ethically

"Against the odds, he won a gold medal in Barcelona; he made a difference. As a commentator with CBC in Athens in 2004, he again made a difference. He was honest, outspoken and articulate—qualities that run through the pages of this book."

Brian Williams, Olympic Broadcaster

"Mark Tewksbury's charisma radiates throughout this poignant story of his life development into an Olympic hero. I found myself riveted with the human drama while gaining knowledge and understanding concerning the struggles and triumphs of the LGBT sports movement. A read that should not be missed."

Helen Carroll, Sports Project Coordinator, National Center For Lesbian Rights (USA)

"Tewksbury opens the *whole closet* for us to view his life of glamour, guts and despair. His story is as much a testimony to the strength of femininity as it is an indictment of the cult of masculinity."

Eric Anderson, Ph.D., Author of In the Game: Gay Athletes and the Cult of Masculinity *and* Trailblazing: The True Story of America's First Openly Gay High School Coach

"Mark takes the reader on an interesting journey of his life and provides insight into the highest echelons of elite sport from many unique perspectives."

Alex Baumann, Canadian Olympic swimming legend and Executive Director, Queensland Academy of Sport, Australia

"This book and the young life it chronicles will open doors to many. I recall the attitudes so pervasive in locker room culture when I participated in the swimming scene. For writing about his personal struggle, Tewksbury should add bravery to his already impressive list of attributes."

Jack Layton, Leader of the Federal New Democratic Party of Canada

"We knew Mark was a great swimmer, but who knew he could write so well! The courage he showed in his competition is mirrored in his book. A great story from a very brave man."

Vicki Gabereau, Award-winning Broadcaster

INSIDE OUT

INSIDE OUT

Straight Talk from a Gay Jock

BY

MARK TEWKSBURY

John Wiley & Sons Canada, Ltd.

Library and Archives Canada Cataloguing in Publication Data

Tewksbury, Mark, 1968-
    Inside out : straight talk from a gay jock / Mark Tewksbury.

Includes index.
ISBN-13 978-0-470-83735-1
ISBN-10 0-470-83735-7

    1. Tewksbury, Mark, 1968-. 2. Swimmers—Canada—Biography. 3. Gay athletes—Canada—Biography. 4. Motivation (Psychology). 5. Success. I. Title.

GV838.T48A3 2006   797.2'1092   C2006-901253-9

Production Credits:
Cover design: Ian Koo
Interior text design: Natalia Burobina
Printer: Transcontinental

John Wiley & Sons Canada, Ltd.
6045 Freemont Blvd.
Mississauga, Ontario
L5R 4J3

Printed in Canada

1 2 3 4 5 TRANS 10 09 08 07 06

CONTENTS

PREFACE

For years various people told me that I *should* write a book. "You have had such an interesting life," they would say. But having an interesting life and capturing that life on paper are two very different things. Every time I made an attempt to write, the project led nowhere. The problem was that I didn't really know where to start, and every endeavour to create ended with yet another blank page and more feelings of frustration. After endless tries I decided to simply abandon the idea.

I had written a book before, a motivational memoir after my Olympic win in Barcelona in 1992, and I knew how difficult the creative process could be. At that time I was a closeted gay athlete sharing his "story," but the story that I was sharing avoided any details about my personal life. It had to. For as long I could remember I had done everything in my power to keep the worlds of sport and gay apart. In fact, this denial of who I was had actually become the very story of my life. It was no wonder I didn't know where to begin.

In July of 2002 I went for dinner in Toronto with a colleague from my former days at *Canada AM*, celebrated author and parenting expert Barbara Coloroso. Barbara is an incredibly persuasive person who does not take no for an answer, and by the end of the evening she had convinced me that I *must* write a book, and that the time was now. Her lawyer was also a literary agent, and she convinced me to have lunch with him before I left Toronto to go back home to Montreal.

Later that week I took the elevator up one of the highest towers on Bay Street to meet with Aaron Milrad, an elegant, charming, distinguished gentleman who told me straight up at the beginning of our meeting that he didn't take any new clients. Then he hit me with another bombshell. "Every one thinks they have a book in them," he told me. "Other than the fact that it's your story, what makes it unique and interesting?" Gulp. Good question. I scrambled to think of something clever to answer his tough question, giving a long rambling response that, by the look on his face, I thought had convinced him not to spend one more minute with me. Instead he surprised me. "I'm not gay, but I am Jewish, so I can relate to what you are saying," he told me. "Let's see if we can sell this story." Maybe Barbara was right, I thought. Maybe it was time.

With my good friend Louise Lemelin, I prepared an outline, and over the next several months Aaron sent it to every major and minor publishing house he knew. Polite decline followed polite decline, until finally we all abandoned the project for the short term, essentially leaving me right where I had started, only this time with a slightly bruised ego.

Two years later the phone rang. It was Aaron. He had met a great couple who worked with authors and publishers to get their projects ready for production, and he had a feeling that we might work well together. I met with Ron and Adrianna Edwards shortly thereafter, and although I had the lowest of expectations before the meeting, I left it highly encouraged that this partnership might actually work. Intelligent, savvy, and supportive, I could sense that they got what the book was about. Within a month I had a new outline. Within three months I had a publisher. And six weeks after I sat down to start writing, I had a first draft. "That came so easily," everyone said. Yes, six weeks and *seven years* in the making, I thought to myself.

I am indebted to many people for making this book a reality. To the early support of Jennifer McGuire, Benjamin Kiss, Jacques Legris, and Henri Davies for believing I had another book in me even when none came. To my friend Alexander Chapman who reminded me to stick to my stories and I couldn't go wrong. To Bertrand Pappathomas, the first person to read this manuscript. As I finished each story, it was

Bertrand who encouraged me when I sometimes felt overwhelmed, and inspired me with his enthusiasm when I wondered if anyone would care. Thank you to Thomas K. Dolan and Debbie Muir for your authentic leadership. And to the amazing team at Wiley, led by Karen Milner, who made turning my ideas into a product more enjoyable than I had ever imagined possible.

This book is literally inside out—an insider's perspective on Olympic politics, media, fame, gay life, friendship, family, and leadership. "Straight talk from a gay jock" is, on one hand, a play on words. But talking straight was essential to me, as this is the first time I have ever told my whole story, not the abbreviated motivational memoir typical of many athletes, including myself the first time around. Inside are stories from my life, which in the telling includes stories about people who have helped shaped my life in one form or another. To the best of my ability I have reconstructed events from my past, catching the spirit of a conversation if not the exact wording. People's names, other than public officials or my family, have often been changed to protect their identities (as indicated by an *). I appreciate that just because I was ready to write about my life, it doesn't necessarily mean that everyone wants their lives to be written about. To the thousands of people who have made each part of my life so rich and colourful, I am deeply indebted to you. I hope you recognize yourselves in some of the stories within.

For years I lived with an intense feeling of difference, desperately wanting to be something other than what I was. It is a feeling I believe that is shared by millions of people around the world. As hard as that was, I am enormously grateful for the first-hand understanding of what it is like to live as a person of diversity. My own circumstances have allowed me to move ultimately to a place where I am not only open in my life, I am truly proud of who I am.

To this day there are still no 'out' gay male professional football, soccer, baseball, basketball, or hockey players competing openly in their sports. In the end that was what Aaron decided made my story somewhat unique. I have seen first-hand the climate of shame that comes from silence and secrets. As I have moved beyond this in my own life, I appreciate that the real shame is that this cycle continues. I hope that in another ten years, straight talk from a gay jock will just be a simple accepted reality of the world we live in. But until then, I hope this story does its own little part in changing that. Enjoy the read!

ACKNOWLEDGEMENTS

I was on a promotional tour in Vancouver following the 1992 Olympics when my path crossed with another celebrated athlete, rower Silken Laumann. Looking at me she could tell something wasn't right. I went with her and her partner at that time, Olympic champion John Wallace, for a drink. I couldn't stand the burden of carrying my secret anymore, so I finally shared my real story. They were both incredibly supportive. Silken would later write me a letter that I would keep for years.

At that time in my life, I did everything to cover up the fact that I was a gay athlete. CBC Radio's award-winning Inside Track did a story on gays in sport, and I participated, but on the condition that my voice be disguised beyond recognition. It worked, but I was still terrified that someone would figure out it was me. I have remained friends with the executive producer of that show to this day, so intense were her feelings of responsibility to keep my secret.

Sylvie Bernier, the Olympic champion diver, came to me in 1996 when I was no longer an athlete but still very much involved in amateur sport on the political side. She was open and frank, and wanted me to know that she was there if I needed to talk to someone. Marnie McBean, Olympic champion rower, was proudly in the audience at my stage show when I publicly came out.

Unfortunately, over the many, many years that I was involved in the world of sport, the people that I felt I could speak to about such a sensitive issue can be named on one hand. If homophobia is going to leave the world of sport, then a lead role needs to be taken by our coaches, teammates, officials, and administrators who can openly promote a positive space for all to participate. Issues of difference are not necessarily easy to deal with at first, but before something becomes a non-issue, it must first become an issue. And not necessarily for long.

This book is dedicated to those individuals and organizations brave enough to make this change; to speak about the unspoken; to take away the stigma of being gay in the world of sport.

CHAPTER ONE

CHILDHOOD SECRETS

GRANDMA'S CLOSET

It was the summer of 1975 and Grandma McDonald was preparing me for something. My usual two-and-a-half-hour trip south to Lethbridge, Alberta had taken on a special significance this year. For as long as I could remember I had boarded a Greyhound bus every summer to spend three to four weeks with both sets of my grandparents during my summer vacation.

It had started after my brother, Scott, had been born. My younger sister, Colleen, and I had both been adopted, so the birth of Scott was a pretty big deal in our family. To give my mom some time to recover and adjust, Colleen and I had been sent to stay with our grandparents for a short period.

Colleen hated being away, but I loved it. In fact, the only way I could be coaxed home to Calgary was with the promise that I could come back to visit any time I wanted. For the next twelve years I made good on that promise. But this particular year was different. Grandpa McDonald had died in the spring, and this summer I was determined to spend more time with Grandma McDonald to help ease her loneliness.

Grandma McDonald and I had always been close. I was her eleventh grandchild, but there was something about me that Grandma recognized as different, and she did everything possible to encourage that difference to flourish.

One of my earliest memories is of visiting her and Grandpa at their condominium, which had a pool, during the brief time they lived in Calgary. I had learned to swim in Dallas the previous year when my father had been transferred there with the oil company he was working for, and every time I saw Grandma she would encourage me to join her for a swim in the condo pool. We would spend about fifteen minutes swimming, and then spent just as much time prepping to go back to see the family. Grandma would wrap me in a towel that was so big it would cover me from just below the armpits all the way to the floor. She would then dry herself and wrap a towel around her head, like a turban, and would watch me watching her do this. "I think you need a head wrap too," she told me as I sat transfixed by her getup.

There was spunkiness to Grandma that I was completely drawn to. A woman who was fun everywhere but church, she wasn't afraid to push boundaries as long as she felt she was allowing her grandchildren to express themselves. It didn't matter that her husband as well as my father looked horrified when they saw Grandma and Mini-Grandma arrive looking like twins. We were both in our element and that was all she cared about. I publicly credit watching the 1976 Olympics as a major inspiration for me to eventually become an Olympic Champion, but if I am to be totally honest, being dressed from head to toe like Grandma was what sparked my love of swimming in the first place.

This particular summer visit with her was like a test for me. Since her husband's funeral, Grandma had obviously been contemplating her own mortality, and when I arrived at her apartment I learned that she had begun the process of placing small white stickers with names on them on the back of all of her possessions to be clear who got what when she died. My first exercise after I arrived was to pick out something that I would like to remember her by when that fateful day arrived. Although this was slightly morbid, I understood what Grandma was asking me to do.

My grandfather had been a successful businessman, owning a local car dealership that continually blared their last name and made both him and Grandma celebrities in their community. In their lifetimes they had acquired many beautiful things, most of which were now crammed into Grandma's swanky one-bedroom apartment. There were expensive antiques, including a stunning grandfather clock, and a massive wooden console with a television built in. In her bedroom there was a solid set of oak furniture that included a king-sized bed, a vanity, and chest of drawers complete with a solid sliver brush set that must have been worth a small fortune.

After much contemplation I narrowed down my finalists to two items. The television console was still unspoken for, and as a seven-year-old I thought this was pretty impressive. But there was one other item that really captured my imagination. It was a black-and-white picture taken of my mother and her sister as little girls that had been hand-tinted to give it color. My mom was about the same age that I was at that time, and I thought it would be great to have that in my house one day.

I finally decided to go for the picture. I knew that Grandma was expecting me to ask for the television, but I thought this picture was the one thing that was truly irreplaceable.

Grandma was surprised by my choice, but completely delighted. Going for something of sentimental value as opposed to material worth made a lasting impression on her, and from that moment on Grandma and I were closer than ever before, if that were possible. Whenever someone came to visit, the first thing she would tell them was that I had chosen the picture over anything else, allowing her to beam with pride at the sensitivity of her young grandson. To this day I still have that picture hanging in my office.

During my visits I would share her massive king-sized bed with her. She would crawl into one side, taking up the smallest amount of space imaginable. In the morning she would still be in the exact position she had started in the night before, a little lump in the sheets the only evidence she was still actually there. I would sleep on the side of the bed closest to the large mirrored doors of her closet.

One morning the mirrored closet door was open just a crack, and I awoke to a creepy, white, disembodied head staring out at me. I was startled and really freaked out. "Grandma, what is that head doing in your closet?" I asked. She smiled a big, reassuring, toothless smile at me. Then she got out of bed, popped in her false teeth, and opened the door to expose three heads with wigs that she once wore to make her more glamourous. "My beauty hair," she called them.

At one point I think my grandma had been quite a socialite, paying a lot of attention to her clothes and how she put herself together. But by my time, I knew her as more of a sensible pantsuit kind of gal. That morning, because I had opened the topic, she took me on a trip down memory lane. Grandma pulled out her wigs and put them on one at a time, and talked and laughed at how they made her look.

Since it was just the two of us, it didn't take long before she wanted to see what I looked like in her wigs. It didn't end there. Grandma had never had her ears pierced, and before you knew it we were clipping on earrings of all shapes and colors to go with the wigs. Then she pulled out some of her old dresses, with a bit of jewelry, blush, lipstick, and face powder as the finishing touches.

I will never forget sitting at her dining room table at 10:30 a.m. on a Tuesday morning in conservative Lethbridge eating breakfast in full-blown drag. I was a seven-year-old drag queen! We were laughing the entire time, playing like we were two ladies in a cafe in Paris, asking the other if they might be kind enough to pass the jam, pass this, pass that, and then cracking up as my bracelet fell off when I reached.

Always up for an adventure, Grandma decided after breakfast that she would pull a prank on one of her friends, Irene, who lived in the same apartment building. We went running down three flights of the emergency fire stairs to Irene's floor. Grandma made me stand in front of the door while she knocked and then ran around the corner so her friend wouldn't see her when she opened the door. The result was hysterical. Irene didn't recognize me at all, and was trying to figure out who I was after I called her by name and asked about her grandchildren. Grandma couldn't stand it anymore and came running around the corner with tears of laughter streaming down her face. Irene was let into the joke and we all went inside to have tea together. On one hand, it was a strange thing to do, but it was done with such a spirit of fun that it all seemed just like a game. Grandma had such a sense of pride, showing me off to her friends, that it was easy for me to just go with it.

My dressing up became a huge hit with the older ladies of Lethbridge. It became something of a ritual and a high point of my visit for Grandma and me. At least once every trip we would spend the afternoon dressing up. Then we would play cards and talk at her dining room table. Every summer before I arrived, Grandma would get on the phone and start calling her friends to organize the big tea party that we would host. I was the official server in all of my finest, roaming the room with twenty of these senior ladies, all of us dressed to the nines. It was a chance for them to revisit their past.

It was also a chance for me to explore my future—a part of me that only Grandma was willing to acknowledge. There was no way that she knew that I was gay. Her generation didn't think in those terms, but she did know that I was different from any of her other grandchildren, and this was her way of saying it was okay.

She also knew the limits of this fun. At the end of every summer trip we put all of the clothes back into a box that would then be put back into the closet, where they stayed until the following summer. Although she was willing to share this with her friends, it was our little secret. No one from the family ever knew about this. Keep it in the closet. Even at this young age I got the message loud and clear.

CONNECTING THE DOTS

The most colorful person in my childhood was my Auntie Dot, although it would take me years before I came to understand just how truly original she really was. Grandpa Tewksbury had two Dorothys in his life; one was his wife, the other his younger sister. Because Grandma went by Dorothy, I came to know my great aunt—my grandfather's sister—simply as Dot. She was a tall, strong, vivacious woman with jet black eyebrows, shocking white hair, and an unforgettable laugh that started as a chuckle deep in her belly and ended with both of her shoulders rising and falling, all connected by the biggest, most adventurous spirit and compassionate heart imaginable.

Until the age of seven I not only had all four grandparents in my life, I also had one great-grandparent. Grandma Coupland (my grandfather's mother) also lived in Lethbridge, but I was always a little afraid of her because she was so old and frail. As a young child I found visiting her creepy because her house smelled of mothballs and impending death. She was wheelchair bound, and couldn't communicate clearly anymore. When I went to kiss her goodbye, I had to avoid the drool that is an inevitable part of a very decrepit elderly person's life.

The saving grace was that when I saw my great grandma, I also saw Auntie Dot. A military woman who had become a much loved and celebrated teacher, Dot was the only one of her siblings without a family of her own, and she had committed herself to taking care of her mother.

In the summer between grades three and four, Dot planned a huge family reunion to bring all of our extended Tewksbury family together for perhaps the last time in Grandma Coupland's life. That year two significant things had happened to me. First, I had won the part of Prince Charming in my elementary school's production of *Cinderella*. I was pretty proud of that accomplishment, but truth be told, only three guys had tried out for the part, and I won simply because my voice was the loudest. My entire performance consisted of singing two lines that I remember to this day. "Try on the shoe, oh Cinderella; try on the shoe; it might fit you." When the shoe fit, I rejoiced, "The shoe, the shoe, her foot fits the shoe." Because this came near the very end of the play, I also doubled as one of the horses pulling the carriage to the big ball.

The other memorable moment that year was watching *The Sound of Music* on television. It was one of my mother's sentimental favorites, and although the movie finished airing close to 11 p.m. and my bedtime was usually 9, she decided that on this one occasion it was worth letting me stay up late.

Somehow these two events collided that summer through my Auntie Dot. I was sitting outside in our backyard when Dot approached me. She had a recording device in her hand and a mischievous look in her eye. "I heard you are quite the singer." I blushed and then said that sure, I had been in a play, but I only had a couple of lines. She then played my own voice back to me. Unbeknownst to me the play had been recorded and she had the evidence. Then she asked if I would participate in a production later that summer at our family reunion. She had always loved the song "Edelweiss," and wanted to know if I would be willing to sing it. It would ultimately become a lasting memory for the attending adults when I forgot the words halfway through the song and my other great aunt, Aurora, started singing from the piano for support, exactly as Julie Andrews had done in the movie. I stood there traumatized, wishing it hadn't been so impossible to say no to Auntie Dot in the first place. Not that she would have taken no for an answer anyway.

Dot was the glue of the Tewksbury side of our family, undertaking whatever was necessary to bring people together. You never knew what to expect when going to her house for a visit, but you could be sure that something interesting would happen. The minute you arrived, she assigned everyone a specific task to get some part of the meal ready. No sitting around idly at Dot's house. She was one of those people who made things happen.

Her legend still lives on in Banff, where she once poured an entire bottle of bubble bath into a whirlpool tub and left the hotel room to get some soda, only to return to find a trail of bubbles leading out of her room and halfway down the hall. When her school's summer trip to the Calgary Stampede was canceled, it was Dot who rented a van and said to her students, "To heck with it, we are going!" She was the one who taught my younger brother to use a jigsaw, took me hiking in the mountains, and got my sister on a two-person bike. She was unlike anyone we had ever met, and we adored her.

For many years Dot had lived with another woman, Jean, who had rather seamlessly become part of our family. I don't remember the day Jean appeared for the first time or ever thinking twice about who this Jean person was. Ever since I was a little boy I had watched Dot take a caregiver role, and I, like my family around me, never thought twice about Dot looking after this lovely older woman as she neared the end of her life.

Jean was older than Dot by many years, and where Dot was extremely modest in her appearance, Jean was a glamour puss. Giving Jean a greeting kiss meant avoiding the bright red rouge on her cheeks and getting a lovely whiff of expensive French perfume. They were the eccentric pair in our conservative group.

In my early twenties, Jean died, and not long after, Auntie Dot became very ill and was hospitalized in Calgary. A simple cold had turned to pneumonia, which had serious implications given Dot's age. To me, that was a signal that it was now time for someone to do for Dot what she had done for others. I decided that I was going to visit Dot regularly and monitor her progress. But from the moment I entered her hospital room I knew that something wasn't right.

For the first time in my life I saw that the enormous spirit that I had associated with Dot was missing. She lay in a sterile white bed with her white gown and white hair and was so small and washed out that at first I didn't even recognize her. She looked completely worn down and defeated. I tried to talk, to get her to laugh, to show me anything that would help me recognize the woman I so adored, but she barely made eye contact with me. I had a sense she had given up on living, that she didn't seem to care if she survived this, and it terrified me.

When I went back the next day it was the same thing. I didn't know what to do, and I actually ended up getting angry with her. "Dot, you don't seem to care about living right now, but I am coming back here tomorrow, and I'll be back the day after that, and you had better still be here when I arrive," I yelled at her. But I still didn't know what to do. I left her room, went to my car in the hospital parking lot, and burst into tears. What was going on? Where was the Dot I knew? How could this illness have taken away her will to live? Here I was, urging her to live, when she was always the one we all looked to for inspiration.

It would only be many years later that it dawned on me that perhaps Dot lost her will to live not because she was ill, but because Jean died before her. These two women had shared a one-bedroom house and were inseparable for many years, yet I never thought twice about the nature of their relationship. None of my family had. We all just assumed that when Jean died, Dot lost a friend, but perhaps the pain Dot was feeling ran much deeper than that. Maybe she hadn't just lost a friend. Maybe Dot had lost all that she had in her life. But there was no place for that kind of admission at that time in our family, no place for her to share that kind of information with anyone. I was a young gay man at the time, and even I didn't consciously clue in to it. I was part of a family, like many others, that was well-trained to see only what it wanted to see.

I went to see Dot every day for the next couple weeks. She finally went on to recover, finding her fighting spirit once again. It was slow going but her trademark deep laughter finally came back, so much so that even the hospital staff were sad to see this fun-loving character leave them. Auntie Dot would, thankfully, go on to live for many years.

When she did eventually die, this woman of seemingly modest means, who only wore second-hand clothes from the Salvation Army and drove the same car for decades, left close to a half-million dollars in savings to be shared by all of her remaining family. Just another hint of the many hidden surprises Dot kept so masterfully from us during her incredible life.

BARBIE IN THE BATHTUB

Spending time with my Grandma and Grandpa Tewksbury was always interesting, but it was also slightly confusing because they called each other mother and father. And as a small child I could never work that out, especially if my own mother and father were there.

My grandparents loved to pack picnic lunches and go to parks and exhibits, play eight-track tapes and Frisbee, and hang out, but at the same time they were incredibly rigid in their opinions of what was right or wrong. Theirs was a black-and-white world. I saw this early in my childhood when we visited the zoo. After seeing the elephants and giraffes, we headed over to the monkey house where on this particular day the baboons were giving us a show. With each step we took toward the cage, a new baboon would swing against the glass wall to show its big, red swollen behind to us. It was monkey mooning. The other baboons would make a screeching, laughing noise, and then another would do the same thing. I was in hysterics being mooned by the baboons when my grandma freaked out, screaming, "Oh, Father, this is awful. This isn't right behavior at all. We have to get out of here now." My Grandpa responded, "Absolutely Mother," grabbed me by the arm, looked into my eyes, and with the most serious look said, "We don't ever do this kind of thing." Not that I was thinking of running into the wall bare-ass naked, but it was good to have clarification. This incident would later give me great insight into the ways of my own father. After all, these were the people who had raised him.

The only thing I could count on in childhood, at least until age eight, was moving. I was always the new kid at school, and just when it seemed like I was making friends and getting settled, we moved again.

When I entered grade three that changed for a while. We found a three-bedroom bungalow in Calgary that had everything we were looking for in a house. It was yellow, which was my mom's favorite color. It had a big backyard and deck, which my dad liked. And finally there was enough space for every child to have his or her own bedroom. Unfortunately, there was a catch. I slowly came to realize as we were taking the first tour of the house that a three-bedroom bungalow meant there were three bedrooms upstairs. There was one for my younger brother, one for my younger sister, and one master for my mom and dad. That was when it hit me. Gulp. Where was I supposed to sleep?

Down the stairs into the basement, in the absolute farthest corner of the house, too far for anybody to ever hear anything should someone break in through the window that was located directly above where my bed logically should go, was my room. I hadn't laid eyes on it for more than two seconds when I burst into tears—those huge crocodile tears you only cry when you are a really upset child. "Why do I have to stay down here by myself?" I blurted through the tears. "Because you are the oldest," my mother replied.

She tried to point out all the great things about the room. "You get this big sliding closet all to yourself." Sure, but it was the scariest closet in the world because it was so deep and big that no matter how hard you tried you could never get light into both ends of the closet at the same time. I spent years thinking someone was in there, jumping from side to side, hiding from me, and waiting until the middle of the night to get me. "You get your own bathroom." Sure, a bathroom with two doors, one side connected to a laundry/storage room, which was a perfect place for some fiend to hide and attack me in the middle of the night.

My dad had listened to my mom's niceties long enough. "Stop your crying. You are the oldest and you should be happy that you finally have your own room." I just cried harder.

As the only girl in the family, my sister, Colleen, had inherited the bedroom set that my mother had been given by her father when she was ten. It was lovely, with a big double-bed frame made of the same wood that matched the dresser and vanity mirror. I would come to know it well.

Night after night I stayed downstairs, feeling safe in my bed as long as I heard the television set in the recreation room outside my door. Without that noise I lasted maybe thirty minutes before I would so terrify myself that I would run and join Colleen in bed upstairs. We came to have a very close bond in those years, not just because we slept in the same bed, but because everything we did drove our parents crazy.

Maybe it was because we both had been adopted, but Colleen and I both sucked our thumbs at night. We did this until really late in life, like still in grades three and four. Our favorite thing to do was to get our pillows nice and cold in the summer, and then as we placed our faces down and heated the pillow up we sucked away on our thumbs. It was better than chocolate and ice cream.

When Mom and Dad found us in the morning sleeping together in the same bed with our thumbs in our mouths, all hell broke loose. They tried everything to get us to stop. The worst were these iodine-like drops that tasted like sour acid on your tongue. But Colleen and I were both very determined, enduring the really disgusting seven-minute tortuous ordeal it took to dissolve the foul fluid to make it through to our nightly ritual.

The only thing that drove my dad crazier than the bed-swapping and thumb-sucking was my playing with Barbie. As fate would have it, my sister Colleen was a girl who could care less about dolls and girlie things. I was a boy who *loved* Barbie and girlie things. A match made in heaven, or so it would have seemed.

A tradition began when I was just a kid visiting Grandma Tewksbury that every night I could take a bubble bath and spend time playing in the tub. Grandma had a set of plastic animals that entertained me for years. But as Colleen became an age when Barbie entered her life, I set my sights on a new bath mate in Calgary. Barbie could bend and click, and that hair could entertain me endlessly. Getting the Barbie away from Colleen wasn't the problem; it was making sure Dad didn't catch me.

It became clear pretty quickly that my love of Barbie was not a good thing. In my dad's bipolar good-and-bad universe, boys with Barbie equal bad. Period. One day he saw me playing with the doll and it was too much for him. "Boys don't do this, Donna. This is not for him to play with," he told my mom. I think my mom on some level, even though she loved me dearly, agreed. But once you've had Barbie, it's impossible not to go back.

Many hours of my life were wasted on figuring out how to get Barbie, and then how to get her back without getting caught. For a long time it was easy because nobody cared about Barbie. I would casually carry her out under my shirt, and return her when I had finished playing later in the day. It became much more complicated when my sister and I turned the ages where brothers and sisters no longer enjoy sharing things, such as the back seat of the car on road trips—and Barbie. So, even though Colleen didn't want to play Barbie herself, she would tell my dad if she found Barbie missing just to see me get in trouble. My dad would grab the wooden spoon, his favorite weapon of discipline, and let me have it.

There were some very close calls. Sometimes, when I got older, my family went out and I stayed home alone so that I could take my bath. One day, when I had finished and Barbie still had wet hair, instead of putting her back I decadently decided to watch some Saturday afternoon television and dry her hair in front of our fake glass fireplace. Her hair dried much fuller looking that way.

Between the TV and me in my faraway Barbie land, I didn't hear the car drive up or the front door open. Then, all of a sudden, I heard my father's footsteps coming down the stairs. I stood there with a towel over my head, one wrapped around my waist, and Barbie with her half-dried hair. I was so shocked that I turned in the direction of the noise. Barbie's perfect face hit the glass plate of the gas fireplace. Part of her face melted and a good patch of her long, blond hair was singed. The room smelled like burning plastic, and there was a long, black, streaky patch on the glass. I had maybe ten seconds to recover. I whipped into the bathroom, threw Barbie under the sink, opened the door on the other side, and met my dad there to help put away the groceries. Although I denied any knowledge of the black streak burned onto the glass plate of my dad's sacred fireplace, it was only a matter of time before Colleen discovered the burned Barbie and my dad put two and two together. I got a whooping that broke the wooden spoon over my behind.

I was only caught with Barbie in hand once more, if you will. I was in the middle of taking a bath and in came Dad through the door on the recreation room side, so I had a split second to hide Barbie. I shoved her as far under my butt and between my locked legs as possible. My dad sat down on the toilet, bottle of beer in hand, and decided it was time to have a little heart-to-heart on this glorious Saturday afternoon. I was about twelve. As I listened to him talk I could feel the air bubbles collecting under my legs. I was doing everything in my power not to budge, but in spite of my efforts, my legs slipped on the bare porcelain tub and midway through my dad's sentence, up popped Barbie. He was so shocked he just looked at me and left. Well, maybe gave me a look is a better way to say it. That time I escaped a physical beating, but got one with his eyes instead. It was the last time I played with Barbie for a long, long time.

THE ROCKY HORROR PICTURE SHOW

It came as a shock to my parents when I finally told them that I was gay, which came as a shock to me because I thought they must have figured it out along the way.

When I visited Grandma McDonald for one of the last summers before I had to forfeit my trips to Lethbridge in order to continue with swimming, something very strange happened. Grandma eventually developed serious Alzheimer's, and I now realize that this must have been the beginning of her forgetfulness. I was around fourteen, and it had been a year or two since we had done dress-up. I had begun to bring friends down with me when I visited, so some of our rituals had to be adjusted slightly.

But at the end of my trip, as I was leaving her apartment and my friend was already on the way to the elevator, she pulled me aside and said, "Take these old things home with you." She handed me a brown paper bag filled with two wigs and dresses. I was shocked, but thrilled. For years she knew the rule, but she seemed to have forgotten it herself this time. The clothes were let out of the closet, and with it my sexual exploration had been unleashed.

* * *

I think the only thing we boys spoke about at that age was sex. Well, we were teenage boys, after all! At school it was all about how far you could go with what girl, and at the pool there was this wild untapped energy from a bunch of teens running around half-naked and physically exerting themselves.

Needless to say, my sexuality was awakening, and at the same time it wasn't able to express itself in a typical way. None of the guys were talking about how far another guy might go, unfortunately. Like a godsend these clothes arrived, and I found a new way to express myself.

I was fascinated with dressing in Grandma's clothes. It was different from when I was younger. Then it was just play. Now they became sensual, sexual. And even better, now that they were mine I had the freedom to use them when I wanted—well, up to a point. I still had to be careful.

I used to look forward to Saturday nights because often my parents would go out, and I would lock myself in their bedroom and play dress-up for hours. My brother and sister would be downstairs watching *Charlie's Angels*, *The Love Boat*, and *Fantasy Island* on TV while I was living my fantasies upstairs. I would put on this blue, low-cut, busty dress of my grandmother's that made me look really sexy.

I would fish through my mother's jewelry box, although I was limited to necklaces and bracelets because she had pierced ears. She worked at Shoppers Drug Mart and had every beauty product imaginable.

At first I would put on only the clothes and jewelry, but with time I graduated to makeup. I would pull out the elegant, long, black-bristled brush and gently apply powder, then do my eyes, with lipstick always last, just like Mom. The wig was always the final touch.

Although I would eventually become a very hairy man, I went through puberty quite late, and I was smooth-skinned and looked very pretty all made up late into my teens. The years of swimming, however, had left me looking muscled and strong.

I would look at pictures in a magazine, imagining these guys wanting to sleep with this woman I saw in front of me. Dressing up was a thrilling outlet for me to explore. Somehow I didn't think of myself as gay because I was fantasizing about having sex with a man while being dressed as a woman. For me it made sense, although I also knew it was a dangerous game.

I might have stopped there in the privacy of my own home had it not been for a fortuitous intervention. At that time a big hit song was "The Time Warp" from the movie, *The Rocky Horror Picture Show*. It starred Tim Curry, who plays a transvestite. I went to see this movie with my swim team, and we all loved it, but nobody loved it more than I did. There on the big screen was someone acting like I did in my parents' bedroom, but for the whole world to see. And everyone loved this guy. From that moment forward, I put all of the energy that other kids were putting into flirting and fooling around into *The Rocky Horror Picture Show*. Because it was such a cult classic there was a soundtrack and even a picture book complete with the comments the audience yells at the screen throughout the movie. Finally I was not alone.

I only knew "fag" and "gay" as being ugly, bad things because already at school, people were calling me these things and treating me like crap, but through this movie I transformed. It was like a Transsexual, Transylvanian seal of approval. Not only is it okay to be different, it's a full-blown blast! In a sense I came out through this movie, although that hadn't been my intention.

How could I not participate in a movie that was all about interacting with the crowd and getting dressed up? I picked a scene from the movie when we first meet Dr. Frank-N-Furter in his laboratory. The camera shoots the scene upward, giving the perspective of someone entering the space above them via an elevator. We first see high-heeled shoes, then fishnet stockings, then a green laboratory jacket, then this over-the-top made-up face with wild, curly, black hair. Dr. Frank-N-Furter breaks into his first song, which is the one I would stand in front of the audience and perform. The show only came to town on long weekends, and Easter was just a few weeks away. Now I just needed a plan.

Because I didn't consider this a gay thing, I asked for help. I needed some fishnet stockings and makeup, which two girlfriends from Bishop Carroll High School said they would take care of for me. They said that I could get dressed at their house, because their parents were going out for dinner that Saturday night. Perfect. A friend from swimming whom years later would come out as well offered to go with me. He had a car. I desperately needed a car. I didn't know how

I would have used public transportation. Imagine sitting in full drag on Calgary Transit for an hour to go to the theater. Imagine the stares. Imagine the comments.

The only other challenge was my curfew. I had to be home by midnight, but that was exactly when the movie started. Another friend from swimming, Jonathon*, was living with his divorced mom, who wasn't very strict about what time he got in at his house. I arranged to stay there after the movie. Everything was in place.

All that was left to find was the green hospital smock. I remembered that my mom had something that might do buried in the back of her huge walk-in closet. There was this nasty looking green dress that I had never seen her wear. Under the chiffon was a layer of green plastic that would be a perfect double for the surgical gown. One night a few days before the weekend I took a pair of scissors and cut all the fabric away. What I found was that the seam in the waist was elasticized, creating an hourglass shape. That was less than ideal, but I took it anyway. It was better than nothing.

In the end, it turned out I didn't need it. When I got to my friend's house she had a real hospital smock, and when my makeup was done and my outfit was on all she could say was, "I hate you. I would kill for your legs." The years of swimming were good for something, I thought.

I went to the cinema and joined the other people dressed up in line. Not everyone dresses up, but at least a good quarter of the audience had some getup on. I wasn't the only Frankie, but was the only one dressed from the laboratory scene. My heart started racing as my part came up in the movie. "Am I really going to do this?" My friend gave me a bit of a nudge. I swallowed hard, stumbled to the front of the theater in my heels, and lip-synched the part, stretching out my hand to the crowd just like Tim Curry was doing behind me in the movie. It was terrifying but when I later arrived at Jonathon's, I was still shaking with excitement.

The next day was Easter Sunday and Jonathon lived up north by the university, which was a fair commute, so I called my mom for a ride home. I called in the early afternoon so I'd have time to get home for the big dinner. I was still high from the experience the night before, amazed that everything had come together so well. When my mom answered the phone I could tell immediately that something was wrong. Her voice was small and strained. "Mom, is everything alright?" "Yes," she replied, but so quietly I could barely hear her. "Where do I come again?" I gave her directions to Jonathon's place.

Forty-five minutes later we were on our way home when my mom pulled the car over and broke down sobbing. Her face was teary and blotchy. I tried to imagine how she might have found out about the night before, but I couldn't. "How could you?" she demanded and started crying again. I was freaking out inside but wasn't willing to come clean. "What, Mom?" I whispered. There was a dramatic pause before she responded. "How could you cut up the dress that I wore as a bridesmaid to my sister's wedding? What possessed you?" I sat stunned. I had really screwed up.

The bridesmaid dress she wore to her sister's wedding. Gulp. No wonder it was so nasty, with all that chiffon and plastic. But I had no idea that dress that I had never seen outside her closet was so deeply meaningful to her. And in the end I didn't even use the damn thing. What a waste!

I didn't know what to say. This was Easter, not Halloween. Where do you begin? There was no place for me to begin, I couldn't even think of any lie good enough to make sense of this. I was stuck and speechless. "What is going on?" my mom demanded. I stayed silent.

My father was equally unimpressed. Instead of facing him I went straight to my bedroom and hid my head under my pillow in shame. After about twenty minutes my sister came to get me for Easter dinner. Even she had a mixed look of "what have you done?" and "poor you" on her face. My mom had cleaned herself up but still looked like she could burst into tears at any moment. My dad was waiting for me at the head of the dining room table. The look of disgust on his face was deeper than any I had ever seen before.

He was positively perplexed by my actions. "Look what you have done to your mother," he hissed at me. I hated seeing my mom so upset. I was sick with guilt, but could offer no explanation or excuse that they would understand. My mom started to cry, and so did I. "I am really sorry, Mom." But my dad continued, "Do you have anything to say for yourself?" I didn't. Not really. How could I begin to explain? What could I say? The truth? I wasn't even sure what the hell was going on myself. How would I start? "Well Dad, I think I like boys but since I can't find any to play with, I dress up like a girl and then get aroused because I imagine the guys I like will have sex with me now because I am a girl and that is good because in conservative, moral Alberta boys only sleep with girls." But I thought things were bad enough as they were, so I didn't say anything.

My silence was interpreted as contempt, making my apology ring insincere. I really meant it. I was sorry for everything. Sorry for ruining my mom's dress. Sorry for ruining Easter dinner. Sorry for being a boy who dresses up like a girl. Sorry that nobody seemed to understand me at all.

There had been a chance to get the truth out. Certainly the window of opportunity was there, but nobody was ready to take it, so no one spoke. The inevitable question didn't get asked, and nothing further was offered by me. It was one of the most painful holiday meals I ever sat through, just the clanging and scraping of knives and forks on plates and the quick exchange of looks, followed by the asking of permission to leave the table. We never spoke of this incident again, which speaks volumes about our family relationships and my secret.

CHAPTER TWO

SEE MARK RUN

The Three Musketeers

I had a great start to junior high school. I had moved with my family to a brand new development in southwest Calgary, so new that none of the houses on our cul-de-sac had a lawn and most were still un-inhabited. Across from us lay a vast area of undeveloped land, more wide than deep, that bordered an Indian reserve. The transit system in Calgary at that time left something to be desired; buses didn't come out as far as our house yet. To go anywhere you had to order a mini-bus, which meant a one- to two-hour wait for the 45-minute shuttle that took you to a centralized hub, where you could connect to the limited 1980s bus network.

I went to a new school in the area, a large, rectangular slab of concrete, with different wings, some portables, and a playground with new grass that hadn't quite settled yet. I had been in the public school system until now, but there had been a teacher's strike, so my mother decided to pull her Roman Catholic rank and got all of us kids into the Catholic school system. This was not only a new house in a new area and a new school; it was also a new education system.

At this new school I became friends fairly quickly with a great guy named Matthew Brown*. Matthew was a tall, thin, but remark-ably athletic guy. He had dark hair and pale skin and was smart. We hung out throughout grade seven, and slowly became part of a larger clique of guys at our school. This was where Jim Stone* entered the picture. Jim was the real classic jock among us, playing quarterback and having the build of a young, muscled athlete early in life, surrounded by a kind of Clark Kent exterior, complete with glasses and floppy hair.

The fact that we were all athletic created a bond. I had started to swim six years earlier, but the irony was that on land I was completely physically challenged. I was enormously clumsy and my accidents often meant stitches, along with having twisted ankles and an oft-bumped head. But because I was a good swimmer and a fairly good runner, I was welcomed into this group of jocks.

Entry came with a challenge. For as long as I can remember, whenever I get startled, or tickled, or surprised, I make this shrieking, girlish, high-pitched noise. Once I have made it, it is guaranteed that someone around me will make a comment about how a man like me could make a shrill noise like that. This was the unfortunate sound I made in grade school whenever any flying object came speeding toward me, such as volleyballs, basketballs, and especially footballs. I would shriek before I could stop myself.

This certainly marked me as different in redneck, suburban, teenage, '80s Calgary. One reason that Matthew and Jim left such a lasting impression on me was that they looked past that high-pitched noise and spent hours at Matthew's house throwing me a football, trying to teach me how to catch and throw and respond more normally. It never really worked; I still shriek to this day, but their efforts were greatly appreciated.

By the beginning of grade eight the three of us had all become very close friends. There were other people in the clique, like Bob Harvey*, Chris Marcil, Donny Little*, and with time, girls. That year saw the beginning of weekends with house parties and "sexploration" games like Truth or Dare, testing how far we could go with a girl. It was a fun time, with a good group of people. Life couldn't have been better. And then came Halloween.

Jim, Matthew, and I were going as the Three Musketeers. We dressed for school that day in our costumes and after school were going to hang out at a party then sleep over at Jim's house. It was quite a day. At one point I remember feeling absolute bliss—my teenaged life in the suburbs of Calgary was perfect. I had my friends and we had such togetherness, like the other musketeers. We were literally "all for one and one for all."

After school we met other people from our clique, including the girls that we were dating or flirting with, at one kid's house. Jim, Matthew, and I were each "going out" with someone, which in my case essentially meant there was a girl I would dance with when a slow song came on. Our teenaged games included kissing, sometimes deeply, accompanied by a little petting but nothing more. The Halloween party was charged, raging with hormones, and you could feel the sexual frustration in the air when the room of teenagers was told it was time to go home.

When we finally ended up at Jim's house it was around 11 p.m. We turned the recreation room area in the basement into a large bedroom for all of us, and as we got our sleeping bags ready, I stopped briefly in Jim's room to say something.

I had always thought that Jim was a great guy, but since the beginning of the school year earlier that fall I had started to develop strange feelings toward him. Earlier that night at the costume party I found myself staring at him as he was kissing a girl, feeling something confusing like envy, not because Jim was with a girl I wanted to kiss but because I wanted *Jim to kiss me*. I pushed the thought out of my head, trying to ignore it. But then something happened that I could no longer deny.

Jim had grown hair under his arms, which hadn't happened yet to any of the other guys. He was very self-conscious because he was the first, primarily because he didn't want to smell. As he was talking to me he lifted his arm to put on deodorant, and I caught a very slight smell of him. Forget musketeer, Jim was the musky-teer!

I had the most intense chemical reaction to his scent, like a bomb went off in my stomach. I think I did a good job of hiding it, but it was mortifying. I didn't want to feel this way, to have this kind of reaction. I wanted to forget that I had these strange feelings for him. But there was no stopping it. As we went back to the group all I could think to do was to keep my distance, which I did.

Later that night we all slept by the dim flickering light of a gas fireplace while the radio played. At one point we were all conversing, but a few minutes later I realized that I was the only one still talking; everyone else had fallen asleep. I sat up and looked over and saw Jim. He was lying on his sleeping bag in his underwear, arms raised with his underarm hair exposed, and I couldn't take my eyes off of him. I just wanted to go over and cuddle with him, smell him, touch him. I stared for a moment and then, like it or not, my body moved toward him of its own volition. I hovered over him for a moment, wanting to play my own "sexploration" game, but before I went too far I forced myself to stop.

I remembered the flushed feeling I had when I saw Jim changing for gym class earlier in the month. I tried so hard to keep away that feeling of being attracted to him, but no matter how hard I tried, it just came back stronger than ever. And it came from the inside, out of my control.

I went back to my sleeping bag but didn't sleep a wink that night. There was nowhere to hide from the fact that I was in lust with my best friend, the quarterback jock who was the pride and joy of our Catholic school in conservative suburban Calgary. What the hell was I going to do?

A KISS OF FATE

People often ask me when I first knew I was gay. For a long time, I didn't know exactly what it meant to be gay. Nobody ever spoke about this word in my world, except when thrown around as a form of slander. If you did anything out of the ordinary, or something that people thought was stupid, then people would say you were being "gay." It would be years before I understood the literal meaning of this word. But for a long time I sensed that I was different. As I was discovering sexuality with my adolescent peers around me, I was always the one who seemed to push things too far.

In grade school I fooled around with my neighbors, a set of twins who lived across the back alley from me. We used to play spin the bottle or wrestle, stripping or rubbing our bodies next to each other under the auspice of fun and games. That in itself was not so extraordinary, as many guys fool around in some way with other guys when first discovering their sexuality.

What made it so confusing for me was how disappointed I was when the session was over. Where the other guys would switch instantly to something else, say, going to play sport outside after five minutes of fooling around, I would secretly wish it would last for hours. Before we played together I would pray that the twins would be horny and something would happen. Thankfully in those days my prayers were often answered.

One afternoon we were downstairs in my basement bedroom fooling around. This had been going on for a few months, and as the stronger twin wrestled me to the ground I could smell his hair and sweat as he pushed himself against me. I could feel the warmth of his cheek against mine.

I got lost in the moment, and before I knew what I was doing I gave him a kiss. It felt like the most natural thing in the world to do. Not so for him. He stopped dead in his tracks. "What the hell are you doing? Boys don't kiss boys! What is wrong with you?" It was a fair question, but at the time I didn't have an answer.

I always regretted that kiss. It was the kiss that sealed my fate, crossing a line that exposed me as different, a place from which I would never be able to return. My friendship with the twins was never quite the same after that day. Whenever we saw each other we were embarrassed and uneasy. The distance between us began immediately, forever replacing the closeness that had been what I cherished about our friendship.

This change in how I related to my friends would become a problem for me in my formative years. The closer I became to certain guys in friendship, the more emotional I felt about them. Instead of responding like a friend in situations, I would act more like a spurned lover, needy and possessive and jealous. The more my inner feelings showed, the stranger I seemed, and the greater the distance grew between my former friends and me.

In the weeks following the Halloween party, my feelings for Jim became impossible for me to keep under control. Once I identified the fact that I felt something for him, I was desperate for him to feel the same way about me. Unfortunately that would never be the case. Instead, my stares and demands and obsession remained unreturned, and my strange, new behavior took its toll on the clique.

Sensing that something about me wasn't right, my friends began to withdraw. One Friday afternoon late in the autumn of grade eight, I became terribly upset when I learned through the grapevine that there was a party at a friend's house and I hadn't been invited. Nobody had told me about it, including Matthew and Jim, as if they had forgotten about me, or worse, didn't want me there.

As I was being cut out, I watched Matthew and Jim, my two former buddies, become closer and closer. I was completely beside myself, wishing I also could have the close relationship Matthew had with Jim. I coveted them and became jealous, envious, and insecure. I wanted *so* badly to go back to the way things were, to be a part of what they were doing. To be invited to play ball, to hang out, to sleep over on the weekends. But there was no going back.

And no matter how hard I promised myself that I would change, that I wouldn't feel this way about guys, that I would act normally like the other guys at my school, I couldn't. The harder I tried to be accepted, the more my friends pulled away. Finally I gave up and withdrew. It was just easier not to have anything than to constantly want what I couldn't have.

I became a loner during this part of my life. I hated going to school. I constantly felt like a loser, someone who had been on the inside but now was out. But I found ways to make the most out of it, to minimize the damage. I lived only a five-minute walk from the school, so I would arrive just before school began, go home for lunch, and leave right at the end of the day, usually because I had swimming anyway.

Every once in a while there would be situations where I had to interact with my fellow students, like in the locker room at gym class, in the science room, or the industrial ed lab. Those were the moments I hated most, because those were the times I would see just how alone I really was.

It wasn't being gay that was killing me, it was the loneliness and isolation. I felt vulnerable and freakish, like I was the only person in the world with this affliction. It was an awful place to be, feeling like a sitting duck in the vicious land of junior high, waiting to be attacked by one of the many jerks I so carefully tried to keep from noticing me.

In the spring as we were heading into the homestretch of grade eight, I made a joke to one of my classmates while another student, Billy Runninghorse*, was speaking. I knew Billy for some time. I had gone to Fairview Elementary School with some of the Indian kids from the nearby reserve, and they had transferred to St. Cyril the same time I did.

I was a casual friend of Billy's cousin, who was a celebrated hockey and football player and who had a certain amount of respect for my swimming, but Billy was another story entirely. He was not a fan and was always trying to pick a fight with me in school. Today he was going to see his mission through.

As soon as the teacher left the classroom, Billy pointed to me and blamed me of disrespecting him by laughing while he was speaking in front of the class. He challenged me to a fight after school. I tried to blow it off, nervously laughing, but he pounced on me, starting the fight right there. As he hopped over two rows of desks to take a punch at me, a student yelled, "Teacher, teacher," and Billy was forced to back off. But in his mind the fight had already begun.

For the rest of the afternoon, every time I passed him in the hallway he would yell at me, "You're fucking dead. I am going to fucking kill you after school. You better not chicken out. You're dead." The tension was thick. I was sick with fear. Billy was a tough guy, and was at least two years older than any other kid in grade eight. His bite was three times as bad as his bark.

It was one of the longest afternoons of my life. I didn't hear a single word that any of the teachers said. I just thought about how I was going to get out of this without getting seriously hurt. I tried the diplomatic approach and asked Billy's friends to please have him reconsider. Yeah, right. I saw Billy spit on the ground when they whispered in his ear.

I thought of going to a teacher but that would just make it worse. Then I would have been a tattletale and a coward. At least there was starting to be a buzz around the school that there was a fight and that I was going to get my butt kicked. Other students were looking at me and sizing me up, and then laughing. I hoped that if this kept up the teachers would get wind of it and stop it.

Then it dawned on me that not one single person in this whole school was coming to help me. Not one. I had no friends. None. I was a total loser. I was filled with fear, but at the same time had no feeling. The pain of the situation numbed me. I was in another place anyway, trying somehow to get myself mentally ready for the fight I seemed destined to fight. Alone.

Later that afternoon there was a big circle of kids gathered around waiting for the fight to start. I was there, feeling petrified but sticking it out. I saw Jim and some other former friends on the sideline giving me a sign like I would be okay, but it was too little, too late.

It didn't matter anyway. There wouldn't be a fight. One blessed teacher had given Billy detention, so the fight was off for that afternoon. The next day Billy wasn't at school, and the anticipated brawl simply fizzled. But even that, in its anticlimax, made me look like more of a loser. There was no winning anymore.

FAG

At the end of grade eight things went from bad to worse. It started one afternoon early in June as I arrived at school for class. I had left home late, not really worried about missing a few minutes of school. Being late meant there would be less chance of running into someone.

As I arrived at my locker, which was situated in the hallway between the science room and the industrial education lab, I saw that my lock wasn't properly closed. I immediately felt sick to my stomach. Oh no. Please don't let this be what I think it is.

I took off the lock and opened the door, and there on one of my blue binders was the word FAG written in black felt pen. One little word, but one that was loaded with enough hate that it brought my entire world tumbling down. I stared, seeing for the first time this ugly slang written about me. Of course I had heard it before, in the hallways, and I always wondered if people were saying that about me. But this was different. To me this said, "YOU ARE A FAG." It was devastating.

My secret was now in the public domain of St. Cyril Junior High School, and had instantly become my reality. I was THE fag. Period. I hated myself so much in that moment. I wished I could be different than this. I was tired of being alone. I was tired of feeling like a freak. A fag. The easiest target in the school.

Whatever spite the person had who did this to my locker, it couldn't come close to competing with the depth of my own self-hate. I imploded. I reacted by destroying my own locker. I ripped the remaining binders and folders apart. I ripped all of my notes in half. I wrote *fag* on the door of the locker, and on the back. Finally there was a place for all my self-disgust to manifest itself, and I completely lost myself in it.

After the high of the shock and adrenaline had worn off, I immediately left school. I ran home and trapped myself in the wooden garbage storage unit outside the backyard of our house. It was built into the fence, and since I had stupidly locked myself out of the house, today of all days, and it was raining, this was where I could stay somewhat dry until my parents came home. It all seemed perfectly fitting—the garbage cans, the rain, and my despair and self-disgust.

When my parents finally arrived, it was incredibly embarrassing. I had to tell them what had happened. I couldn't even say the word *fag* I was so beside myself with disgust. I told my mom, "Someone broke into my locker and wrote awful names about me." I left out the actual word itself. I burst into tears because I felt so ashamed and awkward. My mom whispered, "What did they write, sweetheart? You can tell me." She coaxed me, and eventually I said it. She went white. Then she told Dad. She told me not to think about it. Those kids were just being mean and jealous. She was very supportive. But she didn't know they were right.

I don't remember Mom, Dad, or me actually talking together about the word *fag* in great detail, except when we met with the principal. This was the next day, after school had ended, and there were very few students around. I felt conflicted about what had happened, humiliated, but also a bit guilty because I had blown what had happened out of proportion with my follow-up actions. I had no idea what would come next. Everything happened so fast.

When the principal suggested I could transfer schools, I was surprised. I hadn't really thought of that. My parents looked to me.

"What do you think, honey?" my mom asked. All I could think to do was run. Get as far away from here as possible. I can't ever come back here again. "Yes, that sounds okay," I squeaked. There was still a chance. A new school. New people. A new life. I was sure that if I ran away then I could leave all of this mess behind me. I was so wrong.

I picked a school halfway between my house, in the far southwest part of the city, and the University of Calgary, situated in the northwest, because I had started spending more and more time there, swimming. It was the second week of June when I arrived at the new school, very late in the year, and it made people curious. That was my first strike.

I started hesitantly telling people that I came from Cedarbrae when they asked, and I could see from their faces that they had no idea where that was. So I became a bit bolder about sharing my information. That was strike two.

Then I met Clyde*. Clyde was one of the class bullies, but in a less obvious, softer kind of way. He was born bad, a big guy with long, sandy blond hair, already expelled from another school in another part of Cedarbrae. For a tormenter, he was deceptive. He was very personable and easy to talk to. Which led to strike three, although I didn't know it at the time, and it meant I would soon be out. He asked me what school I went to. I told him, "St. Cyril." "I know people there." In that moment my fate was sealed, this time without the kiss.

The next day Clyde approached me just before the school day began. He said that he had heard that my locker at my former school had "FAG" written all over it. I felt the room spin. I thought I was going to be sick. I couldn't say anything. I fell into a desk chair as the class started, with a pasted-on, plastic smile to hide the utter devastation I was feeling. There was no escaping this.

I watched as Clyde told some other students. They were whispering, and I watched as the gossip spread through the class. There was a group of jocks at this school and they were very big guys, like fifteen-year-olds in twenty-year-old bodies. They all knew Clyde, and by the afternoon the story had reached them, too. They took this information and ran with it.

My freedom, my fresh start, had lasted less than two days before it came crashing down around me. Where whispers in hallways had followed me before, now the attacks and discrimination were a full-on daily assault.

This was the beginning of my double life. I would go swimming at the University of Calgary, and because I was talented, and was doing something challenging with other people every day and excelling, I was accepted. At school I was a loner who skipped as many classes as possible, going just enough to get decent grades. I tried for a while to lose the label that haunted me, but no matter how hard I tried there was no escaping it.

I thought that some of my success in swimming might translate into some goodwill and respect at school. At that time there was an incredible documentary movie made for CBC of Alex Baumann and Victor Davis called *The Fast and the Furious*. It follows these world-class athletes' journeys from the World Championships in Ecuador to the Commonwealth Games in Brisbane. It shows both Alex and Victor overcoming all odds, breaking world records, and winning against the best in the world.

In order to give some insight into what I was about I arranged to have a special screening of the movie at my school. I watched with excitement as all of the jerks that made my life hell every day came to the screening. I thought that finally, after this, I would get a break. How wrong I was.

The only information that seemed to resonate with the bullies was the fact that swimmers shave their bodies to compete, which they thought was the gayest thing imaginable. Instead of acceptance I was greeted with "Hey fag, shaved your legs lately?" A month later I had a profile in the local paper, the *Calgary Herald*, and the next day the guys thought I was an even bigger fag because I wore a Speedo.

No matter how hard I tried, the label of fag stayed with me all through junior and senior high school. Once a fag, always a fag, as far as these guys were concerned.

But thankfully, my swimming improved as each year passed. In that world I was not only accepted, I was celebrated. And for me, being identified as gay in this world just wasn't an option. Although it was impossible to completely repress who I was, for the most part my sexuality was put out of sight and out of mind.

I threw myself into swimming and reaffirmed my commitment to be "normal." I knew from the life I faced at school that the consequences were too great if the swimming world found out I was gay. I spent an enormous amount of energy pursuing my goal at that time— not to become a great swimmer, but to make sure that no matter what happened, my worlds of swimming and school never collided.

CHAPTER THREE

PLAYING STRAIGHT

THE WALK OF SHAME

It was the younger sister of my friend Jerri-Lyn who was bold enough to first confront me about being gay within my swimming world. My pact to keep my two realities apart had gone remarkably well, and I had done a great job of playing straight to my swimming friends. Or so I thought.

Once afternoon I was being silly with Jerri-Lyn at her house and was laughing, reacting to a story she told me by screaming, "Oh my God!" It was my mother's favorite expression, and until then, I used to say it all the time.

Jerri-Lyn's sister looked at me with the most disgusted look on her face and said, "You sound *so* gay when you say that." I stopped dead in my tracks. Feeling flushed, slightly embarrassed, but angrier than anything else that she dared speak about this, I challenged her. "When I say what?" "*OH MY GOD!*" she replied, mimicking me in the most over-the-top way.

I told her to shut up, but in my head I made a promise to myself never to say, "Oh my God" out loud again. She knocked the wind out of me. There was no hiding from the truth. And she wasn't alone in her repulsion of what I was.

Although hard to imagine today, there were periods of my life when I was consumed with the thought of killing myself. The intense and relentless bullying and ostracizing had taken its toll, and there were times as a teenager when I really thought about ending it all. Suicide rates by gay teens are still high today, and I sadly understand the reality that at this time in life, as a teen, there seemingly aren't many options available to deal with intense issues of difference. Unaware of choice, life can seem very black and white.

There were a few times when I would take a long blade from the kitchen, the only weapon I knew, and locked myself in the bathroom. I would never actually hurt myself, but the depths of my self-loathing and desperation in wanting to be something different than what I was pushed me dangerously close. I stayed alive because somewhere deep inside me I knew that I had too much to live for. I had my family, and my swimming, but I also knew that I had this awful secret, and I decided early in my life I would do whatever I could to hide it.

It started simply by lying to myself. I was going to do everything possible to be normal in order to fit into the straight world in which I was living. I was going to ignore this gay thing, hoping it was some strange phase that I would eventually outgrow. I was going to have a girlfriend, fall in love, get married, have kids, and live happily ever after. That was what everyone around me was doing, and that was what I was going to do, too.

I dated girls. First there was Tara, a beautiful, tall, young swimmer from Vancouver. We kissed and petted but never got any farther than that. Then there was the stunning Australian, Joanne, who was absolute perfection. Had it been possible to have my sexuality reversed, she should have done it. I remember thinking to myself that it was such a shame that this feminine beauty was wasted on me. Later, with Fiona, came full oral exploration, which was an odyssey I am grateful to have taken, but would only too happily and quickly leave to my straight friends. I remember looking in Fiona's eyes, prepping to go down and then popping back up. She screamed, "Don't kiss me!" Neither of us was quite ready for the experience.

With Charlotte* came my first sexual intercourse. It was the fall of 1984 and she had joined our swimming club after competing at the Los Angeles Olympics. We had beautiful, open, adventurous sex, but right from the beginning something wasn't really right. I was a virgin, and we were at a house party before going to see *The Rocky Horror Picture Show*. Charlotte pulled me into one of the bedrooms and said, "How about a shag?" I was a bit taken aback, but ever the adventurer, I said, "Sure, but it's my first time." "Really?" she asked. It was. Twenty minutes later I still hadn't had an orgasm, and she was astonished. I wouldn't climax that night, which Charlotte found hard to believe for a virgin, but she would still be my first, just on the second time. But with Charlotte it was more than sex. I had found someone to share my real feelings.

Charlotte had traveled extensively and experienced so much life that I would listen to her and simply open up. One day we began talking together about this guy on our swim team, Paolo*. Charlotte found him sexy in a strange kind of way. "I know what you mean" came out of my mouth before I could stop it. "You find him sexy, too?" As hard as I tried to play straight, gay often just came out anyway. "Yeah, I do," I admitted, heart pounding with adrenaline and sexual tension as I owned my truth for a moment. "Wow," Charlotte said, "that is cool." Within seven weeks Charlotte and I ended up with Paolo at the pub at the university. After some exciting flirting where Charlotte laid the bait, the three of us ended up fooling around in a bathroom on the third floor of one of the dormitories. Very bad idea.

It remains for me a moment that is frozen in time because of the sheer excitement of it. We were in a public place, Charlotte started kissing me, and then she started kissing Paolo, and then I hesitantly went to kiss Paolo. And incredibly, Paolo kissed me back. Really kissed me, before abruptly stopping and going back to Charlotte. We all had had just enough to drink that none of us were completely aware of what we were doing, but we were all still sober enough to be able to do it.

It was around the time I went down that the lights flicked on outside the cubicle, and as we emerged out of our own erotic bubble realized that a mob had gathered outside the door and were waiting for us. The tenants of this floor, who had been watching television when we had arrived, had put two and two together and realized that none of us lived here. They were outraged that we were using their property, and we could hear them telling each other incredulously, "They're having sex in there!" They demanded that we come out of the cubicle this instant.

The walk of shame was dreadful. We opened the door and there were at least fifteen people waiting to confront us. To make matters worse, one of the most innocent swimmers on our team was among them. The look of shock and then immediate repulsion for what we had done overcame the group as they watched one, then two, then three of us empty out of the cubicle. I was last out, bringing up the rear, so to speak. My first impulse upon seeing my naïve teammate was to break the ice and say "Hey!" but that impulse died the moment I saw his eyes.

This hadn't turned out so well. After dropping Charlotte at her place that night I drove home with Paolo because we lived close to each other. We didn't say a word about what had happened. We never did again, silence being a standard response to anything remotely gay in this conservative environment of 1980s Alberta. As far as Paolo was concerned, this had been a one-time deal. Charlotte and I broke up shortly thereafter, her sensing that perhaps she didn't have what I was looking for in a partner. She went on to a long-term relationship with another teammate. I never had a girlfriend again.

The line between my worlds started to become blurred. The older I got, the harder it became to repress my sexuality. At a training camp I made a pass at a poor guy when he was wrestling with me. He didn't appreciate it but thankfully was too embarrassed to expose my indiscretion. Another time I was hanging out in Vancouver with an Australian swimmer and, descending the stairs at a house party, fell onto him. The way he caught me gave me the impression he might also be gay, but when I boldly lunged to kiss him I could see in his eyes that he wasn't. I recovered quickly enough to save that situation, but whether I liked it or not this gay thing came out, making my promise to myself of normalcy impossible to keep. Playing straight wasn't really working. It was time for Plan B.

THE BACK-UP PLAN

Plan B was simple. As it became obvious to me that I was different, I turned to the women in my life to act as my accomplices in keeping my secret. The wonderful byproduct of being gay for me was that I attracted really great, lifelong female friends.

Way out in the suburbs, far away from everything, we lived beside the Clarkes. Although Mr. Clarke was a career military man, between his wife and their three daughters there was so much feminine energy pumping next door it was only a matter of time before I sought salvation there.

Tyrell was the middle daughter, and we were inseparable for years. We spent hours talking with each other, slowly opening up and sharing the most intimate details of our lives. With the free time you only seem to have as a teenager we came to know everything about each other.

She knew what had happened at my school. Her cousins went to St. Cyril, and the fag story had gotten around. She said her family felt really sorry and sad when they heard what happened, but didn't know what to say or do. It was a breath of inspired compassion at this difficult time in my life.

Tyrell was another person who opened me to new things, introducing me to alternative ideas and experimentation. With her

I learned to meditate. I entered ballroom dancing competitions. I snuck hot chocolate with a pinch of rum and Baileys over to her and we drank together in her basement and talked. She was an artist and I posed naked as her model, and when her mother found the drawings she accused Ty of corrupting me. If only she knew who was corrupting whom.

In Tyrell I found salvation. When my dad grounded me on Academy Awards night, I snuck to Tyrell's to watch the show. When my hair was horribly cut at the height of 1980s wickedness, it was Tyrell, on the night of her own art opening, who fixed it.

Our solidarity to each other was real. Once, when I went to a swim competition out of town, Grandma Tewksbury was visiting and she stayed in my room. When I left I realized that I had stored a *Playgirl* magazine under my mattress, and that when my grandma went to make my bed she might have found it—and then probably dropped dead on the spot. I was so terrified that I had done this that I called Tyrell long distance and asked her if she would pick me up from the airport, because I didn't want to face my family in a public place. I had called home and my parents had seemed distant, although I could hear Grandma in the background. At least she was still alive.

By the time I got home I had convinced myself that the magazine had been discovered. I decided if that were the case, I was moving to England. I had just come back from a swimming tour in Great Britain where I had seen openly gay people on the London streets, and the idea of running away to make a go of it there was thrilling. It didn't matter that I had no money or no job; I was willing to make a go of it somewhere I could at least be myself. Tyrell was ready for change, too, and after hours of talking up our courage and living this intricate fantasy in our head, decided she was coming with me. We called the airlines ready to go. It was 7:15 p.m. and the next flight wasn't until the following evening, nearly 24 hours away. I would have to go home and face the consequences and a day of hell before finding my freedom. I was strangely disappointed when the *Playgirl* magazine was where it was supposed to be, untouched. Ty and I stayed in our Calgary suburb, and life went on. But we would continue to develop a lasting commitment to being there for each other in a heartbeat.

On the swimming side of my life there was Andrea. By the time I was in my late teens I had been to Australia and New Zealand, across the United States and Canada, and to Sweden. I had seen London, East Berlin, Paris, Moscow, and Tokyo numerous times. I had a busy traveling life, spending four to six months a year on the road. As hard as things had been at school, there was this incredible opportunity through swimming to see the world. In many ways this was part of what saved me. Around the world I saw that people live life in many different ways. By seeing numerous cultures and customs I found signs of hope that it was okay to be different. For much of this travel my friend Andrea was by my side.

Andrea came to swimming in her teens and literally burst onto the national scene with her talent and speed. Within a few months of serious winter training she was on the national and then international scene. Andrea had come from a small town in Alberta, and had the most beautiful eyes and broadest shoulders you have ever seen. We were close in age, could make each other laugh easily, and became each other's accomplices for many, many years.

At first it was easy, because when teenaged boys and girls hang out together, people rush to make assumptions. It was natural to assume that we must have had something going since we spent so much time together. But we didn't. The great thing about Andrea was that she wasn't interested in many boys from Calgary or even the Canadian National Team. Her crushes tended to be on foreigners. And who could blame her when the gods of France, Germany, and Spain descended upon the pool deck. At home we spent tons of time together, and abroad we would both disappear into our own worlds. We were the perfect couple.

Unfortunately for me as we got older, our little charade became impossible to keep up. It was only a matter of time before Andrea needed to really date, and suddenly the illusion that we were a couple evaporated. But by then, in my early twenties, it didn't matter anymore. I had already mastered the art of lying in all of its forms, from silence and omission to self-deception and misrepresentation. I was willing to do whatever it took to survive.

WOW: The Women of the World

The world of high performance sport is intense. When you aren't buried deep in training, you are traveling all over the world competing. On the World Cup circuit we raced two days on, one day off for a six- or seven-city whirlwind tour. One year I started in St. Petersburg, Russia and arrived seventeen days later in Paris, France, having hit five other cities in between. What kept these trips bearable was the company I kept.

My roommate was Marcel, a married father of two who had defected with his wife to Canada from Czechoslovakia a few years earlier. On each stop of the circuit we would invite people over to our room to hang out together, spending many hours getting to know swimmers from other countries. In all of my years I never met another gay swimmer, or any gay athlete, for that matter.

We spoke about a lot of things, focusing largely on sport, which was the thing that bound us together. When the subject turned to sex I would go quiet, or find some excuse to leave the room for a few minutes so that I could escape the possibility of being questioned about my private life. With these friends I had a relatively safe place to be, ironic given that sport remains to this day one of the last environments for people to openly be gay.

But things were hardly perfect, like the time after I broke the world record during the World Cup circuit of 1991 in Sheffield,

England. I was talking to some friends when I learned that the most beautiful Italian swimmer, Lola DiCiaporro*, had decided that she wanted to sleep with me. Lola had the kind of beauty that ensured that whatever Lola wanted, Lola got. I must have had thirty guys come up to me and congratulate me, not on breaking the world record, but because Lola wanted me. If only they knew.

I was beside myself. There seemed to be no way out of this one. The hottest woman in the pool had publicly declared that she was going to have sex with me. I was the envy of every guy, but I would do anything to lose my seat in this game of musical chairs. Please choose someone else. You don't really want me, Lola. Trust me! But it was too late. She had made up her mind.

I started drinking that night in my hotel room with my teammates as they saluted my good fortune. My former accomplice, Andrea, gave me a sympathetic look. Even she could do nothing in this case. I was on my own. We arrived at the pub before the Italians, and I just I kept drinking. And drinking. And drinking. I remembered being in this awful situation before in my life, and knew that the best way out of it was good old-fashioned drinking until you got totally plastered.

Everyone was sympathetic. The guys understood your need to drink to calm the excitement, and the girls understood that you were an idiot and left you alone. In the end I paid the price physically, suffering a hangover from hell, but I had avoided an embarrassing moment with the Italian stallion-esse. All things considered, it worked out in my favor.

Of all the women of the world, it was the East Germans that I hung out with and was most connected to back then. There was something about these strong women's curious mixture of masculinity and femininity that I could relate to as a gay man from Calgary.

In February of 1990 I was in East Berlin for a competition when I received an invitation from three Olympic legends to be taken out for a birthday lunch. The Wall had come down in Berlin a few months earlier and not very much had changed yet in terms of the typically barren communist lifestyle of my friends. I have to admit that my expectations for the meal were not very high, but since nobody else was offering anything better, it was an invitation that I proudly accepted.

After preliminaries the next morning I hopped into Cornelia Sirch's Lada, the mass-produced square box that was one of the perks awarded to Soviet Bloc champions. Where the public waited seven years for one of these beauties, the champs went straight to the front of the line. Kathleen Nord, an Olympic Champion from the Seoul Olympics, sat in the passenger seat. Astrid Strauss, all six feet of her, sat next to me in the back.

We arrived at a restaurant that was like few I have ever seen. It was old European glamour, and an elegant maitre d' sat us at a booth. The glow of gold was all around us, from the mirrors and light fixtures to the stunning picture frames around masterpieces above our heads. I was given a menu, which Cornelia made me put down, telling me that this was their treat. As she ordered for all of us in rapid-fire German I understood a little of what she said, but was still astonished at what came next.

A full champagne service arrived, followed by soup, a large salad, and the most delicious roast beef I think I've ever had, which says something coming from beef country. A five-layered chocolate cake arrived for dessert, and finally came coffee with a large snifter of cognac. I sat in the middle of this swanky, elegant, regal restaurant, surrounded by the elite society of East Berlin, including three legends of East German swimming. I would have never imagined this in my wildest dreams. I took a moment. Happy birthday to me!

During coffee at the end of the meal we were in the middle of a conversation, Astrid to my left, and Kathleen and Cornelia in front of me. Kathleen started to speak in German, and she spoke so fast that I didn't understand what she was saying, but I could tell from the tone that she was getting upset. She would look to me and said my name from time to time, which was causing me some concern. Finally, after Astrid intervened, Kathleen burst into tears and jumped from the table.

I sat there quietly, waiting for some kind of explanation. Cornelia put her hand on mine from across the table, and said, "She can't handle this right now. It is too much for her to comprehend. For years she was told that westerners were bad, and today she is sitting here with you and she is laughing and sees for herself this is not true. She is coming to understand that everything she used to think is now gone. She doesn't know what to believe anymore." Given the confusion I was experiencing in my own life, I could empathize completely.

THREE'S COMPANY

My first gay relationship came during my first year of university, following a succession of one-sided infatuations with straight guys. My friend Ted was one of the last. He had big brown eyes, full lips, floppy dark hair, and a wicked sense of humor. I met him through friends at university when I was in my last year of high school.

Ted's family was prominent within the Conservative Party of Canada, but for a young man with such strong right-wing ties, Ted was really good about me being gay. It had remained unspoken for the first part of our friendship, but eventually we found ourselves in an awkward, lopsided three-way love triangle that involved a woman. Denise* wanted me, I wanted Ted, and Ted wanted Denise. And nobody was happy.

At that time I didn't admit to being gay. Not exactly. I admitted to having "feelings" for Ted, which I could admit might *seem* homosexual by nature but I told Ted I wasn't sure if that meant I was actually gay. It was just for him. Good try. But then I did something dubious. I asked Ted if he had feelings in return for me. It was a no win for him, because of course he had feelings; we were good friends. He tried to be clear that he didn't have any feelings like *that*, but he did have feelings. The last part was all I heard. I hung onto those words, desperately hoping for more than two years he would return my advances.

I don't know how Ted withstood it. At first I was hanging around so much that even his father joked that we were gay. Ha, ha. Hilarious. But he could see that I was intense. It was such a good feeling to be around someone for whom I had such strong feelings. But it was also frustrating, because ninety percent of the time all I could think about was how I could get Ted into bed. I never did, but you have never seen anyone try harder.

One night I went out with a girl from my swim team to give Ted a break from me. She had asked me a few times before if I wanted to go with her to a gay alternative bar in Calgary that was cool, but I had always declined out of sheer fear of being labeled again. We had never discussed me being gay, but she knew I had some artsy, cultured friends and was into the alternative scene. That night I finally got the nerve to go, and since I was going with a friend, and I knew her fairly well, it made the whole experience way easier.

My heart pounded out of my chest as we drove up to the bar and circled the block to find a parking spot. My sweaty palms made parallel parking a nightmare. But for my friend this was no big deal, and I played along like it was the same for me.

First entering the bar, I was struck by the elegance of it. The Parkside Lounge had booths and these stylish, green couches everywhere. There was a drag queen at the door to greet us, and I finally discovered what real drag looks like. My friend and I settled into a booth tucked away in the back part of the lounge where we felt safe.

It was thrilling to get in, to be in this space. Usually I went to pubs or bars around the university where stale beer and popcorn created the atmosphere. Here it was like being in another world with fashionably dressed people drinking cocktails from martini glasses. I felt like I had entered a secret underground world, and I loved it.

I danced to the great music, the whole time looking around and absorbing the atmosphere of the club, and that was when I saw him. Standing at the bar, about halfway down, was a beautiful man leaning over the counter whispering something to the bar man. He stopped and turned to look toward the dance floor. We made eye contact, and I couldn't stop staring. This was the most handsome man I had ever seen in person. He broke the stare first, looking away, embarrassed. But then he looked back really quickly. I flushed a bit and it was my turn to look away.

When I glanced back again he was gone. As I danced, I searched for him everywhere but I couldn't see him. He had vanished as quickly as he had appeared. As the next song came on I looked at the DJ booth. I saw the DJ placing records, but he was talking to someone in the shadows beside him. It was him! There was my beautiful guy.

I went for a drink at the bar when Mr. Beautiful appeared. I said hello. He said his name was John, and told me that his boyfriend, Rudy, the club owner, was spinning. He mentioned that they hadn't seen me around before. "No, this is my first night out," I replied. He wrote their number on a card and said to give them a call sometime if I would like to go to a movie or something. I called a day later on Monday morning. It had been the longest twenty-four hours of anticipation I had ever experienced. We set up a meeting for that Friday night, the three of us. It would be the beginning of a relationship that would last more than three years.

Rudy was the more mature of the two, at thirty-four when we met. He was a self-made entrepreneur with a heart of gold. Rudy could build and fix anything, spin records, finance the operation, and charm the pants off anybody he met. He was outgoing, generous, and kind. Rudy had a huge sense of family, taking care of his mother and father until their dying days. He was an Aquarian like me, which sometimes made life difficult for the two of us.

John was twenty-six when we met, a freshly graduated law student from the University of Alberta who had to article before passing the bar exams. He was intelligent, cultured, and extremely good looking, but he had the curse of insecurity, being a beautiful person who struggled to accept his own beauty. I spent a good deal of time trying to help him see himself differently so we could finally have sex.

In a way it was a perfect life. In terms of sex, the three of us were only sexual together a handful of times over the course of three years. It was more like there were a number of relationships made up by the three of us. There was John and Rudy; Rudy and Mark; Mark and John; and Rudy, Mark, and John.

There was a lot going on. John and Rudy loved architecture, gardening, records, food, clothes, collectibles, and anything camp. I learned about sex, and specifically about safe sex at a time when I might have done something stupid. I watched *All About Eve* and heard stories about Bette Davis and Judy Garland. I listened to all of the divas from Grace Jones to Maria Callas.

It was introduction to gay culture. I went to art openings and barbeques with gay and lesbian Calgarians—they did exist! I drank martinis and helped host dinner parties. I watched dirty movies and ate out at restaurants. I even got up early Saturday mornings to scavenge through second-hand stores for collectibles. Here I found myself part of a community where I could openly be myself, at least to a point.

I tried to compartmentalize my life, but my emotions didn't turn off so easily. Many times the residue of what I was feeling with John and Rudy would follow me into the pool. Often in this relationship I would feel insecure, and if I wasn't careful, I would find myself in a cycle where my insecurity spawned a need that wouldn't be met, which just made me more insecure. Standing on the starting blocks beside the best swimmers in the world was not a forgiving place for those with insecurity.

This relationship was kind of ironic, because I was from the world of competition, and yet was in a situation where I could never win, coming into this relationship where two people already had eight years together. Sometimes I felt lost in all of that history, slightly jealous and sad that they would always have something I would never and *could never* be a part of.

The thing about three people in love is that love doesn't ration itself evenly. Little things became real explosive issues, like where do you sleep and who sleeps with whom? Wanting a king-sized bed was one of the main frustrations of my life. We always talked of it, but for a long time I would sleep on a futon beside the bed watching John and Rudy sleeping and cuddling. Some nights I would have the taste of bile in my throat because I was so upset, feeling left out. I was in this relationship, but on the sidelines at the same time.

I was at the Seoul Olympics in 1988 when I realized how secure I had become in my insecurity. I was in the ready room before my 100-meter backstroke final and realized nobody had to beat me; I had already beaten myself. I had no confidence, no strong sense of who I was, or even a clear idea of what I wanted there. It was like I was watching my life unfold, and watching it through someone else's eyes. This was not how I dreamed I would feel before the supposed biggest race of my life. I ended a disappointing fifth, far removed from the medal I had hoped for.

John and Rudy always had the best intentions for me, and knew that this relationship wouldn't last forever. It would hurt at first when they encouraged me to see other guys, but they were right in their support. When I finally did leave, a year or so later, John acted very strangely. Rudy pulled me aside. "John's just not ready for you to go yet." I had come to have a close relationship with both, but Rudy and I really understood each other's drive and entrepreneurship. "If you think it is time, it is time." But this time, no matter what happened, I would never be entirely alone again as a gay man in Calgary.

CHAPTER FOUR

FAIRLY STRAIGHT FORWARD

SAY IT ISN'T SO

I never told any adult or person of authority in my life that I was gay until I was well into my twenties. The few close friends that I had told over the years had accepted it, but only after an initial period of wishing it wasn't so. My life, as compartmentalized as it was—given who knew, who didn't, and who I thought couldn't know—held together remarkably well for a long time. That would all change in 1991.

I had a good start to the year at the World Championships in Perth, Australia. My path crossed again with Debbie Muir, a legendary synchronized swimming coach from Calgary. Debbie had a Midas touch; everyone she worked with seemed to win Olympic or World Championship gold. We spent a lot of time together at this competition, and for the first time ever I won an individual medal at a major world meet, only six one-hundredths short of the gold medal. "What a thrilling race!" Debbie exclaimed when she saw me after. With eighteen months to go before the Olympics, everything seemed to be on track. My life was working.

The bomb hit later in August of that year, just eleven months before the 1992 Barcelona Olympics. Jeff Rouse, the swimmer I was chasing to be the best in the world, dropped 1.3 seconds from his World Championship final time, and in that one instant destroyed my dream. My seven years of small improvements, added together, equaled 1.2 seconds. Now I had eleven months to make that much improvement again, at the highest level of sport possible, if I still wanted to win the Olympics. Odds were very much against me. And to add salt to the wound, Rouse's record-breaking race had taken place in Alberta. My family had all been in the stands, witnessing my stunning defeat in person. It was only a race, but I had thrown essentially everything I had into it, and it was my whole life. I was struggling hugely with the place I found myself in.

A month later at a friend's wedding I ran into Debbie. "How are you?" she asked me. "Okay," I half-heartedly said. "Okay?" she questioned. "You are never just okay. What's going on?" "You really want to know?" I responded. She did. I told her that I had my butt kicked by Jeff Rouse, that I had to make seven years of improvement in one year, and that it looked like all of that work and progress of the past three years was for nothing. "It's not over." she said. "You can lose that much time if he has dropped it. You can learn to do some of that underwater stuff."

I could see in her eyes that she was off, her mind spinning with possibility. That was what made this woman so incredible. For Debbie there was no such thing as can't. It was just a matter of figuring out how. She had a natural gift at connecting individuals to their best. "You want to have lunch?" she asked me. I grinned from ear to ear. I left the reception with Debbie's phone number in my pocket and a bounce in my step.

We met the next Thursday, treating ourselves to the sanctuary of one of Calgary's finest restaurants for a late afternoon lunch. I laid my heart out for Debbie, finally feeling I was with someone I could do this with. I told her the situation I was in with Rouse, and how badly I wanted to win gold. She was the only one around me who actually knew what it was like to win Olympic gold. I told her that I had no money, and no spare time because I was already training up to six hours a day. And then the unthinkable happened. She asked if she could help.

Within days Debbie and I began working together a couple of times a week. One day after a set of underwater swimming for close to twenty-five meters, Debbie asked me how I felt. I almost choked. It was one of the first times in my career I had been asked and *not told* how I felt. There was an honest exchange between us. She was tough, pushing me hard physically to excel, but we were doing this together. In working together we completely clicked.

We connected on a human level. Debbie and I started hanging out together and slowly became very close friends. Our connection in the pool led to long discussions at dinners, or movies, or coffees stolen in the middle of the day. With Debbie I didn't have to censor who I was. I could just be. It was freeing, but as we spent more and more time together, and became closer as friends, I realized that I was going to have to share my secret with her. If I didn't it could jeopardize our friendship, and, besides, I didn't want to hide anymore.

We were at a cafe downtown on a Saturday afternoon. One of our favorite things to do was to go to funky shops and wander around the city. We were going to really treat ourselves and go to a matinee movie but decided to grab a quick bite first. Sitting across from each other in a booth, after we had ordered, I told her I had something I thought she should know, something that I needed to tell her.

I felt excited, but nervous. I had a feeling Debbie already knew, but we hadn't ever gone there. "What is it?" she asked. I paused. Saying those words was so hard. The air suddenly grew heavy. She pushed a little, asking again, "What is it?" I looked her in the eye and said "You know." She said that she thought she knew, but she needed to hear me say it. After a bit more resistance, I said, "I'm gay." I said it so softly that she didn't hear it the first time. I was already starting to go red and reacting to having said the words out loud, but I had to say them again. She got very teary eyed when she heard it, which scared me for a moment because I interpreted this as disappointment. I waited anxiously until she said, "It must have been so hard for you here."

I felt like the world had been lifted from my shoulders. I broke down and started crying tears of relief, and Debbie joined in. I still had my best friend. And even better, we were chasing this dream together more than ever.

THE MORALITY CLAUSE

There is a popular but incorrect belief that when someone wins a medal at the Olympics they make millions of dollars. From my silver medal in Seoul I earned $200 as the starter of a road race. That was the first and the last of my great Olympic earnings. There is usually one Olympian who benefits greatly from the games, and in 1988 it was rightfully Carolyn Waldo, double gold medallist in synchronized swimming. For the rest of us, we had to return to our lives and find an income.

Returning back to Canada as an Olympian was tough at that time. Ben Johnson's positive drug test following his winning the 100-meter dash put a dark cloud over all of us. Sometimes at public appearances you got the sense that the public's frustration and disappointment could inspire more egg throwing and jeering than cheering.

The 1988 Olympics ended in October, so going straight back to university was not possible. Instead, there was a chance to take a real break from school and swimming for the first time in years. I jumped on it and was like a lazy hibernating bear. John and Rudy were away, I had the run of their house, and I would lie on the couch, pop some of my mom's hors d'oeuvres in the oven that were left over from my welcome back neighborhood party, and watch sagas like the Godfather videos. It was an uninspired life. Until the phone rang one morning.

Diane Jones Konihowski, a legendary pentathlete, was looking for me. She was offering me a public speaking course. With no impending appointments for the next two months, I thought, why not? It was a weekend Toastmaster's crash course, and I was one of ten athletes taking this class. After it I decided it was useless to learn this skill and not do anything with it. Diane was developing a program to take athletes throughout the province to schools as public speakers, and I became the guinea pig. I would start the following week.

We arrived at the first elementary school on Tuesday. I really didn't know what I was getting myself into. I was waiting outside the gymnasium with Diane and the principal, and I could hear the kids entering from the other side of the door. The noise was increasing rapidly. One-hundred-and-twenty kids from grades one to three were in there waiting for me. I had butterflies and sweaty palms and felt I was going to faint, but thought, "How hard can this be? This is elementary school."

This was still one of the toughest crowds I've ever worked. It was a miracle to get them quiet, which quickly became surreal because this was not a crowd that should be quiet. No need to worry, it didn't last long. A little boy started to cry, some girls started talking, and one adventurous kid even crawled to my feet. I did my show anyway, getting varying levels of attention, but was able to hold the stage for twenty minutes. It felt like an eternity. The teachers were entertained, which meant good reviews, and for the next few months I took the show on the road with Diane. She would introduce me, and I would present to thousands and thousands of kids over the next months.

Word got out that I could speak well publicly, and eventually a friend asked if I could come and speak to his company, Investors Group. There wasn't really a payment involved, just a chance to do something in front of a corporate crowd.

I wrestled with how to alter the presentation I was giving to elementary school kids for these adults. I remembered that a Dale Carnegie class I had taken taught that you have earned the right to tell your own story, and the most effective speakers spoke at a grade four level. Since I had been speaking to grade four students and they loved it, I decided not to mess with success and I didn't change a thing.

The corporate crowd gave me a standing ovation. They thought I was animated, passionate, and enthusiastic—all the things in high school that had gotten me pegged as gay now were being celebrated. That speech was a big one for me in more ways than one. Not only would it give me a strong sense of self-confidence, it would lead to financing my Olympic dream in Barcelona.

The general manager of this branch of the Investors Group had children in sport, and understood completely how challenging it was to chase your dreams. He was willing to do something about it while he had the opportunity. He invited his boss to hear me. His boss then took me to his boss, who then took me to the CEO and chair of the board. Eighteen months after I first spoke to this company I had a six-figure, two-year deal that would ensure that all of my needs as an athlete working toward the Olympics would be met.

But there was a catch. With every corporate contract I signed there would be some morality clause spelling out what would happen should I be caught in any act that would bring ill will or public disdain against the company. It was put there due to the unfortunate climate of suspicion throughout corporate Canada following the aftermath of the Ben Johnson affair. But as a gay man this clause haunted me.

I had become very good at keeping my lives separate, my gayness unmentioned in the swimming and corporate worlds, but the stakes were becoming higher and higher each step upward I took. I struggled. Even though I was a good speaker and would deliver on the contract, I felt deceitful. I was everything they thought I was, and not what they thought I was at the same time. My needs overruled my moral dilemma at this time. I had financially supported myself for a few years already, and really needed the money to swim, so I signed.

That night I went for a drive with my dad, as we had so many times going to and from the swimming pool when I was growing up. I broke the news to him that I had a sponsor, and it was one of the most genuinely happy moments I ever had with him. I hadn't lived up to his expectations as the stud jock son in so many ways, and although he was not an overly materialistic person, this sponsorship deal gave me great value in his eyes. He was very proud of me, beaming. It made me feel great. Finally I seemed to be making good with Dad. And I was certain that I didn't want to do anything to screw this up.

Do the Hustle

I was beginning to juggle many balls in my life. At swimming I was now an Olympic medal contender, I had sponsors and the beginnings of a public life, and I was a young man in my twenties with no outlet for sex. It was nearly impossible to fulfill my sexual needs as I neared the pinnacle of my athletic success without giving myself away. I was single, had no girlfriend, but didn't want anyone to know that I was gay. I went out sometimes with teammates to the straight bars, but it was too hard to navigate the horny, drunken women or the too-often violent men.

I was as creative as I could be. Debbie would take me in her tinted-windowed car down to the gay bar, for example, and I sat in the back and tried to poke my head up to see what was going on without being caught. The tint worked so well that not only could no one see me, I couldn't see them either. It was hilarious and pathetic all at the same time.

In the summer of 1991, after I was beaten by Jeff Rouse in my race, I had to be in Toronto for some public relations work. I was staying in a hotel in the downtown core, and I was desperate—to escape the nightmare of Jeff, to connect with a gay person, to feel alive for a moment. I was slowly going crazy in my hotel room, knowing there was a thriving gay scene somewhere close by but feeling isolated and unable to be a part of it. I was held hostage by my fame, or at least by my own fear of what might happen if I got caught, of what I might lose at that time if the truth came out.

Later that day I left the hotel and went for dinner on the fringe of where I thought the gay scene was, and I saw a gay newspaper in a box on the street. I grabbed one and snuck it under my shirt to take to the hotel. I tried not to run.

Back in the privacy of my room I stumbled upon the advertisements at the back of the paper for massage. For a fee someone would come to see me. I could have interaction, and as terrifying as it was to imagine a complete stranger coming to see me, it seemed to be one of the few options available. It would be a bit strange paying for sex, but with payment came a contractual obligation, and a promise of discretion. My business contracts with a morality clause had led to the idea of sex with a confidentiality clause.

There was one guy who sounded great. Before I could stop myself, I called him. He lived two minutes away, but preferred if I went with him to his place. He would come and get me. He told me to look out for the blond in the green khaki pants. "Oh my God," I thought to myself. "This is really happening."

When I saw all six feet three inches of him, my heart missed a beat. He was strapping, with a strong jaw, beautiful big blue eyes, gorgeous with an intensity that was electric. He took me up to his loft through an alley. It was spacious and sparse, very hip and modern, with a futon on the floor, lots of white, and a *Globe and Mail* and *Vanity Fair* sitting on a workbench waiting to be read.

His name was Daniel*. He had been an intellectually gifted child, which had left him a bit of a loner. He had ended up at an Ivey League school, had a degree in applied science and had worked at impressive organizations early in his life. I would slowly get to know more about him the more I visited.

One night I was at Daniel's and the phone rang. He answered, and immediately turned his back to me and kept his voice down. He pulled the extension as far away from the common area as possible and spoke for at least fifteen minutes before rejoining me, lying on the futon. "Who was that?" I asked. "I can't say." I was glad that was his answer, as that was what I thought was part of the deal. "But I will say it was one of the top three box office stars in the world that I met while working in the United States." I always had my suspicions of who had been on the other end of that phone, especially given the media and denials through the years, but it would never be confirmed. That was what I liked about Daniel. Although he was a hustler, he was still a man of honor.

With my limited access to other gay people, and my intensity of feeling, it wasn't long before I fell in love with Daniel. I saw him many times over a period of months, but the more I saw him the more distance he put between us. He was working after all, and love from his side was an occupational hazard that he couldn't afford. This only served to make me try harder. I put myself in some dangerous positions, like running from a public relations event to a public phone so that I could make an appointment to meet with Daniel that night. I told myself it was exciting, but in truth it was becoming harder and harder to keep everything under control. This was just a little taste of what was soon to come.

THE READY ROOM

The Olympic year of 1992 was the first truly empowering, freeing time in my adult life. Working with Debbie throughout that year had created for me a friendship where I could completely be myself, and although that space was small, it helped me expand in confidence a thousandfold in and out of the pool. I opened up and discovered different ways to connect with guys, as if some kind of survival mechanism kicked in, and some innate dormant skill set came to the surface.

I would walk down the street and notice another man looking at me. To a straight person this wouldn't have struck them, but the look was just a little too long, and my inner "gaydar" went off. Sure enough, I would glance back and find the man looking back at me, too. Debbie was fascinated with this gay vibe, and how quickly two men could exchange information and identify one another.

And just like I associated my hustler friend with integrity, Debbie would show me that she also valued my newly developed skill. She recognized that something important had happened that year. Through our relationship I had been able to change how I felt about myself in terms of being gay. Where in the past I had wasted a lot of my energy by keeping a secret and hating myself for it, with Debbie I was completely open. I could focus my energy much better, had significantly more self-esteem, and was much more open to life in general.

In the final weeks before leaving North America for the European training camp leading up to the Olympics, the Canadian swimming team gathered for a few days of light training in California. Debbie came down to work with me one last time on my underwater starts and to help me have a couple days of fun before the final few serious weeks before my race.

We were staying at a new hotel, and one night coming back from dinner we noticed this handsome young man working at the concierge desk. As we passed him he looked at me just a little bit too long. My heart pounded stronger. I shared with Debbie that I thought he might be gay. She smiled and asked me what I was going to do about it.

I came up with a plan to find out if he was gay or not. I was with Debbie in her room, wrestling with the idea of doing this. I kept thinking, I can't do this, I'm part of the Olympic team. I can't try to pick this guy up. Then Debbie would taunt me, "Oh, come on. You're not going to miss the opportunity to meet this guy, are you?" She watched me get up enough courage to get to the door, and then take a few steps back, filled with doubt. Finally, after a couple of times, I made it into the elevator. As the doors closed there was no going back.

When I arrived downstairs, luck was on my side because there weren't any swimmers, coaches, or team managers around, and

Shane*, Mr. Handsome, was still at the desk. As I approached, our eyes met and we couldn't break each other's gaze. There was electricity in the air, attraction at first sight.

I had brought down a poster tube that Debbie had in the room, and asked how much it might cost to send this to Calgary *special delivery*. He smiled at my last two words. In order to connect, I had to talk a kind of double talk, a language filled with innuendo obvious enough for the other person to see, but not obvious enough that I gave myself away as gay in case he wasn't. But he was. We spoke for a few minutes before I realized that some of the swimmers were beginning to arrive back from dinner. I grabbed the poster tube, and told him I had to go. "I get off at 9 p.m.," he said before I rushed off.

Back in the room I told Debbie I had been right. We screamed together. In that time it was such a thrill for me to take a risk and have it pay off. Fortunately, my gaydar tended to serve me well.

I met Shane for a drink off-site, and the next day we had a dinner date. We ended up in my hotel room but were never quite comfortable; me because I was bringing a man into a hotel filled with my Olympic teammates, and he because he was an employee breaking the rule of visiting a guest's room. But we were so turned on by each other we risked it. His getting out of the hotel undetected was the climax after the climax. For me it was a much needed release before what lay ahead.

* * *

Arriving in Barcelona for the Olympics was exhilarating. There was something about the city, the history, architecture, and the Spanish lifestyle and culture that created an irresistible combination for me. I felt good the whole time I was there.

The Olympic Village itself was stunning. It was built close to the sea, so there was water and beach within minutes of our residences. The cafeteria was part of a center that included computers to communicate with other athletes, retail stores, and a post office. There were bowling alleys, chill-out music lounges, even a cinema with multiple screens. I felt solid and focused in the days before my race.

The Olympics is a game of waiting—first for the competition to start, and then for your event on the program. I didn't race until day six, which meant that night after night I went to the pool to watch the finals. It is an all or nothing game, and being the best swimmer in the world is not actually enough to win the Olympics. You have to be able to connect to your highest possible performance on the day, in the moment. This is what makes it so exciting—you never know for sure what will happen, and the finals are always full of surprises.

I watched the 200-meter backstroke where Spaniard Martin Lopez-Zubero won, but he looked labored, like the pressure of the world was too much for him. The same heaviness was plaguing my Canadian teammates, only we weren't winning. Although we had many swimmers make it to the finals, by day five no one had made it to the medal podium.

Like it or not, there was a pressure that built as each day passed, and I would need a big surprise in my swim if I was to win, because I was certainly not the favorite in my race. I watched night after night as my teammates left the pool with broken dreams, and paid close attention to comfort them but not take on that feeling myself. I had to be in a different headspace entirely. It would be Debbie, once again, who would give me that kick.

A few weeks before I swam my race in Barcelona, a package had arrived for me from Canada. Getting mail was a highlight of the day, something to break the boredom. The package was from Debbie and it included some CDs, pictures, and a letter, but the letter was marked "not to be opened until day before your race." I tucked it away, curious but following the instructions.

It was July 29 at around 9:30 p.m., and my roommate also had to swim the next day, so we started to get ready for bed. I spent time opening all kinds of mail that had come in, and our team manager dropped by to say good night. I remembered that I had an envelope from Debbie, and when my roommate went to brush his teeth, I opened it. I started to read.

"Remember when you were a little bit younger (about twenty-nine days younger)? You went up to the front desk of the hotel you were staying in to get some change and your special friend helped you. You looked at this person and thought, Hmmmm, I'd like to get something going with you ... *and so you did!*"

There had been a "just do it" Nike ad campaign at that time, and Debbie used it as a prototype to send me this message at the Olympics. She continued, "You put it all on the line then and now here you are again. That nervous/scared feeling is back. WOW—what fun! You get to go out on a limb again, take a risk, and feel the thrill of going for something you really want but don't know for sure if you'll get. You're going for the win (did your stomach just flip?) and in the fifty-odd seconds you are out there, you will love the thrill and excitement of this performance. And at the end of the day when all is said and done just remember that you have learned more than just how to swim fast ... *you have learned to live your life with passion!!*"

Debbie made me laugh. Only she could turn a hotel pick-up into such inspirational fare. I cried when we spoke on the phone the next morning after heats, because of her letter but more because we both had this feeling that I was going to win. But neither of us spoke it for fear of jinxing it. We just knew.

Thirty minutes before the final of my race at the Olympics I entered the marshaling area. I would have no contact with anyone outside, just my competitors and the officials. The eight guys from around the world who would be competing sat in what is called the ready room, with chairs, four walls, and one doorway. After this final resting pit, the wait is over; the chief marshal arrives and it is your turn to do battle in the Olympic pool.

With me I had my tracksuit, goggles, lucky towel, which I had used whenever I had broken records, and the letter from Debbie. At one point I was sitting there, facing all of my competitors, thinking about how I had gotten to this point. It was out of character—I wouldn't have expected to think of this—but as I looked at the seven other guys I realized that we *all* had swum up to six hours a day, missed school, made sacrifices. So what distinguishes us? What makes me different?

I gazed around the room slowly. The best swimmers from Russia, Cuba, the United States, Spain, Germany, and France were in front of me. And I *was* different. I was *the fag*. And in that moment I owned my truth completely. Holding Debbie's letter in my hand inside my tracksuit pocket, I thought, "If these guys knew how hard it was for me to get here, they wouldn't believe it. They have no bloody clue what I have been through. Or how strong I am."

I felt energy pulse through my hands and into my wrists and forearms, creating a pins and needles effect. I had to take a break. I took a slow breath, not too deep. I would need to conserve this energy for my upcoming race. But the transformation had happened. In the last minutes before the biggest moment of my life, all those years of feeling like crap changed into a positive force. I had never felt so alive, so completely primed with energy.

I went out and swam, dropping more than 1.2 seconds from my personal best, and out-touching Jeff Rouse from the United States at the wall by six one-hundredths of a second to win the first gold medal for Canada in Barcelona. It was a Thursday night. I'll never forget it.

During the race I had that feeling again, like I knew I was going to win. It started in the last ten meters when time became very slow, even though we were swimming fast. I just felt like I had never felt before at the end of a race—strong, charging, focused. I wouldn't be sure until the results came up on the big screen.

When I saw my name blink first, which meant that I had won the race, I simply reacted, jumping and screaming out of pure joy before any conscious thought. Then it started to hit me. I won. I had WON this race. I HAD WON THE OLYMPICS! All I remember was thinking, "OH MY GOD!" as the shock took over.

CHAPTER FIVE

BAM!

THE GUY FROM *TIME*

My life began to change almost instantly after I won the gold medal. The world press descended, firing questions at me in the interview room immediately following the race. I struggled through my surprise to answer. The next night my parents and I had a long, live interview on national television that included watching the playback of the final moments of my race. I received very intense attention for a day or two, but then the enormity of the Olympics took over, thankfully, and the news media was off chasing the latest mcdallists from that day. The machine moved on. Still, it was becoming clear to me that things would never be quite the same as they were before.

Finishing competition after the first week meant I could enjoy the second week of the Games. My favorite thing to do was watch the athletics competition, and it was at the track one night that it all hit me. I burst into tears during the playing of the national anthem for one of the women's events, partly out of happiness for the winner, but mostly from realizing that this had also happened to me a few days earlier.

As the days passed, I would be somewhere and suddenly remember, "Oh my God! I've won the Olympics." I was just in the beginnings of adjusting to this reality when I also saw that I would have to adjust to how other people responded to me.

One day I was walking through the Village and two Canadian athletes stopped me to ask for my autograph. It was such a surprise to me. *My* autograph? I never thought of myself in those terms. I remembered prior Games, seeing Carolyn Waldo play this role, and I realized this time was my turn. But I still didn't quite expect how much people would respond.

When I went outside the Olympic Village, someone, almost always a Canadian, or a Spaniard who was a Lopez-Zubero fan, or a really radical swimming fan who knew everyone, would suddenly call me by name. People greeted me with such genuine congratulations, which I responded to, but I could see already that life was going to be much different from before.

I had always promised myself that after the Olympics I would finally invest time in my personal life. I wasn't willing to continue keeping separate lives, especially after the freedom and empowerment I had experienced through my friendship with Debbie. I had reached my dream and I really thought I would finally focus my energy on other parts of my life. I was completely naive. It wasn't going to be that way at all.

My first steps out of the Olympic bubble and back into everyday life happened at Gatwick Airport as we flew back to Calgary through London. Everybody was making such a fuss about me that it was embarrassing. There was even a woman from Canadian Airlines to greet us at the plane.

I had grabbed the first flight out, coming straight from the closing ceremonies. I had hopped on the bus with my bags in the wee, wee hours of the morning to wait in line for my seat on the plane. This was the normal routine of an athlete anyway, and it was fun to see that even Lloyd Robertson, one of our television anchormen, had to wait in line.

But in London all of that changed. I was whisked to a lounge, and brought a hot breakfast, complete with eggs, sausage, tomatoes, and beans. As I got on the plane with my team manager, Ann Schulman, one of the stewardesses said loudly enough for the whole business class section to hear, "Oh, it is the guy from *Time*!" I almost died of embarrassment but muttered that yes, it was me.

I had seen the international edition, which had an article inside about upsets at the Olympics and a picture of my victory in the 100-meter backstroke. The flight attendant brought me the Canadian edition, which I hadn't seen yet. If I hadn't already been buckled in, I would have fallen out of my seat when I opened it. There was my face staring back at me from the magazine cover. Gulp! I was on the cover of *Time*! Beside me Ann let out a shriek, and I promptly did the same.

After the initial excitement, slowly came the dreaded realization. For years I had always promised myself that the sacrifice I had made in my personal life for my swimming career would be settled after the Olympics were over. I would focus on a relationship and building a life. But now, how?

Happily Ever After

To say life was frantic when I got back from Barcelona in 1992 would be an understatement. Somehow in between everything else that was going on, a friend convinced me to go see a unique bungalow with magnificent city views on a golf course five minutes away from downtown Calgary. It was put on the market by the architect who had designed and built it.

I fell in love at first sight and I had to have this house. It had the potential to become my home, which was a major priority for me at this time. I had grown up seeing my parents, and then John and Rudy, creating homes and happy lives. I longed for a relationship, a home, building and sharing a life with someone, so on top of all that was happening, I bought this house.

I took possession at the end of 1992. Unfortunately, as a newly crowned Olympic Champion, demand kept me mostly away from home. Quite frankly, during that time, I didn't know where I was half the time when I woke up, let alone have any idea what home, security, or routine felt like.

I was in Toronto meeting with agents on Monday, driving to Barrie, Ontario to give an inspirational speech about healthy living to high school kids on Tuesday, meeting on Wednesday morning with potential corporate sponsors in Montreal, on a plane to Halifax for a speech for the Special Olympics on Thursday, back to Toronto for a taping of a television show on Friday morning, and trying to get to Calgary for the weekend. I was living on planes, trains, limousines, and taxis.

I crisscrossed the country, but spent the majority of my time in Toronto, and it was here that I reconnected with an old friend from swimming, Rhonda*. Post-Barcelona there were very few people who I felt I could really open up with. My life seemed so great, which it was, but mostly it was complicated. Rhonda understood a lot of what I was going through because she had been a closeted gay woman who had been in the Olympics. Now she invited me into her world.

At the time Rhonda was dating Joan*, who was managing a successful restaurant chain. One night I was talking to Rhonda about my desire to build a life with someone, and about how, given my new reality, I didn't know how I was going to find someone. Joan said to Rhonda, "What about Peter*?" Rhonda was surprised. "Peter is gay? Peter from King Street? Six foot three, rower, big personality? No!" Joan grinned, "Yes, he's gay, silly. What do you think about him for Mark?" I was all ears by now. I sat upright, thinking that it didn't really matter what Rhonda thought, he sounded good to me.

We went to the restaurant the next night Peter worked. I sat staring at him every time he walked by. He was cute, tall, strong. I had butterflies in my stomach. After work he came with us and we got along well and had a good time. Peter was a bit younger than I and was new to the gay scene. I was new to it, too, in a way, certainly in Toronto. But something happened to me almost immediately after meeting Peter. I knew that I wanted to be with someone, and I didn't know how to meet people, other than hiring them or through my limited network of gay friends. Peter was funny, extroverted, athletic. He was externally exactly what I had always dreamed. Before getting to know him at all, I very quickly—*too quickly*—saw a future with him. I had it all mapped out. My delusion was deep, as would be my denial that anything was wrong.

Our timing was the first bad omen. We met in the fall of 1992, and Peter was leaving after Christmas for a European trip that had been a long time in the planning. We took advantage of the time before he left, including bringing in the new year together at a dinner party at my house in Calgary with friends. That didn't go so well. I had the beginnings of the flu. Peter got obnoxiously drunk, swung from the chandelier, and squeezed Debbie so hard I feared for her life. It was the beginning of trouble but I didn't want to see it.

When you live in a self-imposed prison, afraid to be who you really are, there is a natural fear that envelops you, limiting your perception of choice in life. Being thrust into the public eye closed me down. The steps I had taken to be open and free with Debbie the year before were gone, as if I had reverted to my old, scared ways. I was so deeply closeted at this time that it never occurred to me that if things didn't work out with Peter I might find someone else.

Security, in my mind, depended on keeping things right with the guy in front of me, so I didn't let myself see the flaws. I had a good time with this guy, you would never guess he was gay, and I was going to spend the rest of my life with him. It was that simple. It wasn't necessarily based on love. It was primarily based on filling a need. I wanted someone in my life. I needed a way to fulfill my sexuality and relationship fantasies. I didn't want to go to gay bars, to hire hustlers, to put myself in dangerous positions anymore. This was a safe and comfortable option, providing me security and home amidst a chaotic life.

Poor Peter. I hit him like a wave. He wasn't anywhere near this thinking. He was having a good time, a young guy in Toronto discovering a new side of life he had denied for years. I was in Calgary, feeling our conversations becoming more and more banal, but not wanting to acknowledge that something was wrong or simply missing. There was too much at stake, and to endure the endless publicity tours that were still a part of my life, I had to believe that soon I would create a steady home with this guy.

Peter left for his three-month trip and I immediately began planning for the apartment we would find in Toronto when he got back. I was going to split my time between Toronto and Calgary. I didn't realize just how desperate I was, how out of touch. I had our whole future mapped out as if it was some race at the Olympics. I just needed room to live my gay life on one hand, but still carry on being that guy from *Time* on the other. I needed to be with someone who could help me bridge that gap. I convinced myself that Peter could do this for me. But I hung all of these needs onto Peter without knowing if any of this was what *he* needed. As far as I was concerned, he just needed to get back from Europe so we could start living happily ever after.

A Day to Remember

I always promised myself that I wouldn't choose some major holiday, like Christmas or a special birthday, to come out and tell my family I was gay. I always had a sense it would cling to the occasion, and could even leave lasting damage, so that every Christmas from that one forward would be remembered first as the day Mark came out, and then as Jesus's birthday, as the day Santa's coming, and all that jazz.

I woke up on a perfectly clear November day in 1992 and received my daily call from Peter. We were in the final stages of getting ready for his trip, and things in his life were changing rapidly. He exploded over the phone the moment I said hello. "I just told my parents I am gay," he said. Long pause. He continued, "I just couldn't stand it anymore. So I told them everything, including you. They were surprised I am gay. They were surprised you're gay, too." It was a good thing he felt like talking, because I went into shock and couldn't respond anyway. Peter told his parents that he was gay. I couldn't believe that he had come out to them. We had talked about whether we would do it sometime, but more as a philosophical idea than an action plan. And then for good measure he told them I was gay, too. *My* parents didn't even know yet. But on this day that was all about to change.

For many years the talk about women and marriage and kids, all those little pressures to have a family, were put aside as I journeyed toward the Olympics. I had thought that my parents weren't pushing the issue anymore because they had clicked into the fact that I was gay. I couldn't have been more wrong.

My mother and father were in complete denial. They had eased back because they knew that I had no time for a serious relationship at that point in my life. But shortly after Barcelona, after moving into the new house on the golf course, my mom came over. As we walked around looking at the sprawling decks that circled the property, she very causally said, "This would be a beautiful place for a wedding." It was the way she said it. I knew what she meant was "This would be a beautiful place for *your* wedding." I stopped in my tracks for a moment, feeling a bit winded, like she had snuck a rabbit punch when I wasn't looking.

I really thought that the time of innuendo and double meaning was over. But now, post-Barcelona, it was back in full force. So on this particular November day, I decided it was time to let people in my life know the whole story, and I came up with a plan. First I'll tell my family. Then I'll tell my agents. Then once and for all we can make it public.

I started the coming-out process that day by telling my sister, Colleen. I called her over to my house and, after two-and-a-half cups of tea and lots of reminiscing, I got the words out of my mouth. It was still early in the game of declaring my homosexuality. I said it with no pride at all, more of a sheepish embarrassment, squeaking out "I am gay" in barely a whisper. But she was terrific. She was honest, said she had wondered, then hugged me.

My being bullied at school had a direct impact on my relationship with Colleen. I understood the expression "a cycle of violence," because every time that something awful happened to me it was only a matter of time before I needed to take that out on someone else.

Colleen was an easy target, only in that she was there, not because she was weak. On the contrary, she was one of the toughest people I knew. Colleen once kicked a hole in my parents' bedroom door after I picked on her so much she exploded. I had locked myself in there and she was coming to get me, very much like Jack Nicholson in *The Shining*. I called her the nastiest names. She threw hot tea on me. I smacked her face.

For a few years in our teens we were the worst of enemies, taunting each other every night at the dinner table until either my mother or my father broke it up. Over the years we had become closer again, but there was still a slight distance, and my news helped Colleen understand how this had affected our relationship.

After the initial emotional outburst, Colleen said, "You have to tell Mom and Dad." "When?" I asked. "Now," she said. I freaked out but before I could stop her she called our parents and told them we were driving over and that I had something to tell them. I wanted to kill her, but I was on a roll; my truth was in motion, and suddenly the moment that I had always been waiting for was here.

Both of my parents were excited to see me. Around that time I seemed to be awarded a new title every week, from athlete of the year to an inductee into some hall of fame. I am sure that they thought I was there to share some breaking good news as the Olympic year drew to an end. They seemed to be expecting more of an Order of Canada kind of announcement rather than the real-life drama that was about to unfold. They really didn't see it coming.

I asked them to sit down, which started to shift the feeling in the kitchen. My parents looked a bit puzzled, because this was more serious than they had expected. Colleen remained standing behind me, with Mom to my right and Dad directly ahead of me at the kitchen table. "What is it?" my mom asked. I was finding it hard to say anything. There was a sick feeling deep inside my stomach, but also a strangely thrilling sensation, as if I was so scared I couldn't wait to alleviate the fear by finally getting this secret out in the open. I was past the point of no return, but I will never forget how hard it was to finally say those three little words. "I ... am ... GAAAAAY." The words flew through the air, the entire scene captured in my mind in slow motion, watching as the connection of what I had just said and what it meant hit both my parents at the same time.

I had told people already, but this time the words took on a heaviness that made time stand still. Both of my parents had intense emotional reactions. Their eyes filled with shock and then tears. Their faces looked beaten, as if I had hit them with my words.

I expected my father to take it badly. He actually surprised me a bit by whispering through his tears, "I still love you." It was my mom's reaction that was devastating. She just kept saying she couldn't believe it. "Are you sure?" I followed her into the dining room where she whispered questions to me through her tears, shaking her head as she asked, "What will people say?" She had this look in her eyes that was deeply sad, but at the same time distant, like in this moment of truth I had betrayed her. We had been so incredibly close at one point in my life. It killed me to see her so distraught.

Thirty minutes later I sat staring at the steering wheel of my car, outside my parents' house in Calgary. "Gee, that went well!" I said sarcastically to myself. Colleen had stayed behind to calm my folks. I had always thought that telling my parents that I was gay would somehow make us closer, make up in an instant all of those years that we had been estranged. It was a foolish thought. After all, it had taken me years to accept it myself, and even to that day I wasn't completely comfortable with the thought. I had come a long way from the time when I first saw two guys kissing and it made me feel sick. But that was part of the problem. Because I wasn't completely comfortable in my own skin, I wasn't really looking for understanding. I needed my parents' support, solidarity, and strength. Instead they were inside sobbing, complete wrecks at the news that their medal-winning, speech-giving, award-receiving, dress-cutting son was gay.

It wasn't until later that evening that I realized that it was November 11th, Remembrance Day. How appropriate, I thought. A day none of us will *ever* forget. My earlier plan had been so simple. First I would tell my family. Then I would finally talk to my agent. Then the general public would know. After Mom and Dad, the conclusion was simple. Abort plan!

THE TRAIN DERAILED

About a year and a half before the Barcelona Olympics, a friend of mine introduced me to an agent with the International Management Group (IMG). I met him for lunch while at a swim meet. We talked about the possibility of him representing me. Public speaking had become a full-time source of income for me, and if I was to have any chance of focusing on becoming an Olympic champion, then I needed some support managing the business side of my life.

It was a strange experience, because it was like an audition. I needed help, this guy had the means to help me, and I had twenty minutes or so to make my case. "Usually IMG wouldn't really be the right fit for a swimmer without a world title or record, and even then the market is small," he started. "But seeing as you already have a sponsor, and your public speaking is something we could really help you manage, I think this could work." It was the first step.

Many weeks later he would meet my mom and dad in Calgary, the last formality before we put pen to paper. It was exciting, especially for my dad. This was business, and my dad liked that I was being represented by this agency. He asked some questions, but clearly gave me the look throughout the meal that he was impressed. My mom thought my potential agent was a nice man, and that this was a great thing.

When I went into the Toronto offices of IMG to sign the contract, Brett Hull, the hockey star, was also visiting that day. I am not a big watcher of professional sport, but even I knew this guy because he was on commercials at the time. He was rock solid, and very intimidating, but I butched it up the best I could to be in the same stratosphere of masculinity. The place was bursting with macho power, titans bringing the worlds of sport and business together. I officially signed as one of their athletes. And so it began.

IMG created a well-crafted marketing and sponsorship plan that took my public profile to a new level leading up to the Barcelona Olympics. First they signed me a modest contract with Speedo, a natural. Then came a contract with clothier Bugle Boy. This deal was also modest, but included a bus shelter campaign that would run across the country and it came with bonuses. This turned out to be a great experience, but I have to admit, it was kind of strange to be waiting for the bus beside a blown-up picture of myself. Then came a not-so-modest contract with the Canadian Cattlemen's Association, the beef people. A renegotiation with Investors Group followed. IMG was busy making me busy. They organized photo shoots and business deals for me, got me interviews and profiles in the *Globe and Mail*, the Canadian press, *Maclean's*, on CBC and on CTV. IMG was doing a great job, but a lot was riding on my Olympic result.

Almost immediately after winning the 100-meter backstroke in Barcelona, the IMG machine kicked in to take my already high public profile even higher. I arrived home in Calgary to a spectacle of T-shirts, cameras, and friends. Requests for speaking and interviews came pouring in and we just kept saying yes to them all. It was like a train that had left the station but I only had one foot on it. I was trying to keep my balance but it was becoming harder, largely by my own doing. I made the mistake of thinking I could do it all. From Toronto to Calgary to Fort McMurray to Regina to San Francisco back to Toronto in five days. Two days off and then I would travel across the country all over again. "Sure, I travel all the time like that with swimming," I said. But I wasn't thinking. I didn't know how hard it would be, especially given that I had a secret that could bring the entire machine crashing down if exposed.

Fame made living a double life doubly hard. Increased recognition had started with the win and the cover of *Time*, but then came a commercial for beef. Once on TV, even if it is just a commercial, I was amazed at how people suddenly react to you. The recognition factor multiplies by a thousand. (Although I did a commercial for beef, it was interesting to see how many people thought I was doing something for milk. Wrong part of the cow!) A book deal with Penguin came next, followed by a line of clothing with Sears, then a twelve-city speaking tour with David Chilton, the wealthy barber. It didn't ever seem to end.

Instead it started to crack. Rumors were starting to circulate that I was gay, and it was becoming a problem.

It started with a *Frank* magazine article. *Frank* was a monthly publication from Ottawa based on rumor, speculation, and part truths. It had a small but influential readership. Some of those who read it could move and shake, and articles sometimes had a nasty way of creating media buzz. In the fall of 1992 there was an article about Svend Robinson and me being seen together at a local gay bar. At that

On Bondi Beach in Australia. I visited in 1993 and moved there
in 1994 for 2 years. I studied politics by day, and at night felt
liberated to finally explore being gay.

Courtesy of Mark Tewksbury

With my dear friend
Nola, in Australia.

Courtesy of Mark Tewksbury

Tattooed, blond me in 1998, screaming
to come out, despite myself.

Courtesy of Mark Tewksbury

My partner of three years, Benjamin. It was with Benjamin's support
that I came out publicly in 1998.

Courtesy of Mark Tewksbury

That's me in the middle, out and about in full-blown drag, Halloween 2001. Once was enough!

Receiving the International Person of the Year Award at the Pride Parade in São Paulo, Brazil, 2005.

Running a half-marathon with Megan Fowler, my friend from the Canadian Olympic Committee. This race would be a precursor for my 2003 dream of finishing the New York City Marathon.

© Marasport

With Angelica Huston at the Kentucky Derby. Look at the hat!

Receiving an honorary doctorate from the University of Western Ontario in 2001, recognizing my ethical leadership and active humanitarianism. This was a huge honor for me.

Courtesy of The University of Western Ontario

A simple speech to a grade four class in 1988 would lead to a professional career for the next 18 years and counting. To this day, speaking to a live audience is one of my favorite ways to make a living.

Courtesy of Mark Tewksbury

Carrying the torch in the pre-Olympic relay, leading up to the 2004 Summer Olympic Games in Athens. These Games would bring me full circle, being at the city we chose when I was part of the IOC commission, but doing CBC prime time television swimming coverage during the Games instead of politics.

In my role in the "other" sports movement, as Co-President of the 1st World Outgames, Montreal 2006. Pictured here in Montreal with, left to right, Gerald Trembley, the Mayor of Montreal; Lucie Duguay, Co-President of Montreal 2006; and Louise Roy, CEO.

© Olivier Sanson

The logo for the 1st World Outgames, in front of Montreal's City Hall. We have had unprecedented support from LGBT sport, government and tourism officials.

Courtesy of Mark Tewksbury

Back at home in Calgary with my family in 2005 for my birthday. Megan, my niece, has brought the whole family closer together than ever before.

Courtesy of Mark Tewksbury

time Svend was the first openly gay parliamentarian in the House of Commons. As nice as this might have been, it never happened. But of course the article wasn't intended to reveal that particular truth, it was about the other one. This was the first time my sexuality hit the public domain this broadly.

My agents at IMG had flipped out when they heard about the impending article. They had my lawyer write a letter to the publication threatening them if they printed this story, but they neglected to tell me about it. Of course, none of us wanted to talk about "this gay thing," but it was getting more and more difficult to avoid having a conversation about it.

The word on the street was starting to get around that the Olympic swimmer was gay. In a way it was crazy that it didn't break completely, because I had been out in Calgary with John and Rudy years earlier. But it didn't come out that way. It was something else entirely.

Toward the end of 1992, I traveled down to New York City with one of my agents to film a commercial for the Dale Carnegie organization. We arrived the night before, shooting not starting until the next afternoon, because we wanted to have a bit of a night on the town. We stayed at IMG founder Mark McCormack's private suite at the exclusive Mark Hotel in the Upper East Side. The apartment had two suites to it, so both my agent and I had our own apartment within the apartment. I jumped in the shower to freshen up. Done in an art deco theme, the bathroom included a steam and multi-headed shower. The place was loaded with little touches of luxury.

At around 8 p.m. we headed over to the Royalton Hotel, where we were going to have dinner in the famous lobby restaurant. At that time there were certain landmarks that you went to if you were gay, and the Royalton was very high on that list. A hip, progressive, open concept for a lobby functioned as a restaurant, meeting place, and cocktail lounge all in one. It was second only to the surprise waiting for you in the men's bathroom, where you relieved yourself into a falling shower of water. I was thrilled that this was where we were going for dinner.

The place was hopping, and I was happy to be with my agent. He maneuvered, and played every card to get what he wanted. We ended up at a center table smack in the middle of the room, feeling all dressed up and "somebodies" at the center of the New York universe. We were completely delusional.

High from the buzz of the room, we talked and talked and talked, about the past year, the build-up of the Games, that our dreams had come true. And then my agent shared how unhappy he was sometimes with his job, his life. I don't know whether it was the setting, or the opening that he gave me, or the fact that everywhere I looked I saw beautiful gay men, but I simply blurted out, "You know I am gay, right?"

He wasn't the least bit shocked. He thanked me for finally telling him. He told me he knew but he wanted to wait for me to tell him. I asked him why they denied me being gay in *Frank*. He told me that it was for the sponsors, to give them leverage if anything happened. "But you lied," I said. "Technically we didn't," he replied. "We had never talked about this before, and we just answered on your behalf." "But you didn't ask." Nor would they. Never. "I know this is harsh," he continued, "but you are never to talk about this again. If we are going to represent you then you have to give us this guarantee."

That night I went out walking the streets of New York alone. Dinner had ended well. My agent was a good guy; he was just caught in a machine. But so was I. I went to a gay bar in the Village in Chelsea, but I wasn't really there. Surrounded by all of these gay people I still couldn't shake the feeling of being terribly and utterly alone.

CHAPTER SIX

POST-OLYMPIC DEPRESSION

MY LAST HOPE

For the first nine months upon returning home from the Olympics it appeared from the outside looking in that I was living a dream life. I was busy traveling the country and was being celebrated at each stop. I had won the Canadian Press athlete of the year award, as well as receiving other honors from the Governor General and Canadian Olympic Committee.

What I had never understood before was how isolating fame was. How could I? I had never really been famous before. Suddenly everywhere I went I found people reacting to me, but it was not me, Mark Tewksbury the person, to whom they were responding, but to more of an idea of what I represented. That made for exciting twenty second exchanges of, "We think you're great!" but made it difficult for any deep, meaningful connections.

So many things had changed. I have very few regrets in life, but if there were one thing I could change it would be how I left swimming. Instead of being overtaken by touring schedules and agents, I would have competed for one more winter season, easing myself out of my sport and my long established way of life.

Not only had I left my routine at the pool, I had left behind my teammates and coach, with whom I had shared years of intimate moments in pursuit of my dream. They were back at the pool carrying on toward future Olympic glory. I had already reached mine, but it was a strange thing to have achieved my dream, my intense busyness hiding the fact that I was completely lost, not knowing what to do now that my lifelong goal had been fulfilled. That reality itself was lonely, but over time, the combination of celebrity and hiding a secret, thrown in with the strained relations around me, pushed me to the limit.

On the family front, my parents and I were still struggling to find common ground to salvage our relationship. It would take years for them to come to their own terms with my sexuality. The first months were not fun. It was a period of enormous awkward silences, with feelings of intense discomfort made even more unbearable because the closeness I had once held with my family, especially with my mom, had shifted to total estrangement. We would meet for dinner at a restaurant and sit in silence, except when the waitress would come and speak with us, taking our orders and asking how things were. It was brutal.

On the work front, I was hanging on by a thread. Keeping up the image of Canada's boy next door, while feeling a lot like the girl next door, too, wasn't very easy. What saved me through this time was that I knew that Peter would be coming back from Europe soon, and we would start to build something together, giving me a place to find comfort, support, and strength. Where I had lost the support of my mom and dad, and of my agents, at least I still had Peter.

In March the big day arrived. Peter had returned from Europe a couple of days earlier, and I was heading to Toronto to see him. He met me at the airport with his parents' car, and we went to the hotel downtown where I was staying. It had been a number of months since we had been together. We had sex, but it was awkward, more bumping into one another than love making, and it was over very quickly. I remember feeling very disappointed, an omen of what was to come.

Peter wanted to get out of the room immediately and go for a sauna and swim upstairs. It was still a time when entering a public swimming area meant instant recognition for me, and I much preferred to stay in the room. But it was clear that Peter wanted to go, and before I could talk him out of it he was out the door. I threw on my bathing suit and followed.

I imagined when he came back that we would spend hours talking, not knowing where to start with each other. Instead, he completely withdrew, leaving me insecure in everything I did or said. Each minute felt like an eternity, every movement measured, tense, unnatural. We were in the sauna on opposite sides of the room when I tried to get things going one more time. "How was your trip?" "Fine," Peter answered. Three months and I got a fine. "You must be tired still, I guess," I said, alluding to the fact that he didn't seem to want to talk to me. "Not really," he replied, and then got up and jumped in the pool.

That night I met his family for the first time. Although our private time together hadn't gone as I had hoped, the fact that I met his parents made me feel slightly better about things. Peter still lived at home, which was why I was going to surprise him with the offer of moving into an apartment in Toronto together.

We had a nice meal with his family, but the distance that I had felt from Peter remained. What was going on? I was getting all kinds of mixed messages. To me, meeting me at the airport meant he cared. I thought bringing me to dinner with his parents meant he was serious, but I felt like I was in a room with a complete stranger. I had hung all of my hopes on us having a relationship together, and was desperately waiting for a clear sign that everything was okay.

When Peter's dad drove us back to the hotel, and Peter brought his backpack to move in with me, I felt relieved for the first time all evening. I had met his family, he was coming back to my room, his dad drove us—things were okay. We went up to the room, and I was all excited about the night and started to engage Peter in a conversation.

He cut me off mid-sentence with the words "It's over with us. I am sorry but I don't love you, I don't think I ever loved you, and I came back because I wanted to tell you in person, and I didn't want to waste any more time." My face dropped. Abrupt was one way to describe it, but this was also unfeeling and cruel. I could sense that he wanted to run out of there, as if had he hurried he might still catch his father for a ride home. The initial stun wore off remarkably quickly, though. Then I was just furious. By the time I had asked if he was sure it was over and he had said yes, I attacked him.

I had hung on to the idea of his return month after month, promising myself everything would be better once Peter came home. When everyone around me seemed to distance themselves, he had become my last hope. As I realized that he was leaving me, that this was over, I snapped.

It was a final rejection I just wasn't prepared to deal with. I grabbed him and threw him across the bedroom. He pushed to move me out of the way, and I was momentarily brought back and ashamed of what I had done. But I couldn't stop yet. I was so fucking frustrated; it hurt so much. We were huffing and he looked a bit scared of me. I screamed "Noooooooooooooooo!" into my hands.

I saw him there, against the wall where the television unit was. I couldn't force him to stay. I couldn't make him love me. I was defeated. It got really quiet. We agreed it was over. He said, "I'm going to go home now," and took his things and left. I sat there stunned by what had happened. And even more suprised by my reaction to it.

The silence of the hotel room became magnified when Peter left. I noticed it before the sobbing began, which successfully filled the room with noise until I cried myself to sleep. I woke up in the morning as the sun rose, the bed still made, my teeth not brushed, and my clothes still on.

Rock Bottom

My training as an elite athlete had prepared me to withstand enormous pressure, physically and mentally. I could withstand deep, deep pain. But nothing had prepared me for this period in my life. Being dumped by Peter was the straw that broke this camel's back. It pushed me over the edge of what I could cope with, and started a dangerously dark downward spiral in my life.

I tried to reach out, to talk to people about what was going on, but it was very difficult, especially since ninety-nine percent of the world thought I was straight. One April day about a month after Peter dumped me, I was struggling and just barely able to pick myself up to get out of my stinky pajamas and out of the house. I went to a party for a friend, and her mother came over and told me how wonderful it was to see me, and how exciting my life must be now.

I was bordering on massive depression, and I knew this woman was a social worker, so I took this opportunity to speak frankly. I replied, "Actually, I am having a really hard time. I feel really empty, lost, and depressed." Her face went from sugar to vinegar in about two seconds flat. "You ungrateful person. You have every opportunity in the world and you have the nerve to stand there and tell me how hard your life is." My mouth fell open. She continued, "I work with people who have *real* problems. Maybe you'd like to trade shoes with them." Gee, that went well. I was so glad that I opened up. It was like coming out to my parents, except that this time the plan was to ask for help. Abort that plan, too!

My life was like that at the time. Even if I could talk about my hardships openly, nobody wanted to hear about them. I was the poster boy of success. Who wants to think that something is wrong in Disneyland? Somehow I had come to represent motherhood and apple pie, and those things don't have hard times. So instead I started to keep things inside, which didn't go very well, either.

As I traveled and gave my speeches, I was starting to become more and more depressed. I could still perform my speech, not unlike an actor that has done three thousand shows of the musical *Cats*. I would go on autopilot and be able to do it, but then I would go back to my hotel room and close down, getting stuck inside my head, the self-loathing starting to take over again. Slowly I couldn't draw the line anymore, and that destructive voice took over even when I was working, ensuring that nothing positive made it through my filter.

After I gave a speech many people had something nice to say, but for every nice comment I would have a negative one in my head, unable to take anything they gave, because at the end of the day I had my own disclaimer. "You are a great speaker." *If only you knew who I really was, then would you still say that?* "We are so proud of you!" *Really, I am a fag. Still proud?*

In my black-and-white world, there was only one option to get me out of this mess: Peter needed to take me back. Then things would be alright. I was alone in my hotel rooms, holding onto the idea that I needed a relationship; that I couldn't go out to bars for fear of being exposed; that I wouldn't meet other people because even my gaydar was off—many men were looking at me simply because they were sport fans, not because they were gay. It was Peter or nothing. A whole world was out there and I had tunnel vision. My narrow mind had nowhere to go but obsession.

It would be Peter's mom who finally got through to me. When I called once too many times, she told me, "You had better think about moving on because I am sorry to say this to you Mark, but Peter isn't coming back to you." Ouch. That was when the real craziness began.

My depression had been building for months, perhaps years. The toll of living this gay, secret, double life was bound to erupt eventually. I hung up the phone from talking to Peter's mom and lay in the fetal position. I couldn't move, not even to walk across the room.

In my paralysis I had remembered one thing Peter had said to me, in passing, at the beginning of our relationship. "You have more body hair than anybody I've ever been with," he had said. I needed to have a reason to justify Peter leaving, something had to be wrong with me. Body hair became the new weapon, instead of gay, that I used to torture myself.

I had had a bit of a complex about my body hair in the past. As a swimmer I was always the hairiest guy on the team. I almost died of embarrassment the day a fourteen-year-old girl on my team noticed I had a few hairs on my back. She screamed, "Look everyone!" while jokingly pulling one out. That just made me want to crawl out of the pool like a Neanderthal. It made me very self-conscious, like the girl whose boobs get big first. Smooth bodies had ruled the '80s and '90s, and they were everywhere around me. Why couldn't I just be smooth skinned like everybody else?

My mind needed to identify some reason that I was alone. I am a hairy man, but I am not *that* hairy. I just saw myself that way. That was where my thinking was back then.

It was like my junior high school locker all over again. I felt so isolated and had so much self-loathing that I needed to find a place to focus all of those feelings. I was an adult now, and instead of just exploding at the locker, I imploded on myself.

I left no stone unturned on the path to destruction. I played the "you are too hairy, you are too hairy" tape through my mind as if I got a royalty for every time I said it. But no matter how hard I beat myself up, or waxed, plucked, shaved, or trimmed for that matter, I would never be smooth or have silky haired skin.

One morning I was giving a speech to the McDonald's corporation and was sitting at the VIP table with the CEO and senior executives. I was exhausted because I had mastered this cycle of abuse where I focused on my body hair until the wee hours of the morning, and then switched my focus to how little sleep I was going to get and how exhausted I would be the next day, which of course became a self-fulfilling prophecy. Completely sleep deprived, I sat for breakfast beside the CEO of the company, the man who had brought McDonald's to the Soviet Union. He was sharing some of his insights into life and business. Here was a legend sharing his secrets of success next to me and I didn't hear a word he was saying. My attention was completely consumed by the hair on the back of his big hands that I had noticed when I sat down.

An Unlikely Turner Point

I thought I was doing a good job of hiding my depression from people, but those around me could see that something was wrong. My eyes were coal black, and for the first time in my life I was subdued and unenthusiastic. All of that negative energy was floating around inside me all day. It was surprising to see how it would eventually find its way out, and what seemingly trivial event would eventually break it.

On one road trip where I was feeling particularly distressed, there was a young, handsome man in the crowd that approached me after my speech, and instead of giving me the usual admiring compliment, boldly asked if I was okay. He was a complete stranger, but he asked the right question at the right time, and he got through to me. I said, "Actually, I have been better." The next person moved forward to speak to me, and my stranger was gone.

I saw later as the room cleared that he was waiting for me. He asked, "Would you like to join me in doing something?" I looked at him, surprised. He leaned toward me and added, "It must be hard always being on the road. Don't worry. I don't want anything from you, just maybe to spend some time and talk." I said okay. At that time in my life a close friend had made me an appointment with a psychologist for me to get some help. I had gone once, but never returned. I didn't want to admit that there was anything wrong with me, afraid of yet another stigma. But psychologist or not, I really needed to talk to someone.

I didn't ever find out this stranger's story exactly—if he was gay or straight, an athlete or a sports fan. I just know he was kind, and let me ramble on endlessly about nothing because I was so completely guarded at first and wasn't going to risk telling him anything important. Gay remained my secret. It had been hard enough *not* to share my joy when I was in a relationship that was going well; it was another thing entirely being unable to share the pain of being dumped because people didn't know I had been in a relationship to begin with.

My stranger told me that he knew something wasn't right when I was speaking. This sensitive guy must have been a young gay man reaching out to me, but there was nothing sexual about it. We had a meal. I finally could share a lot of my frustrations about my life with someone, in the end perhaps even more easily because it was with a stranger. My faith in people and life returned a little that night. I began to wake up.

Debbie had assumed the role of taking care of me as I sunk to rock bottom. A woman used to getting results, she was frustrated and at a constant loss because no matter what she tried, nothing worked. I just stayed depressed. Nobody seemed to be able to get through to me. It was like the time when I went to visit Auntie Dot in the hospital and she had lost her spirit. I was gone.

If it was going to change it obviously had to come from me, and I made some significant changes in my life. Instead of staying in the house that I had bought to begin building my life with someone, I moved into a friend's house. She lived in a straight but unconventional setup. Her family had immigrated decades earlier from Holland. My friend, a businesswoman, and her brother, a doctor, both in their forties, lived with their mother, who was nearing seventy. They had a space in the basement for me, and they invited me to come and stay. I moved in for three months.

What I needed was the support of a family unit, and since mine was not able to provide that function for me at the time, this warm, intelligent, generous family became my surrogates. The environment and conversation was so open, a bastion of European liberalism in the midst of conservative Alberta. We talked about many social issues, including being gay, which for them was a nonissue. They had huskies, and although I had not been around animals for a long time, I loved taking their three dogs for long walks. Receiving all of this unconditional love started to bring me out of myself. I was part of a home, of a family, and I became more stable.

I moved back to my own house eventually, taking another step toward recovery, but I also started to realize that unless I could live openly as a gay person, full recovery would probably never happen. There was a connection between my being gay and my being depressed.

Debbie was still one of my most trusted confidantes and we often hung out. One night she wanted to go see the sneak preview of *What's Love Got to Do With It?*, the new movie starring Angela Bassett as Tina Turner. I didn't really feel like it, not being a huge Tina Turner fan, but at the last minute Debbie convinced me to go and we whipped down to one of our favorite cinemas in Calgary to catch the 7 p.m. show.

We grabbed our seats and the movie started. In the opening scene a very young Tina Turner was losing herself, singing in church in a style far too over the top for the choir. After being told numerous times to tone it down, she gets thrown out. Then, when she arrives home, she learns that she has been abandoned by her mother and left to be raised by her grandmother. Something about that little girl and her boundless enthusiasm combined with her difficult circumstance struck me and, in spite of myself, I started to cry. I didn't stop for the next two hours.

I was like a waterfall during the movie, crying so much that I gave up on using paper serviettes to try to keep my face dry. I just let the tears flow and fall where they may. It was a story of survival, of appearing to have it all but dealing with demons and hardships behind the scenes, and then overcoming those odds to come back. It moved me deeply. In the height of my depression my empty feeling took all of my space, and for a while I didn't know anything else. This movie, of all things, broke through that wall. I was hugely inspired and whenever I doubted myself, I would roar, "I, TINA!" as I punched my fist into the air. I felt empowered for the first time in a long, long time.

* * *

A bit of good fortune followed. As if I hadn't won enough in 1992, without even knowing, I had been entered in a contest through my frequent flier program, and my name was drawn for two business class tickets anywhere Canadian Airlines flew. I decided to go as far as I could, to Australia. I hadn't had any money to pay Debbie for her expertise during the Olympic year, so as a thank you for constantly being there for me, I gave the other ticket to her to join me. And off we went.

It was June, the fall/winter season down under, but it was still beautiful. We explored different parts of Sydney, including ultra gay Oxford Street. We saw *Madame Butterfly* at the Opera House and toured the Hunter Valley wineries.

Debbie and I both had a feeling of peace and freedom during this trip. We would take long walks in the afternoon, and then break for a late afternoon coffee and watch dusk descend upon the city. There was a stillness in the air that made it hard for us to believe we were in the middle of a city on the other side of the world. We were enchanted by the endless ocean views, the thriving downtown core, and the laid-back way of life. For the first time in months I forgot to be depressed.

I remember getting on the plane to come back to North America, feeling really good but having a small nagging concern deep inside me, wondering if the depression would come back as I returned home. But the residue of the trip to Australia was strong, and that helped immensely.

I thought about our trip many, many times, and also started communicating with people in Sydney who had become friends. I longed to go back. Almost immediately upon my return I was thrown back into the chaos of travel and promotion. I was much, much better, but I was still unhappy with what I had created in my life. There still wasn't room to be open about being gay, which now was perhaps even more difficult because I had seen how good life could be when your external environment supported you. Thankfully, a series of events would continue to unfold that would allow me the chance to change.

As a former athlete who had received my first breakthrough at the Commonwealth Games, I was called upon to promote the event when it was coming to Victoria, British Columbia in 1994. I went to Vancouver for one of the dog and pony shows, and did my presentation with the small team of leaders who were responsible for this project.

After I finished speaking, a gentleman came over to say a few words. It turned out he was the High Commissioner of Australia, who had been stationed in Vancouver for the last two years, and he was from Sydney. I spoke about my recent holiday, telling him how much I loved being there. And then I casually said, "Oh, what I wouldn't do to live there." He asked me if I was serious. "Absolutely," I replied. My heart began to race.

He told me about a special clause in the immigration process for Australia for people of achievement called "distinguished talent." With certain skill sets that could be proven to bring goodwill and benefit to the country, I could enter an opening in the immigration process. With Sydney bidding for the 2000 Olympics, and my Olympic background combined with public speaking, he thought there was a good chance I would be accepted should I decide to apply. I asked him who approved the applications. "I do," he replied. Music to my ears.

A few weeks later I was en route to give a speech in Red Deer, Alberta, about an hour-and-a-half drive from Calgary. I had been swallowed by my schedule again, still struggling from time to time, but basically I was back on autopilot fulfilling appearance and speaking requests. I put the soundtrack from *What's Love Got to Do With It?* into my CD player in the car, and the minute the first song started I had the same strong emotional response I had had at the theater. I started to cry the moment that I heard Tina sing. I was driving along the highway, sobbing my eyes out, and there was nothing I could do to stop it.

There was a scene in the movie when Tina and Ike were in the back of a limousine beating the shit out of each other. Tina jumped out of the limo in the middle of a freeway and entered a hotel, saying her name, that she had less than a dollar in cash, and that she had a concert that night and needed some help. It was the turning point when she realized enough was enough. She left everything behind for a chance at a new start, and all she carried forward was her name. With that, she could rebuild.

About thirty minutes into the drive I started to look like a blowfish, I was so puffy from crying. As people were driving by me I had to make sure to look slightly away so I didn't scare them. When I later arrived for my speech they panicked when they saw my face, but understood how allergies could be. I had to tell them something.

When I had been in the car, my head had raced as quickly as the tears were streaming. I had thought about Peter, my work, Debbie, my family, IMG, but I kept coming back to what the High Commissioner of Australia had told me. And at some point, it was like all the pieces of the puzzle fell into place and as my tears finally stopped my future lined up in front of me as clear as could be. It was time to get out of here, out of this province where I felt like a second-class citizen as a gay person, out of this country where I felt like I had to constantly pretend to be something I wasn't. It was time to start over with nothing but my name. I was immigrating to Australia.

CHAPTER SEVEN

ONE-WAY TICKET TO AUSTRALIA

QUEEN OF THE DESERT

It was a good thing that I was so clear on my intentions to move, because most people weren't very happy about it when I broke the news to them. Moving to Australia to get sane and reclaim my life just made me look crazy to many people. They thought it was the worst decision I had ever made. My agents were an excellent example. One afternoon in the fall of 1993 I went into their offices in Toronto. I sat them down and I told them that I wanted out. "What?" they asked incredulously. "I am moving to Australia to get away for a while. We have to figure out how to wind things down, because by the spring of 1994 I am planning on living in Sydney." "You're not serious?" they questioned. I was dead serious.

Sport had taught me to take risks, but not stupid ones. In order to ensure this was the best move for me, I planned a sabbatical to Australia for the Christmas holidays of 1993. I decided that before my application for permanent residency came through I had better do a test run, so to speak, just to double-check that this truly wasn't a wrong move. I chose to spend six weeks over Christmas because it can be the loneliest time of the year. I figured if I made it through that then I would move full-steam ahead.

In Sydney I quickly found an apartment complex that rented rooms by the week, complete with kitchen and bath, and it was cheap.

This became my home base for the trip, giving me a sense of living in the city and not just visiting. Coming from Canada, everything was upside down in terms of Christmas. It was hot and the sky was clear. Christmas would be with a barbeque and beach instead of an oven-roasted turkey and snow. But much more importantly at the time, it would be with gay and lesbian people and not straight ones, filling every day with excitement as I discovered a whole new world.

Sydney fascinated me. In a country where men were mates and the women were still sheilas, chauvinism prospered, and yet there seemed to be a magical circle that ran around a part of Sydney and as long as you were in this circle, you were safe as a gay person. It only took a twenty-minute drive and you were out of that charmed, safe circle where gay was normal, and not only were you back to reality, you were back to a reality that was more like small-town Alberta than I would have cared to admit. But in spite of this there remained an oasis in the eastern suburbs where thousands of out and proud gay people lived.

Every three or four months they held big gay dance parties, and the parties were packed with *straight* guys all wearing the gayest out-fits, wanting to be part of this culture. Being down under was all mixed up in more ways than one to me. Here it seemed normal, even cool, to be gay.

As luck would have it, the next big gay dance party fell on the night of New Year's Eve, which was during my trip, so I would get my first real taste of the gay party life. In my first days I had met an Australian man who was actually a big girl with muscles. He opened the gateway for me to be a part of the gay life I had always dreamed of. He took me under his wing and showed me the preparation involved in looking "au naturel" at these gay circuit parties.

If I had thought that smooth bodies ruled in North America, then in Australia the men would have to be described as "baby bottom smooth." They had perfectly smooth skin that made the thought of me taking off my shirt publicly to reveal my chest of fur completely impossible. When faced with this truth my Aussie mentor screamed at me, "Get over it! I've got a girl who will fix you up. Look at me." I did. It was incredible. This guy didn't have a hair on his body. He had his own eyebrows and hair, but beyond that, it was all gone. I guess now it would be called a Brazilian wax, but at that time, it was just called shocking. But the real shock would come with the actual treatment.

With the big dance party coming up in five days, preparation was at its height. In a strange way it had a similar feeling to the count-down to the Olympics, or to a special occasion, where anticipation rules the day. My regimen started with the gym, then the beach, then shopping for the right outfit, then begging for a sold-out party ticket, then hair and wax, and on and on. Although it was a bit ridiculous to have my schedule ruled by an upcoming party, it was thrilling for me, and I would barely be able to sleep at night, like a young child at Christmas not being able to contain myself. I felt a part of something, wondering how I could have felt so alone for so many years when there were all these gay people in the world.

On December 29 I went for my wax appointment, leaving my-self enough time to heal before the dance party. Or so I thought. Slightly burned from the sun already, and tight from pumping up, I had allowed my Aussie mentor to convince me to do a chest and stomach wax as well as removing any hair on my back. I laid down on the paper-lined massage table and Ms. Waxer From Hell started with my back. It wasn't so bad, except that I felt it burn my already sunburned skin.

When she flipped me over it was another story entirely. I realized only after she had poured this gooey, hot, sticky stuff all over my left pectoral, and she had taken the first small strip off, that I was much less hairy on my back than my chest. The odd cluster of hair from the back felt very different from the thick hair on my chest. I had known some serious pain in my life from training, but as the hot wax strip came off, and the tears spontaneously rolled out of my eyes, I had never known such agony.

Ms. Waxer stopped dead in her tracks and asked if everything was alright. "No," I whimpered. "Is there any *other* way you can get that stuff off?" She shook her head no. It looked ridiculous to leave my chest like that, one tit furry, the other plucked, so we kept going even though I knew the sheer hell that lay ahead. I didn't realize that it could get worse. The pain at the chest meant nothing by the time we got to the area below the belly button. I almost passed out from it.

Unfortunately things didn't work out as planned. Although I had spent the past two days diligently putting tea tree oil on my plucked skin, I had this massive ingrown hair smack in the middle of my torso, right above my belly button. It was red and huge with puss forming. It was disgusting to look at, like a one-eyed monster in the middle of my belly. Five days of beauty regime for nothing, I was sidelined the night of the big ball. The only saving grace was that my mentor friend had bought me a matching outfit to his, which consisted of neon green shorts with black trim, and as awful as this big zit was, I was secretly grateful that I couldn't wear this outfit and had to wear an ordinary tank top. I am open for many things, but there were limits.

As we neared the large show grounds where the party was being held I became so excited that I could feel my stomach start to flip. The closer we got, the more people we saw and the louder the bass became from the music inside. I felt like the sidewalk was vibrating. I felt giddy, and wanted to scream, "I am going to my first gay party!" This felt about as far away from Calgary as I could imagine.

The party didn't disappoint. The new year was brought in with a huge stage show that took my breath away. Australia is famous for its drag queens, and one drag queen came on after another, all lip-synching with fantastic outfits. The show kept building and building, and by the end there must have been seventy-five men, women, and drag queens on the stage. My mouth was wide open. A cute guy in our group, Tim, asked me if I liked the show. "Are you kidding, I loved it!" I screamed. "That is what I do,' he screamed back. "You do drag?" I asked. "No, I dress the drags," he smiled.

Tim was five feet ten-ish, had brown hair and green eyes, and freckles on his cheeks and back from too many hours in the sun. He had that raw Aussie male look and loved what he did, but struggled to make a decent living doing it. He was always working, finding materials for the drag queens, sewing outfits, and running around fitting people. Because I had time on my hands, Tim would call me when he needed to take a break, usually accompanied with some kind of adventure.

With Tim I went backstage at the drag clubs, because he would often be involved in making the outfits. I knew Tim wasn't making a fortune, and neither were these performers, yet they had all of these new costume changes every week. I had wondered how they afforded to do it all. "Let me show you a secret, Mark." Tim grabbed the sparkling blue dress that on-stage looked haute couture and showed me it was just a stapled-together, cheap end-piece of fabric that looked great for five minutes and then fell apart. It had served its purpose.

Just as I was leaving Australia, Tim had started working on a movie. He laughed because they had given him the smallest budget imaginable for this picture, but he knew he could work miracles given his background and resourcefulness. The last time I saw Tim was with the rest of the world when he accepted the Academy Award for Best Costume Design for that little movie he had been working on called *Priscilla, Queen of the Desert.*

As I sat watching the awards show, I knew that however misguided my decision to move to Australia might have seemed to some, it was the perfect move for me. Seeing this guy I knew who stapled drag dresses together walking offstage with an Academy Award made me feel that anything was possible.

FROM HERO TO ZERO

There was a reason that I had chosen to live in Australia. It wasn't just about changing geography, running to a new place, although that was part of it. My choice was more about giving myself a chance at a simpler life, one away from the spotlight and into more of a routine. Australia was just about as far away as you could get in the world from Canada. If I was in Europe it was still possible to be brought back to Canada for public relations work, as it would have been in the United States, but to fly me back all the way from Australia was another story entirely.

When I'd left Canada, I had never intended to come back. Getting my life in order to make this change was a huge task that consumed all of my energy. I had to settle all personal and business affairs. I sold my house. I sold my car. I donated hundreds of personal items to a sports hall of fame. I boxed small pieces of furniture and keepsakes to ship. I closed bank accounts, dined with friends, met with sponsors. I didn't stop to think about what an enormous step this was. I just did it.

One February afternoon, as I was doing some office work in my house, the final piece of the puzzle arrived. The package was from the Australian Consulate. Inside was my acceptance letter, instructions for next steps, with my visa and my entry permit card. *Resident Sub Class 125 granted on 03 Feb 94 must not arrive after 25 Oct 97. Multiple travel holder permitted to remain in Australia indefinitely.* Indefinitely! Gulp.

If the permanence of my decision didn't hit me then, it certainly did when I was buying my one-way ticket to Sydney. There was a special program that provided immigrants with reasonably priced tickets if you bought through a particular agency. I joined the long line of defectors, leaving Alberta forever.

In April of 1994 I entered Australia for the first time, claiming my permanent resident status. There was a huge sense of freedom upon arriving, but also a surprising feeling of aloneness I hadn't anticipated. I wasn't alone in the sense that I didn't have people around me, because I did. I was staying with friends. I knew many people living in the city. But in the morning they all went to work, because they all had lives to live there. I didn't yet. I had so much freedom that I didn't know where to start. For the first few days I was just simply overwhelmed, but in a great way. I walked through the streets and searched for an apartment and came to terms with the idea that I actually lived there now.

I eventually settled into a beautiful penthouse suite that I shared with two guys, one of whom I was dating, in the eastern suburbs of Sydney. We had the most spectacular views imaginable, overlooking the Harbour Bridge, Opera House, and north Sydney on one side, and Bondi, one of Sydney's most famous beaches, on the other. Rent was peanuts, but the apartment needed some work, as did I.

To keep busy and to make some spare money I had taken a part-time job catering at the private dining room of a bank. I was the kitchen hand, washing dishes and helping serve food as we assembled plates for the forty-plus people in the boardroom outside. One evening a group of executives was finishing their meals in the dining room and I saw Greg Norman, the golfer, pacing out in the hallway getting ready to speak. I chuckled to myself. That was the place I had often found myself in; now I would be cleaning his dessert plate. I was living a very different life now. That wasn't the part that I found hard.

Upon arriving in the city I had deposited a big check at the bank that represented the proceeds from my car and furniture as well as my savings, and it was to cover me for the first six months in Sydney as I got settled. After making this deposit I applied for a credit card, wanting to have a fresh start in every way, intending to retire my Canadian credit cards. But there was a glitch—I was declined! In spite of the healthy deposit into my bank account, because I had no credit history in Australia I couldn't even get a card with a credit of $500. One long flight and I went from hero to zero in the bank's eyes. I needed to get an identity, quickly.

One day, when shopping at the large department store David Jones, the Australian version of Macy's, I noticed applications for its in-store credit cards. I applied; they accepted. They allowed me a small credit of $300 to begin with, which worked out great because I just kept buying things from their store, charging them, and paying the bill in full each month to build a solid credit rating.

After three months the bank told me I still had to wait another three months before they could approve a VISA. "But I have this account, on top of having had these cards, this credit history in Canada," I pleaded. The bank rep remained unmoved. "Sorry sir, that means nothing here." I had wanted a simpler life. I had gotten it.

CRACKING THE CLOSET

I found it fairly easy to make friends in Australia when I moved, because the people were very laid back and welcoming. One Friday night I had stopped at a good friend's apartment to say hello on my way into the city. There, a man and a woman swept past me heading out the door just as I was entering.

The woman was dressed in jeans and a fitted jacket, but the man made a lasting impression. He wore black leather pants with a crisp white shirt. He had long legs with a slightly shorter upper body; white, white hair cropped short; large nose, ears, and lips; and extremely flamboyant mannerisms. I never forgot that first sighting, thinking to myself, "Wow, this guy is *so gay!*"

His name was Noel, but everyone called him Nola. He was a man of fashion and style, an impeccable host who loved to dance and socialize. Our unlikely friendship began because above all else Nola was a storyteller, and I loved a good story. We met more formally later at a house party where we hit it off. I would spend many hours going to visit him at his apartment, just hanging out.

The thing about Nola was that he was completely disarming. Nobody felt threatened by this big teddy bear kind of guy. It would always amaze me to see how people of all stripes would open up to him, sharing the most intimate details of their lives. The disappointing thing for me was how closed I became when Nola opened up in public.

Years of repressing my own homosexuality had created a dormant homophobia in me that I wasn't aware of until I started spending time with Nola. In the privacy of his home I loved his outrageousness and expressiveness, but in public it was another story.

Even though I was on the other side of the world where very few people knew me and I had nothing to lose, I still didn't necessarily want people to know that I was gay as I was going about my everyday life. Going to a dance party as a big, screaming fag was one thing; going into town to do trivial errands as one was another. For me, the double life that I had lived for so long was not easily changed.

We would get into a cab and Nola would shriek, "Hello darling!" to the driver in the most over-the-top way. As much as I liked him, I couldn't stop myself from cringing when he spoke like that. Part of me died inside for being out with someone so openly gay. I hated myself for being embarrassed, but years of living in a homophobic environment had affected me deeply. I found myself playing straight, butching it up even, trying to overcompensate for this bundle of gayness beside me.

Moving to Australia hadn't suddenly unwired everything that I had learned during my years in Alberta. At first my intense fear of being exposed as a homosexual won out over allowing myself to be open. For so long I had trained myself to fit in, be like everybody else, and that was what I wished for when I went out with my friend. Thankfully, Nola was in his own little world and didn't notice. But as

I rebuilt my life and regained my identity in a new place, I was struck by how hard it was to break some of my old habits. I had started to punish Nola for the very thing that I loved about him. Something had to give.

Thankfully what gave eventually was my worldview, my way of looking at things. Within my first year in Australia I realized that if I cared for Nola and we were friends, then I had to embrace him for who he was, not for who I wanted him to be. This is what people had done to me for so many years. It was time to get a reality check. Everybody loved Nola. What was I so afraid of? What was my hang-up? It was time to let go of my fear. Nola helped me understand acceptance, and also showed me that somehow life has a funny way of working itself out.

A year later when I bought a car in Australia, it was Nola I first picked up for a drive. Nola had never learned to drive, and because taxis were so reasonably priced there was really no reason to. Nola would call a cab and proclaim, "The limousine of the people is on its way, darling!" Now with my own vehicle it was my turn to be the chauffeur. I couldn't wait to show off in my bright orange Volkswagen beetle convertible.

My embarrassment at being in public places with Nola had long made way for pride as my outlook on life changed completely in Sydney. Nola and I went to the movies every Friday afternoon, and met at least once a week to go out.

On this day, fresh from picking up the car, I was simply dropping him for an appointment close by. On our way we were stopped at a traffic light halfway up this very steep hill, with both Nola and I sitting in our seats but leaning backwards at what seemed like forty-five-degree angles. The emergency brake was on so the car wouldn't roll backwards, but the car behind me was on my bumper, giving me no room to err.

I could feel myself starting to sweat. I was driving a five-speed with the stick shift and steering wheel on the opposite side of what

I was used to, and this was my first major outing in the city. I was concerned with how I was going to pull this off, but I didn't want to say anything to alarm Nola. As the car before me started to move, I revved the gas, squealed the tires, released the brake, and jolted forward. Both Nola and I screamed.

When I dropped Nola off I made a similar burning rubber noise as I left him. During that whole ride, Nola had not spoken. When I looked in my rearview mirror I could see Nola trying to distance himself from the car that had made the loud noise. I had a huge smile across my face as I realized that finally it was my turn to embarrass Nola by being *too much* in public.

SEX ED

One of the best decisions I made was to go back to university and finish my education in Sydney while I had the chance, although by no means was it easy. Arriving at the University of New South Wales for classes after having taken close to four years off was enormously intimidating at first. I was twenty-seven years old returning back to campus, listening to nineteen-year-old kids with so much knowledge that I was too afraid to participate in case I made myself look stupid. I had stopped taking classes at the University of Calgary in 1990, partway through a political science degree in order to focus on swimming. I had a sinking feeling that all that I had ever learned was so far gone it would never come back.

I entered final year, advanced courses. It took me most of the first semester to find my way, and my academic breakthrough came almost completely by mistake. I had to review an essay written by Dr. Stevens on Japanese economics and politics, two things I knew very little about. This wasn't such a big deal, because throughout the semester each of my classmates had to do similar critiques of different authors. The challenge rested in the fact that the author, Dr. Stevens, was also *the* Dr. Stevens standing at the front of my class. Gulp. No wonder nobody else had chosen this particular review.

Although I wasn't sure if I completely understood what he was saying or not, I gave my critique while the other students glanced at him, aware of how strange it was to listen to me simplify what our much-respected professor had written. I really dumbed down his text, remembering that trick of speaking at a grade four level that had served me well in the corporate setting years ago. At the end of my presentation there was momentary silence before Dr. Stevens looked me in the eye and said, "I wish I had said it like that." The lesson of speaking at a grade four level continued to pay off. It was a turning point where I started to find my voice and confidence in an academic setting. Just in time, too.

In the second semester a whole new world opened to me. I had enrolled in a class about sex, power, and politics. There were about twenty of us in this class, mostly women, and we came from all walks of life. We studied concepts like the cults of masculinity and femininity, radical humanism, individualism, and objectification. Our discussions were peppered with words like *patriarchy* and *dominant culture*. Classes became heated as we shared our opinions and experiences with each other.

Not talking about sexuality had become my norm for so many years that at first I was very shy to speak. But over time, being in this class gave me a vocabulary to finally start speaking with. I started to understand that society, whether we realized it or not, imposed strict codes of conduct on men and women.

Some authors we read wrote that a gay man was somehow less of a man because he was attracted to other men instead of women. On the hierarchy of masculinity, gays were at the bottom, so to speak. I came directly from living in a place that reinforced this way of thinking. Gay was seen as a liability, a weakness, hence my constant denial of that part of myself. Now I realized that if I bought into that way of thinking, that gay men were somehow worth less than heterosexuals, then I would also have to support the idea that women in general were weaker then men because they were feminine. Given the strength of the women in my class, and the power of their arguments, that way of thinking was finally thrown out the window.

At the end of the second semester I had my degree, but I had much, much more than that. I had written a deeply personal paper sharing my experience of masculinity through sport and being gay that won the *Sydney Morning Herald* prize for academic achievement in political science. Where I had arrived at school too shy to speak, I left solidly finding my voice, and breaking free of some of the deepseated thinking that had held me hostage for so many years. Little would I know how much this time in Australia would shape my life to come.

CHAPTER EIGHT

SEDUCTION

Princely Intervention

When I toured the world with the national swim team, one of the many stops we made every year was in the principality of Monaco. It was one of the best environments of the tour because we were treated to luxury at every turn. Prince Albert himself was usually in attendance, since he was an International Olympic Committee member and a huge sports fan. He gave out the awards for my event, and when he made his way around the pool deck the next day he stopped and made small talk with me for a long time.

Prince Albert and I became friends over the years, in a close but passing way. We had good chemistry together, we moved in some of the same circles, and when we met from time to time we had great conversations. He was the driver of the bobsled team from Monaco, and was often in Calgary for training. We would sometimes grab lunch together at a small diner in a strip mall by the university. We ate chef's salads and talked about issues related to sport, like the fight against performance-enhancing drugs. I was after him about getting the IOC Athletes' Commission to do something about this issue. I spoke openly and freely, comfortable with this unassuming royal whose mother had been Grace Kelly. He recognized my passion for issues, and in the summer of 1994 invited me as a guest for the 100th anniversary of the International Olympic Committee in Paris. How could I say no to Prince Albert?

At one of the many receptions during the week I ran into Carol Anne Letheren, Canadian member of the International Olympic Committee and head of the Canadian Olympic Committee (at that time, Association). She was very surprised to see me there, since she had not invited me as part of the Canadian delegation. When I told her that I was the guest of Prince Albert, I could see that something registered in her eyes. Somehow my value rose and a seed had been planted in her mind. It would be Carol Anne who would eventually dangle the carrot that enticed me to move back to Canada from Australia.

Carol Anne had first entered my life as the chef de mission of the 1988 Olympic team in Seoul, Korea. We had had a team briefing in Vancouver before heading over to the Olympics, and while terribly efficient, organized, and controlled, Carol Anne wasn't the warmest person I had ever met. Carol Anne was the person who had to go and retrieve the gold medal from Ben Johnson after he tested positive for steroids and then, as head of the Canadian delegation, escort him out of Korea. Her masterful handling of the situation as well as her astute political maneuvering ensured that she would eventually become Canada's first female IOC member soon thereafter.

Many months after the Paris meeting I received a phone call in Australia from Carol Anne. She asked me if I would accept being nominated to run for the IOC Athletes' Commission. But the invitation came with a catch. I would be representing the *Canadian* Olympic Committee, not the Australian. If I accepted I would have to leave Sydney. I told her I would have to think about it. It was a very hard decision, but what she was offering me was a chance to get on the inside of the leadership of the Olympic movement, to make a difference. All of the issues that I had spoken about with Price Albert I would now be able to do something about personally.

But before I could commit, I wanted to let her know that there was a catch from my side, too. I had come too far not to be open about my sexuality anymore, and I wanted her to know that I was gay. "I have no problem with that, Mark. Some of my closest friends are gay," she informed me. I told her she had a deal. It took me a while to get my life in Sydney wrapped up, and I headed back to Canada, this time to Toronto, in February of 1996.

POLITICS OF POWER

Ambitious, powerful, and intimidating was how most people saw Carol Anne. That was the facade I had to deal with at first, as well. Consistently voted among the top fifty most influential people in sport by the *Globe and Mail*, and usually cited as the most powerful woman, it wasn't for nothing she made that list.

But I came to learn as she groomed me to become her successor that when she gave you her energy, she was extremely charismatic and engaging. I have rarely seen someone as hard working or efficient, solving a month's worth of problems on an overnighter to Europe. For the most part I believed she was well-intentioned, just slightly misguided by self-interest, which was largely the residue of playing with the big boys.

Eventually she would surprise me by showing me that she could be insecure and vulnerable, which I didn't expect. She had been adopted, like me, and we had an unspoken understanding of that part of each other. It always astonished me when this titan of survival in the old boys' world of sport told me she loved me. I felt like she meant it on one hand, but was trying to manipulate me on the other. That was the contradiction of Carol Anne. At least when I began this relationship I knew what I was getting myself into. Or so I thought.

As I was getting settled in Toronto, I met with Carol Anne to tell her that I was thinking of finally coming out publicly in Canada. I was a different person now, tired of hiding, and as she had said when I first told her, it didn't matter. She listened to me go on, but when I finished she blurted out, "I don't understand why you would want to do that!" I had just spent more than ten minutes telling her why I wanted to do it. "What do you mean you don't know why I would want to do that? You told me yourself before I came back from Australia that it didn't matter," I said. "And I meant it, Mark, it doesn't matter." She continued, "But it would matter if *you* made it matter." I knew exactly what she meant. She had said that it didn't matter, but had meant it didn't matter *to her.* It still mattered big time in the closed, homophobic world of amateur sport, so shut up about it.

There was a consensus from the people around me at that time not to speak publicly about being gay, *ever.* Which meant in a way I was right back where I had started, living a privileged life, this time on the luxurious leadership side of international sport, but at the same cost, perhaps higher. This time it wasn't being something I wasn't. It was not being something I was. I was gay, but I couldn't be. I didn't realize the trap until it was too late.

Since I had come back to run for the IOC Athletes' Commission, this was what I spent my energy focusing on for the short term. For the first time, athletes would be voting for their representatives. The problem was, that's where the democratic process started and ended. Each athlete was given a pamphlet with the pictures, nationality, sport, and athletic accomplishments of all forty-something athletes running for the Commission. There was no position on issues and no chance to hear the candidates. It was mostly a popularity contest, with big countries and sports being favored. Since the decision was ultimately to be made by the athletes themselves at the Olympics in Atlanta, with Carol Anne leading my campaign, I headed south for the Games.

Atlanta was a tough Olympics for everyone. It was extremely hot and humid. A few early screw-ups left the organizing committee collectively blasted by the world press, which led to low morale, which just led to more screw-ups. It wasn't pretty.

I had an IOC accreditation complete with car and driver, thanks to Carol Anne. That was priceless because it gave me access to everything. But even then it was difficult to navigate those Olympics comfortably. The events, the intense security, and the overwhelming size of the venues were enough to discourage you from ever going back. The downtown core was overpowered by commercialism that made the Olympics feel less like a gathering of humanity and more like a sixteen-day carnival that traveled across the country, packing and unpacking the same tacky goods town to town until they were finally all gone.

Much of my time was spent hosting people back at the property the Canadian Olympic Committee had rented for the Olympics just outside the downtown core. All the rooms looked over a central swimming pool. It was like living in our own Olympic Melrose Place. During the Olympics Carol Anne had her birthday, and on that night all of the VIPs gathered to be with her. Carol Anne was a lot of fun to party with, and we were looking forward to her returning from some of her official IOC duties to celebrate.

Although I was still discreet about my sexuality, I always had people around me now that knew me, leaving behind the feelings of isolation over being gay but still feeling compromised by not being completely open with everyone. Thankfully my close friend Megan worked for the Canadian Olympic Committee, and she was my outlet in Atlanta, the person that I could be completely honest with. At Carol Anne's birthday, it was Meghan who covered my ass.

At one point as I was hosting the corporate VIPs, I saw this big strapping guy walking down the corridor on the far side of the pool. My stomach flipped. A few nights earlier, quietly, I had gone out to a gay bar way out in the suburbs. This guy had dropped me here on his way home, and apparently he was here to surprise me. It worked.

I was talking to a very conservative CEO, and I could see that I had a situation here. Megan was a few feet away from me. I quickly excused myself from the conversation and placed my hand with my room key into Megan's hand. I mouthed in her ear, "See the big guy on the other side of the pool?" She nodded. "Let him in my room *now*, okay?" I pulled away and looked in her eye, where the hint of stress was overshadowed by her amusement. She navigated beautifully, saving the situation just in time.

All I could imagine was how Carol Anne's surprise would have unfolded. "Remember that thing you don't want talked about. Surprise! Happy birthday!" But it was becoming like that. I wasn't willing to be a prisoner again, but I still had to hide. And the longer things had to remain hidden, the more prone they were to finding a way to come out.

SITE SELECTION

I was chosen for the Athletes' Commission, but had to step aside because Canada was only allowed one spot, and one of our track athletes got more votes. It would turn out to be a blessing. Carol Anne called me in the early afternoon at the beginning of September 1996. The athlete representative on the IOC Site Selection Committee had had to cancel at the last minute due to family issues. She offered to put me forward for the spot.

"What does that mean?" I asked. "We are the commission responsible for the technical evaluation of the cities bidding to host the 2004 Olympics. There are eleven cities bidding. We have broken them down into four trips over the upcoming three months, as well as a debriefing in Lausanne in January, and attending the IOC Session next September when they will announce the city. Here are the dates." I looked at my calendar on the wall. "We start in St. Petersburg, Russia, in ten days. From there we go to Stockholm, then Lille, France. In

October we visit Seville, Istanbul, Athens, and Rome. In November we visit San Juan, Rio, and Buenos Aries. And in December we finish with Capetown, South Africa."

When I first heard the massive travel schedule that was to begin in less than two weeks, I didn't think I could do it. But in the middle of that night I awoke and knew this was an opportunity of a lifetime. I quickly accepted on the next day. That afternoon I received a note from His Excellency Juan Antonio Samaranch, welcoming me to the Site Selection Commission for the Games of the XXVIII Olympiad and wishing me well in my most important upcoming work. And so it began.

I arrived with Thomas Bach, German IOC Executive Member and head of our delegation, in St. Petersburg, Russia, the first stop of our tour. Police led us as we followed their motorcycle escort to our hotel in a 1960s style limousine. The hotel room that awaited me was bigger than my apartment in Toronto. This was a whole new world.

There had been a working dinner meeting that night of the commission, but I passed out when I got to the room and woke up around 9:30 p.m. I ordered room service and was shocked at the prices. I didn't realize yet that prices didn't matter. I could have anything I wanted.

What happened the next morning would begin a four- to five-day routine that we would repeat many times in the upcoming months. Half the time was spent in meetings, the rest in actual visits to locations and the various relevant venues. The meetings were held in some spectacular rooms around the world and always had an impressive formality about them.

The first part of every meeting was spent introducing each member of the commission and what we did. There were fifteen of us—ten members of the IOC sport world and five of us experts in other areas. I was considered one of those experts. We varied in age from twenty-eight to seventy-five.

Each member of the commission was responsible for at least one of the many files, including security, transportation, and government relations. This was where I started to notice how things *really* worked. I was the athlete representative, and in every single city I was positioned as the most important person on the commission, so important that I oversaw all the files. This was true on one hand. But it was also a clever way of saying that I had no file of my own. I shadowed the Olympic Village and some of the sports, but I was the only commission member with no direct responsibility. Crack number one. \

Essentially we were given a presentation from each city on each file of the bid. Then the commission member responsible for that file would ask questions, and then the meeting was opened to questions from the rest of us. It didn't take long for us to figure out how the process worked. Each section of the bid connected to many others, so if there was a problem with a bid, usually one of us would find it, and from there it would just unravel as we went from file to file, one problem leading to another until the whole thing came crumbling down. For example, differing seating capacities between the numbers listed in the Opening and Closing Ceremonies and numbers for the athletics events, which both used the Olympic stadium, exposed inconsistencies in a bid. This led us to budget problems, as a difference of 20,000 seats over sixteen days had serious financial implications. From there the whole bid would unravel. No amount of gifts could distract us from the facts. But that didn't stop people from trying.

Each city wined and dined us. Russia got us off to a good start, though, I have to say. We had a private tour of the Hermitage and the Summer Palace, and ate where Rasputin was murdered. We had a private classical concert, saw the Bolshoi Ballet, and met the prime minister of the country. Every night there were fresh cut flowers with champagne in my room, along with gifts that represented the activities of that day, like a trinket from the hermitage along with a hard-covered book and fresh caviar. These gifts from each city were then boxed and couriered home for us, often arriving days before us.

In Sweden we had breakfast with the king and rode in boats to the Ericsson mansion. In Spain we had a helicopter ride overlooking Seville, went to a bullfight, and had dinner with King Carlos's sister. In Rome we met movie stars and the president, and the handsome young mayor hosted us at a dinner overlooking the ruins of the ancient city. In Athens we met the president of Greece and toured the Acropolis, being taken directly to the top of the mountain by bus, a privilege very few people enjoy. An ambulance followed us everywhere we went, in every city, just in case.

There were moments when I was reminded of real life. It was easy to forget sometimes, being engrossed in high-level power meetings, endless food, and entertainment, having anything you wanted. It was easy to overlook the endless wasted buffets full of food for the fifteen of us that could have fed the entire hungry staff in some places we went. It was easy to fly first class, to stay at five-star hotels, to take gifts, to become part of a culture of entitlement. It snuck up on me without me even knowing.

In Istanbul, we stayed out by the airport in a Novotel rather than the Four Seasons in the city for a number of reasons. The rooms were fine, but not quite up to the standard to which we had become accustomed. Arriving in the room, I found no gifts, no welcome package, nada. My first instinct was to check out the whole room, because I thought surely there must be some gift somewhere. I looked under the bed, in the closet, I even went and checked in the bathroom. Nothing. I looked around that average little room and thought to myself, "Does this city really think they have a chance at winning?" It wasn't the proudest moment of my life, but I caught myself. How quickly we can lose sight of what it is that we are about. I was becoming assimilated. Crack two.

The Site Selection Commission had been encouraged to become a cohesive unit, and we had come together fairly effortlessly in St. Petersburg right out of the gate. There were a few wildcards, particularly a couple of the older IOC members, but for the most part we worked well together. It became clear in each city that Thomas set the agenda, because we met before the inspection began and he set the tone. To be fair, I don't think it was Thomas's agenda; it was the IOC's. Thomas was in very close contact with President Samaranch each part of our trip. Samaranch knew exactly what was going on, following the plan but giving nothing away to the outside world.

In each city we had a press conference at the end of our working sessions. It was the same speech eleven times, each city deserving a gold medal for their results, and then the mayor or bid leader receiving an Olympic gold medal from Thomas. It was the prototype from the same gold medal that I had worked sixteen years for.

I knew we were doing real work, and that it was valuable, but at the same time I couldn't shake the feeling that it didn't matter that I had spent months doing this; it was already predetermined anyway. That said, we weren't exactly a quiet group, and it wasn't always peaceful within our commission. Different cities hit different buttons with different members of the commission. We were fifteen people with fifteen egos representing numerous countries and constituencies, and even if the result was predetermined, it wasn't going to be easy to keep us all on the same page.

Blame It on Rio

The Site Selection Commission worked very hard, often meeting for ten hours in an official capacity before attending some kind of formal evening function. We took one night off in each city, and that was it. We followed the same routine, city after city, eleven times. Collectively and individually we became better and better at finding the flaws. It got to the point in some cities where we had to hold a special meeting to remind each other the intention was not to leave a city devastated because their bid didn't measure up.

We were never allowed to show how we really felt, which led to some brutal moments. San Juan had coordinated the largest human effort to see us out of the country that I had ever experienced. A line of people six deep in their festive gear cheered us as we left the hotel to get on the bus. The highway was closed to traffic on our side while the other had a sea of people waving flags along the entire drive to the airport. I caught the eye of Carol Anne, and through the plastic smile she flashed me I could see the agony in her eyes. I was smiling and waving but squirming with discomfort inside.

I also felt uncomfortable because the more time I spent with this insider gang, the harder it became not to share anything about my life beyond work. That was what would finally be crack number three and drive me to break. It wasn't enough to be able to be gay. I wanted it to be a part of my life so that I too could talk about my friends and family. Unless you can talk openly, it remains a secret, and like it or not, shame surrounds secrets. But I had agreed with Carol Anne that I wouldn't speak about it, so I didn't.

But people weren't stupid. Very early in the trip one of the IOC members came up to me and point-blank said, "Mark, are you *a* gay?" with his Spanish accent. The way he said "*a* gay" almost made me laugh. He told me he had noticed I didn't sleep with any of the beautiful girls that hovered around us in each city. "Are you a *gay*?" He was kind of kidding, but not. Carol Anne heard the word *gay* from a distance and masterfully appeared. "What was that all about?" she would ask me later, when we were alone. "You are going to have to talk with him. He's onto me." By the time Carol Anne worked her magic I became a part of this Latino IOC member's inner circle.

The environment at top-level sport at that time was hugely conservative. It was rule-bound, smothering, self-serving. My gayness was becoming a liability, but the more I hung around with this bunch, the less I cared. Given the high-flying life I was living, it also became a bit of a thrill to be breaking the rules in a high-flying way. I played the game alongside Carol Anne for many, many trips but something exploded in me in Rio.

The first day, there were a number of IOC people who went to exercise. As I was on a machine I noticed a stunning Brazilian man with short-cropped hair, a v-shaped back, and thick, hairy legs. He didn't seem to have a gay bone in his body, but he kept staring at me. Thinking I was imagining things, I moved across the gym. He followed. I shook with excitement.

I am still not sure exactly how it happened. He didn't speak English and I didn't speak Portuguese, but in the way that used to stun Debbie, in just a few seconds I communicated what hotel I was staying at, and by holding fingers up for numbers, figured out where and when we should meet. None of my IOC colleagues knew a thing. It happened so fast I could barely believe it happened at all. The ride home from the gym was bliss. It didn't last long.

Back at the hotel an emergency meeting had been called while we were at the gym. Before we even had a chance to change, we were told the news. The drug cartels that ruled the streets of Rio didn't want the Olympics to come to the city because it would hurt their sales, so they made death threats against us, the IOC Site Selection Commission, while we were in town.

Thomas Bach made it very clear that we were not to do anything out of the ordinary. This was a serous threat. We had to stay in the hotel. No unauthorized outings. For the rest of the trip we were each assigned security who would be with us at all times, and who would guard our doors while we slept. As this was unfolding I kept thinking about what I had just done at the gym, and I thought I was going to die right there. *What have I done?* I had invited a complete stranger into my hotel while I was with the IOC. And we were supposed to be extra careful here. Oh God.

Eight o'clock, our meeting time, came and went, and no sign of him, much to my contradictory feelings of disappointment and relief. I went to my door and checked outside. There was security at the very beginning of the hallway, far around the corner from my room, but I told them that would suffice.

At around 8:45 p.m. the phone rang. It was him! Gulp. After much disjointed conversation I realized that he was in the lobby and calling to see if he could still come. My heart pounded out of my chest. There was a knock on the door. I opened the door to see him in his business clothes. He was a business executive who considered himself straight but slept with guys sometimes. At least, that is what I gathered from our limited lingual mix. It worked out fine, but I had crossed a line and I knew it. I just didn't care anymore.

It was getting more and more difficult for me to play the IOC game. I was getting unruly, frustrated at feeling like I was wasting my time and not being respected. Slowly that feeling was spreading through our group. There was a growing unrest, and not just with me. Unanimity in our group decisions was getting harder and harder. Nerves were fraying and personalities were beginning to grate against one another. Slowly we were coming undone. Luckily we got a wake-up call in Capetown just in time.

Our world tour ended in this African city, and like South America, this continent had never hosted the Olympic Games. There was a lot of pressure to make sure they made the shortlist.

We started the meeting with a presentation from the president of the country, Nelson Mandela. As he approached the front of the room I was struck by how frail he was. He walked very slowly, and when he made it to the podium he needed thick glasses to read. Much physical damage had been done to him those horrible years on Robben Island. But it was truly something to be in his presence. He spoke about the social impact the games could bring to this part of the world. He challenged us to help him change the next generations' future through the power of sport. It was very moving. But his greatest impact came after the speech, during the photograph session.

For all the talk about athletes being the most important people, I found myself very much on the outskirts when it came to picture time. The most senior and most important IOC members took center stage, and we rookies took the wings. There was great attention given to protocol, naturally. C'est la vie.

As Nelson Mandela watched us lining up, saving the middle spot for him, he looked bemused from the sidelines. When they called him to come in for the picture, he went straight to the back, put his arms around the two least important people, me being one of them, and said he was now ready for the photo. Without saying a word he reminded us how we were acting when we were representing an organization that claims to value youth, fair play, and respect for basic fundamental human values. Mr. Mandela was clear. We are all equal and important here, none more so or less so than others.

At the end of the commission's site visits, I was left with a lasting impression of how much the cities wanted the Games, and the lengths they would go in order to get them. On the last night in South Africa there was a man dressed as Santa Claus who had a laugh I knew. As he approached I realized it was Bishop Desmond Tutu, carrying a sack of presents for us, playing his part to help support the bid. I had to remind myself how easy it was to get sucked into the allure of the Olympic rings.

But as much as the bid cities wined and dined, we on the IOC drank and ate. It took two to tango. I left with an inside view of how things worked. Once you were in, you were a part of the family. By the time my duty to the commission was over I would be the Secretary of the Athletes' Commission for FINA, an executive member of Toronto's bid for the 2008 summer games, and a member of the Canadian Olympic Committee. I had more titles than I knew what to do with.

I was getting in deep, and the deeper I got, the more impossible it was to keep quiet. The "if you get asked, don't tell" policy wasn't really working for me. On one hand, it was an extraordinary challenge and privilege to work at the highest levels of sport, but it was getting harder and harder to not ever speak about being gay.

CHAPTER NINE

RUPTURE

Point of No Return

One Saturday morning in the fall of 1996 there was an extraordinary breakfast meeting at Carol Anne Letheren's house in Toronto. She had brought together three former athletes, figure skating legend Toller Cranston, basketball great Sylvia Sweeney, and me, to discuss going into business together. Carol Anne, her partner, Michael, and my business partner, Jacques, made six at the table.

By the time we left that meeting later in the day, each of us had committed to do our part to build something together under the banner of The Camelot Group. We would combine our respective talents from the worlds of television, speaking, and performing to promote Olympism in a way that had never been done before.

Earlier that fall Carol Anne and I had been on a bus in Athens together. It was the sixth or seventh city on the Site Selection Commission world tour, and we were traveling back after a long day of visiting facilities. We were talking about our futures, after spending weeks in opulence with the IOC. "I need to make some serious money soon. I need to make a killing," Carol Anne had said to me. "I know" I replied. She had everything—power, charisma, intelligence—but the one thing she lacked was wealth. And having been part of the IOC, it was clear to me that if you wanted to move up that food chain, you needed cash. I just hadn't realized that I was part of that equation.

Carol Anne had big plans for me. I have to admit that at first it was thrilling to get her attention. She was such a force, had so many ideas, and was always suggesting things. In the beginning I appreciated her suggestions, but I eventually came to realize that if I wanted to stay on the inside, then I really had no option but to say yes to the things that she put forward. I wasn't particularly happy with this, but learned to live with it.

At that time, Carol Anne was in her early fifties, and the retirement age for IOC members was eighty. That meant technically she would groom me, and I would be beholden to her for another 26 years! The IOC worked the way any closed family operation works; it handpicked its replacements. At that time, the idealism of making a difference on the inside still had a strong hold on me, and I consciously wanted this opportunity. But I was still a little disappointed to see that nothing came for free or was as it appeared in Olympic sport.

One night as we were getting to know each other on a more personal level, Carol Anne came over to see where I was living and working in Toronto. She was kind enough through the tour, but the next time I saw her she *suggested* that Toller help me with my decorating. "Why yes, Carol Anne. What a good idea." Gulp. He came, did a survey, asked my budget, spent three times as much, and surprised me in the end by hanging his art in every room of my house, offering me one great price for everything as a fee for his services.

Decorating my place was just one step in Carol Anne's idea to get me ready to present myself with the kind of sophistication that she thought would be fitting for an IOC member. After the first trip of the Site Selection Commission she had asked Toller to take me shopping because my Armani classics were too "drab" for her liking. So I went. Toller's idea of sophistication was green blazers and blood-red shirts, and Carol Anne was pleased.

I found myself in a difficult position. I had become completely entangled in this life, and although it was different from my experience as an athlete at IMG, I was again part of a machine. The problem I had with the IOC was that it sold itself as a swan, upholding and representing the purest and noblest of ideals, but it was really just a duckling, an international business with many greedy individuals out to make money for themselves. Since nobody wanted to acknowledge this, many things were kept secret.

This culture of secrets hugely frustrated me. Gay was secret. My outside business partnership with Carol Anne was secret. It was a breeding ground for double lives. Everything was under the table, but it was a time in my life when I didn't want to keep secrets anymore. And the layers of secrets and unwanted surprises just kept coming.

One day I went into the office and Jacques and Sylvia pulled me aside. They had some horrible news to tell me. They had found out that our partner, the guy representing Carol Anne's interest as well as being in charge of all financial matters, was being investigated by authorities for "borrowing" a very large sum of money from his clients. This was getting better by the minute. The three of us—Sylvia, Jacques, and I—decided this first project would be the last for The Camelot Group.

When the truth was admitted to us later, I was furious with Carol Anne. She had known when she put us all into business together that this was happening, but she didn't let that stop her. I had even gone for dinner with her one night and told her outright that I had some mixed feelings about the Prince Charming who was representing her business interests. Although I wasn't happy that the price of my involvement in the leadership of amateur sport might mean some personal benefit to Carol Anne, I realized my participation required her support. If I had to go into business with her, I wanted to do it directly and not with her partner. "You know I can't do that, Mark. My partner looks after my best interests," she replied. Very badly, I thought to myself.

The pinnacle came when her partner, out of sheer desperation to hang onto staying in business together, threatened to tell the world that Sylvia and I were gay. He did it with innuendo, like he would hate to be forced to share *"our little secret"* with the press. It was pathetic, especially given that *all of us* except Carol Anne and her partner were gay.

Nothing like a little extortion among friends. Carol Anne and I had passed a point of no return. A trust had been broken that would never be able to be fixed again. But finally I would have the freedom to publicly find my *whole* voice once and for all. It would be harder than I thought.

A WELCOME KISS

I saw a sexy man with a tattoo in the summer of 1997 in Berlin. He was a Swiss actor and former figure skater by the name of Benjamin Kiss. I was visiting Berlin for the weekend of their gay pride parade when I met him. I spent hours and hours talking openly and freely with this beautiful stranger. Our time was intense, warm, connected. I felt something and asked him what was happening. He said he didn't know, but he felt it, too.

Within a month, Benjamin would move with me to Toronto, and we would spend the next three-and-a-half years together. Benjamin was everything I wasn't. He had been openly gay since he was fifteen. As estranged as I was from my mother, he was close to his. Where I was strongly material, Benjamin was strongly spiritual. Where I was structured and organized, Benjamin was creative and flowing. We met in the middle and fell madly in love.

We were different but we fit, partly because we were both intense. Benjamin had had a very interesting but hard life. He had been the victim of discrimination when he was the Bern champion in figure skating. But as opposed to shying away from gayness as I had, Benjamin looked it straight in the face and became rebellious—not against his family, but against society. Benjamin's mom was a free thinker who encouraged difference. She was a proud socialist who brought Benjamin to marches. He had led a student protest at his theater school later in his life. And for all those things I was crazy about him.

Benjamin will always be one of the great loves of my life. He came to Toronto, supported me in every way possible, even traveling and becoming part of my business. The arrangement was that we would try to split our time equally between Canada and Germany, but in the end it was more like nine months based in Toronto, three months in Berlin, with me only there half that time, if I was lucky.

It was incredible to be in Berlin, discovering the city through an extensive route of bike paths by day and cabarets and clubs by night. The European attitude toward sexuality was so different, so open. There was something special about Berlin. The years of occupation created multiple cities, many underground, and we were living through a time when it was all coming back together. East met west, underground came above ground, and we discovered ourselves amid this emerging melting pot.

It was a time of exploration, travel, and questioning. But where artistic freedom ruled life in Berlin, life in Toronto was dictated by the corporate world. It was in Bermuda on the eve of my 30th birthday when these two sides to my life collided, when I knew that things weren't working, and that my life would have to change once again.

As Benjamin and I checked into a hotel for a corporate presentation, the travel agent for the company I was speaking for looked horrified when she saw there were two of us and realized she had booked me a room with only one bed in it. "That will be fine," Benjamin told her. "No it won't!" the woman responded. "We'll have to find you another room." Benjamin looked at me to make an intervention, but I didn't. I wasn't ready to take such a stand.

When we arrived in the room with two queen-sized beds Benjamin was furious. "Why didn't you say anything?" he demanded. "What does it matter?" I replied. "I didn't want to make a big deal out of it." But Benjamin knew the truth and he threw it at me, which is what I loved about him. "You are more concerned about what a complete stranger thinks than you are about us. How am I supposed to be your partner when you would sacrifice our relationship before admitting to being gay?"

And he was right. I was so used to playing the game of silence and omission that I didn't even know *how* to speak out at first. I couldn't even support my partner who *was* speaking out, for crying out loud! Here was a guy who had moved from Berlin, who had made sacrifices to his career as a stage actor to live with me in Toronto, and I didn't even have the guts to acknowledge our relationship.

Asking for only one bed in a hotel was such a little thing, but it was exactly those little things we normally take for granted that were starting to make my life unbearable. *"Don't speak about it, Mark."* Everywhere around me, that was all that I had heard for years. I was still in hiding. But Benjamin was here now. He was out in the open, and if I didn't change he was going to be out of my life. And I was just about to learn how important love and support are in life.

GET HOME NOW

In the fall of 1997 I went home to Calgary for a couple of weeks to introduce Benjamin to my family and friends. It was a big deal because until that point being gay had just been an abstract concept for my parents. They had never met anybody that I was dating, let alone intending to spend my life with. Benjamin coming into their home gave being gay a personality and a face. And Benjamin gave good face.

Handsome, fit, and intelligent, Benjamin was one of those guys who was multitalented and could get along well with just about anybody. He could cut hair, work with handicapped kids, act, paint, even teach aerobics. He was spiritual and sensitive and strong. By the end of our time in Calgary he had cut the hair of half my friends and family. He was a hit.

Toward the end of the trip we had dinner at my parents' house, but it was a Tuesday, the night my mom went singing with her choir. Dad said he would like to barbeque some steaks, so we did an impromptu soiree. My parents still lived in the house where we had moved when I was in grade seven, but what had before been a remote area on the edge of a vast wasteland was now fully developed suburbia. Jerri-Lyn, my old friend, also came over. We laughed, sharing stories of the past with Benjamin.

As I sat in the same seat at the dining room table where I had sat during that dreaded *Rocky Horror Picture Show* incident that Easter dinner so many years ago, I had to smile to myself. There was Benjamin, my boyfriend, sitting in front of me with my dad to my left, and they were both laughing and enjoying themselves. I would have never imagined this possible. My life had certainly changed.

There was something wrong with my dad, though. He was hobbling around, having real problems with his spine and hips. He had been to a chiropractor, and thought that had eased the pain for a short time so he was going to go back. My dad was a fun-loving guy who was famous for being the life of the party, but he was also stubborn and rule-bound. He wasn't willing, for example, to accept a brand new car that his father-in-law had wanted to give him as a wedding present so many years ago. He was still extremely proud, and I knew that he would not share his pain openly. But I could see he was suffering.

A couple of days after I got back to Toronto, I spoke with my mom on the phone. Dad had gone to the doctor and had some routine tests. The results showed some problems but no one was thinking it was that serious. Then, an ultrasound showed growths on his liver and a biopsy was ordered. We were all scared but didn't want to jump to any conclusions. On the day when the results were supposed to be ready, Dad called the medical clinic. "Yes, your results are here and it is cancer," the stranger on the other end of the phone said. "Sorry, I have to take another call," she said, and then hung up.

Dad was self-employed. He and one employee ran the show at a black-and-white photo shop. He was at the shop when I called from Berlin. "Hey Dad." "Hey Mark." He sounded fine. I thought that was a good sign. "How did the meeting go?" "Just a minute, okay? I'm just finishing up with a customer." After a few moments he came back on the phone.

My dad's retail space was tiny; there was only a little closet-sized space at the mall where he could get away from the customers for a moment. I knew this little space was where he was standing. At first, I couldn't make out his words. "It's cancer," I finally heard him whisper. He started to softly cry. I didn't know what to say, except, "Oh God, Dad. I am so sorry." Then he sobbed.

I had never heard my dad cry on the phone. Ever. I had only known him to sob once before in his entire life, at his mother's funeral. I felt so helpless. I asked him why he was working. He told me he thought it would be good for him. I made him agree to go home. The scan had shown spots on his liver, spine, brain, arm, and lower vertebrae. There was so much cancer in his system that it was a miracle his bones hadn't snapped.

It was a turning point for our family. Until that moment my brother, sister, and I had been the kids. Suddenly everything was different. Those who were strong became weak, and the weak became strong. The kids became responsible while the parents fell apart. Roles were played in order to be able to cope. The first one up to the plate was my sister.

The medical establishment was very intimidating for both of my parents. Colleen went to all of the meetings with doctors and specialists and asked questions, insisting that the practitioners answer her in a language she could understand. If a doctor had no time for her, she changed doctors. In the first three weeks she went through four oncologists.

Colleen had always said that her dream was to be a great mom, having a couple of kids and being a caregiver. Not for nothing did she have this dream. But it was still surprising to discover these little moments of inspiration among the gloom. With her directness, her no-nonsense ability to simply get to the facts, she became our surprise caregiver; we had never seen her play such a role. She was remarkable.

Scott and I both lived away from Calgary. I was supposed to be heading to Australia with Benjamin for the World Aquatic Championships to be held in Perth at the end of December. The tickets had been bought in September, and I had to decide what to do about Christmas. Colleen helped make it easy. Scott and Melanie, my sister-in-law, would come for Christmas, spend time, and take the first shift, and I would stick to my original plan, being away and then coming to Calgary in January to take the second shift. Colleen agreed that if things looked bad she would call immediately.

On the second-last night of the World Championships in Perth, the dreaded call came. I was part of the Athletes' Commission at that time, and when I returned to the hotel from the pool late that night there was a message to call Colleen immediately. My heart sank. What was happening? When I spoke with her things didn't look good. Over Christmas, Dad had started radiation treatments and they seemed to be having a positive effect. But that changed almost overnight. His weight had just dropped dramatically, he was weaker than ever, and he asked if I could come home now. I quickly did the math in my head. Getting from Perth, Australia to Calgary, Alberta would take about forty-eight hours. "We are on our way," I assured Colleen. "Tell Dad to hang on!"

When we arrived home I saw a ghost of my father. He came down the stairs with the help of my mom, and I just couldn't believe that this man before me was my dad. He was bone thin, yellow, beyond frail, more like broken. But he was so happy to see me. In the moment we hugged I could feel him squeezing me as hard as he could, which wasn't very hard. I was reluctant to squeeze back given his frailty. It was heartbreaking to see him like that, but both Benjamin and I did our best to hide our shock.

One day during one of his chemotherapy treatments a nurse stopped me as I walked down the hospital corridor. She recognized me, and she wanted to tell me how sorry she was for my family. I shared with her our hope that chemotherapy was going to really work. She was very kind and gentle, and she listened to me as if I was the only person in the world. And then, with that same gentleness and intense gaze, she said to me, "Mark, make sure you spend as much time as you can with him *now*." Her hand softly squeezed my forearm as she said it.

I understood what she was telling me. For many years, Dad and I had run from settling unresolved issues between us. Now we would have to face them, or we would never get the chance. It was a time of talking, of coming to peace, and of trying to let go of past hurt, although it wasn't easy, even when facing death, to let go of some painful patterns from the past.

Give Me a Sign

We spread my father's ashes on a beautiful early summer day. The memorial service had been hard but celebratory, and surprisingly uplifting. My father had been an atheist, and remained a non-believer until the very end. He didn't have any instructions whatsoever for his funeral and yet somehow, for a conservative man, he certainly had a unique farewell. A female pastor delivered the memorial, my mom's choir sang, and we planted a tree in his name.

The emotional toll that the disease had taken on our family was enormous. In the first weeks of diagnosis we spoke about cancer morning, noon, and night. Colleen led the research. She was exhaustive, but we let Dad make his own decisions. We bought him a La-Z-Boy armchair, and planted him in the middle of the family room so that he was a part of things. That was at first.

Eventually the horrible time came when we all realized that Dad would not be getting better. We had tried everything, from visualization and belief exercises to radiation and chemotherapy. We even considered experimental clinics in Mexico. But ultimately we had to face the reality that Dad was going to die.

My father's illness coincided, probably not accidentally, with a time in my life when I was doing a lot of reading and spiritual soul-searching. Perhaps one of the greatest fringe benefits to being gay was that it forced me to constantly question, first myself, then the world around me. I spent many hours by Dad's bedside reading books, being there for the few moments when he would wake up.

Dad was getting very, very sick. He needed help to do absolutely everything because he was so weak and full of morphine. But he was still heavy enough that Mom and Colleen sometimes couldn't carry him. One of the most terrifying moments came when I was giving my dad a bath. I was aghast when I saw him naked. He was yellow and shriveling. When we got him out of the tub he was slippery, and three of us were holding onto him for life, literally. He was so frail I was afraid of what might happen if he slipped.

My mom and dad were sharing a bed the entire time my father was ill, and it was taking its toll on my mom. It was a brutal period. There was so much to deal with. I can't imagine sleeping next to the person you shared your life with and watching this unfold. But my dad had such a force to fight for his life. He was close to death so many times. He was hanging onto life by a thread, but there was no letting go, which was where I came in.

In the gentlest way possible, we needed to find out if there was something we could do to make that transition from life to death any easier for Dad. Unfortunately, my father had lived a closed life in many ways, and in the end he was not able to change that. He didn't believe in anything after life. He didn't care about his funeral, or seeing a priest, nothing. It wasn't necessarily a point of aggravation; he just had absolutely nothing he wanted to say in these matters. Still, it didn't make it any easier to talk about the things that needed to be discussed. I had to find my voice, but in a very different way.

The one good thing that came from the cancer experience was that from time to time my dad talked about difficult issues, even if only momentarily. Not often, but every once in a while, he felt compelled to get something out. On a short neighborhood walk one day, he told me out of the blue that he was worried for Mom's future. He had wished he had spent more time dancing with her. Another time he confessed that he could never understand or accept my homosexuality. He just couldn't get past the fact that two guys were together physically. He hadn't reacted as badly as my mother had to the news in the first place when I had come out in the kitchen in 1992, but he didn't ever come around like she did, either. He told me he still loved me, but he just didn't get it. I still loved him, too, but I did get it. Many men get stuck at looking at being gay as a physical act, and can't ever get past that to understand the emotional and spiritual part that brings two people together in a relationship. But just because I understood his limitations, it didn't make it any less painful to hear he couldn't accept me as I was.

One morning I sat by his bedside reading yet another self-help book. I had just finished *The Celestine Prophecy*, and I teased my father. To break the mood between us I said to him, "I know you don't believe in any of this, Dad, but just for the fun of it, if you get to the other side and there is something, give me a sign, okay?" He rolled his eyes, but betrayed a tiny glimmer of humor in them as he did so.

Dad's battle with cancer was over by the end of May. Now the burial preparations began. One of the favorite things Mom and Dad used to do was go walking near the mountains with their friends. There was a trail around Beaver Lake that they loved, and this was where my mom decided that we were going to spread my father's ashes a few days after the memorial service. It would be a day I would never forget.

It began at a bookstore early in the morning after meeting my friend Debbie for coffee. I had been looking for something in particular, and a saleswoman helped me out. On the way back to the register she asked me if *The Creative Visualization Workbook* was any good. As she was ringing me up, she stopped, leaned forward, and said, "I never tell people this, but I feel compelled to tell you that I almost died a few years ago. I had a terrible accident and I was pronounced dead, but I didn't die. Instead I came back, but I remember seeing the world as a giant mathematical equation and everything made sense. In the end, the world balanced out to all equal zero." She took a breath. "I really don't know why I am telling you all this. But the strangest thing is that after the accident I understood all mathematical equations. My husband is a physicist and I help him now with his work." I stood there stunned by her news, quickly paying my bill before running to my car, where I started to bawl. I was already extremely emotional, and this stranger had overwhelmed me by sharing her secret. I had traveled the entire world seeking enlightenment and here it was in a strip mall in Calgary.

Later that day, when we got to Beaver Lake to spread my dad's ashes, it was glorious. We had taken the bouquets from the memorial service, and added all of the drying flowers into two large, brown paper bags full of petals to spread. The sun was shining, and the air was fresh. There were about ten of us in total, and without a lot of speaking we started following each other into the trees. As we walked we could see the mountains on the other side of the crossing, and hear the flow of water from the dam the beavers had made. It was somber but stunningly picturesque. As we walked we looked for the spot to lay my father to rest. I have to admit, the competitor in me, as well as Mr. Spiritual at the time, wanted to find the *perfect* spot. I was scouring the landscape, saying to myself over and over, "Come on, Dad, give me a sign, give me a sign," when I heard my mom's friend scream, "Over here!"

We all gathered around her and she had found *the* spot, I had to admit. It was a shaded area surrounded by a group of trees, with a bank of grass beside it. You could still hear the running water, and the sun was breaking through the trees to create a large sunny patch, which is where we all gathered in a circle. To make room for everyone I took a step backward and felt my foot hit something. When I looked down to see what was at my feet, my mouth fell open. There was an unopened can of beer. I couldn't believe it. For as long as I could remember my dad had loved beer. It was part of what made him the fun-loving guy of the party. We all screamed as the shaken beer was sprayed around as if it was champagne. Then hundreds and hundreds of flower petals were placed on his ashes. I had wanted a sign from my dad. I had gotten it.

CHAPTER TEN

STEPS TO FREEDOM

TATTOOED BLOND BARBIE

My father's death was heartbreaking and a huge loss, but with it came closure. The house that we had grown up in was suddenly too big for Mom, and it was sold. Memories were boxed; van loads of goods were given away. Scott and I moved Mom into her new condominium. She ended up having a charming place, but for her, Dad's death would mean loneliness and depression. For me it would mean freedom.

The change started from the inside and made its way outward with such a force there was no stopping it, even if I had wanted to. What had begun in Australia, and been nurtured in Berlin, would inevitably give birth to an openly gay life in Canada. But not without its own struggles.

I had never thought about it when my father was alive, but I realized when he was gone that our relationship was a major obstacle in my own acceptance of being gay. My father and I had disagreed on just about every single social and political issue. We had so many heated debates that our relationship had been burned long ago.

But there was an inherent respect that I felt for my father in spite of our differences. He had adopted me, taken care of me, provided for me. Neither he nor my mom had ever made an issue out of the fact that two of their kids were adopted. They had been giving, and I unconsciously wanted Dad to give me his acceptance before I spoke about being gay in public. I knew it hurt him that I was gay, and out of respect I didn't want to cause him embarrassment. When I had come out to him and Mom on that Remembrance Day so many years ago, he had told me something that I had never forgotten. I had asked, "Didn't you have any idea that I was gay?" My dad responded, "A few times I heard guys walk by the store and point to your picture and say, 'Hey, did you know that guy's a fag?'" He was barely audible. I could feel his shame.

I think there was this awful double meaning for my father, having this son who was an Olympic champion, a decorated athlete who should be the definition of masculinity, and yet at the same time I was gay. In his eyes, I was flawed. It was only in his death that I found closure with him on this issue, although in the end closure meant that we would always have to agree to disagree on this particular issue. But with him physically gone I could finally begin my own long process of acceptance.

I continued asking myself a lot of questions about life. The courses I had studied in Australia got my mind probing. *Why was it only in death my dad could cry? Why was he so freaked out that I played with Barbie? Why was he so homophobic, not wanting my brother to go on a trip with a guy my dad thought looked gay because he had long hair?* The poor guy wasn't gay, he was just forever labeled by my dad. *Why, even in the end, was Dad so closed, never allowing his vulnerability and emotions to show?* I was baffled, and at the same time, I understood. His shame had become mine.

The more I looked at my dad, the more I saw a part of myself. I was opening up slowly. At least I could hold Benjamin's hand walking down the street in Toronto, or kiss him in public. At first I was so self-conscious there was really no point because I was too worried about what people were thinking to actually be there and enjoy the kiss. These feelings ran deep. This intense fear of difference was within me as it had been in my father. No matter how hard I tried to fight, I had to finally reconcile these conflicted feelings within myself. It was a matter of survival.

Reconciliation came in strange ways. Benjamin and I had played with a deck of Zen tarot cards from the very beginning of our relationship, and one particular card, the rebel, had always struck me. I hadn't really considered myself rebellious, but at this particular moment it fit. The commentary on the card said the rebel was the master of his destiny. On his shoulder was an emblem of the sun, showing that he had broken the chains of society's repressive conditioning. His very way of being was rebellious, not because he was fighting against anybody or anything, but because he had discovered his own true nature and was determined to live in accordance with it. I got a large sun tattooed on my right shoulder a few months after Dad's death. I felt different, branded, but by my own conscious decision. It was the first step.

Later that same summer, as my business partner was celebrating his fortieth birthday, I suddenly had this compulsion to go blond. Earlier we had gotten onto talking about hair coloring and Benjamin said that if I ever wanted to do it he knew how, since he was a hairdresser. "Really?" I asked. "Really." Two hours later I was in my underwear in the basement sitting in front of my computer answering emails with aluminum foil all over my head, transforming. I had been a kid with dark, wavy hair who had always wondered what it would be like to have straight blond hair (just like Barbie!). Now I would know. When we showed up for dinner at the restaurant the response was overwhelmingly positive, but now it was impossible for people not to see that something was going on with me. That was the second step.

During this time I wasn't thinking about being gay, or coming out; I was just on a personal mission to express myself. Tattoos and dyed blond hair were my way of honoring something within and at the same time revealing something about myself without having to speak about it. That was the beauty. I still wasn't ready, so I didn't have to talk about being gay. Something was changing within me and everyone could see it without me having to say a word, until eventually one day, an old playmate appeared and brought it all out into the open.

One late summer day Benjamin and I were downtown in Toronto, walking along Church Street, and noticed a garage sale table with all kinds of odds and ends. I was rifling through some of the book titles, and looking at various items when I saw her. There was Barbie, lying there wearing these black and white lace panties that rode her ass, with a top that her perfect perky boobs were popping out of. She looked like Slut Barbie. I had to have her. "How much for Barbie?" I asked. "One dollar." I didn't even bargain. Who says a dollar can't buy anything anymore?

That night I had a bath, playing with Barbie for the first time in over eighteen years, loving every minute of it. I looked to the ceiling of my bathroom and said, "See Dad, Barbie and me in the bathtub again." I smiled to myself. I had maybe five more baths with Barbie before she found her permanent home straddling the water faucet, her outfit perfect for the new mission. But with this plastic doll came the third step in my own personal mission to heal and finally accept myself. Every day when I showered, Barbie was there, just a little reminder that I was slowly beginning to wash the years of shame away.

DREADING WEDDINGS

During much of 1998 I felt like a snake that needed to shed its skin but didn't know how to let go and just allow it to happen. The corporate world in Toronto was already stifling, just more so now because I was finally facing my own demons. I didn't like myself as a person very much at this time and I looked for ways to escape. Benjamin and I smoked pot, indulged in sex, drank, ate too much. It was like there was a hole inside of me that I couldn't fill. The intense years of discipline and sacrifice I had known as an athlete gave way to a different kind of intensity as I overindulged, experimented, and struggled to find comfort in my own skin. Years of running hadn't made dealing with reality any easier.

For all that had transpired, I was still living a life with layers of truth. I could speak about being gay in some places, but not in others. And many times when I was brave enough to speak openly my boldness would be met with blunt discrimination.

Benjamin and I went back to Calgary for a wedding. Ted, the straight friend I had tormented with my teenaged lust years ago, was getting married. At his wedding reception I was catching up with Ted's dad when I noticed that Benjamin was in the buffet line. Hungry, I excused myself, and headed over to join him.

As I neared the line, two couples behind Benjamin intercepted me and said, "Hey, *Mark Tewksbury*. Great to meet you! Wow, you look great. What are you up to these days?" I spent a few minutes talking, and then turned to greet Benjamin. I gave him a little hug and then introduced him as my partner to my new friends. If looks could kill there would have been a double homicide on the spot. Bam, the two fags were dead.

They were so disgusted that a gay couple was in front of them they actually left the buffet lineup. I couldn't believe it. Five seconds earlier I had been someone they wanted to know, and now I repulsed them. Discrimination is like that: shocking because you are going along taking equality, respect, and human decency for granted when all of a sudden it is ripped away in front of your face. You are suddenly reminded that no matter how hard you pretend that we are all equal, in the eyes of the ignorant we are not.

But things like this pushed us to action. After this incident Benjamin and I made an agreement that we would live openly in our personal life, even if it meant facing this kind of reaction from people.

It didn't mean that we always made an announcement that we were gay; we would just show up to events as a couple. We didn't have to do anything more. Sometimes less was better, especially at weddings.

My younger brother, Scott, and his fiancée, Melanie, announced after eight years of dating that they were finally getting married. We shared in their joy, especially when we learned the wedding would be held in the more open-minded Miami instead of Calgary, where our last wedding reception had been so harsh.

South Beach had to be one of the gayest places on the planet at that time. There was a strip of art deco hotels across from the beach, and Benjamin and I stayed in the pink one near the top end of the drag. We were there for a family wedding, one of those rare occasions when you not only see your own extended family after a long break, but in this case, also meet a whole new family, Melanie's side, for the first time. Although I had told my mom and dad that I was gay, they hadn't told the extended family yet. Between the location and Benjamin attending with me, they were soon to find out.

Benjamin and I were joined in Miami by many relatives. Aunt Cheryl and Uncle Terry were liberal-minded relatives from B.C. who knew I was gay. Small town Albertan Auntie Jo, the most devout woman you'll ever meet, and Cousin Patty, also somewhat conservative, both didn't know. When Jo saw my blond hair she said, "Oh my," scrunched her face up, and grabbed the cross that was hanging from her neck. She had had eight kids, and most of us Tewksburys had been to at least six of those weddings, so she came with her oldest daughter representing her family.

Uncle Jim, my dad's younger brother, was also there. He didn't know about me either. It was the first time we had seen each other since Dad's funeral, and fragile emotions made the tension high.

Scott and Melanie had the most unorthodox wedding imaginable. The maid of honor was a straight man. Bridesmaids included a photographer, a club hostess, and a tattooed lady. The ceremony took place at a public pool space, which I was certain would be a disaster but turned out to be quite magical. And equally intense.

We arrived at this public pool, complete with a bridge, numerous pools, and an island, where we had the actual ceremony. They kicked the last kids out at 4 p.m., and we were scheduled for a 4:45 wedding. The doors were to be opened at 4:30 p.m. There was not a single dry spot at the entire venue. The wedding party, the parents, Benjamin, and our relatives all swept away the water and set up what we needed for the wedding. The bridge needed to be decorated, the island set up for the ring ceremony, and the reception area set up for the dinner afterwards.

At 4:20 I was swearing to myself and thinking this was the stupidest idea anybody had ever had. This was going to be a complete disaster. A wedding at a pool, what were they thinking? At the height of this insanity someone had touched a nerve with my mom about her being alone now, which left her near tears. Benjamin was taking care of her, because she was so sensitive about being at a family event for the first time without Dad.

But amongst this chaos something happened. Somehow the hundreds of things that were going on and seemed to be going nowhere all came together in a moment. The frantic energy that had been driving this whole weekend broke, and this potentially tacky nightmare turned into a romantic dream.

Something was in the air that night. At the beginning of the trip we had all been worried about what Auntie Jo and Uncle Jim would do about Benjamin and me. When Benjamin was introduced, it was as Benjamin. Period. Not Mark's boyfriend. Just Benjamin. Kind of like how Jean was introduced by Auntie Dot. This is Jean. Period. But of course everybody knew that Benjamin was my boyfriend, just nobody talked about it openly.

At the end of the reception, still at the pool but at that time of day when the sunset casts a glow on everything, Benjamin was out back having a cigarette with the girls when I went to join them. As I approached, Auntie Jo said, "Okay, you two. I need a picture. Come on, Benjamin." Then she really shocked me. "You guys look so cute together!" I couldn't believe it. If I'd had a cross around my neck *I* would have reached for it.

After the pool ceremony, the wedding party moved to a nearby local bar for drinks. Everybody came at that point, but as the night wore on, most of the older generation parted, leaving the wedding party and a few troupers, like my Uncle Jim, to round out the night. We moved onto a club called Liquid, and as we arrived it became clear that there was something special about this particular club. It was gay. As Uncle Jim and I ended up beside each other on a couch having a beer, surrounded by dancing gay men, I smiled and said, "I guess you know about Benjamin and me?" He smiled back knowingly. Finally my secret was out in the open with my family.

SPEAKING ABOUT OUT

My father's death marked the beginning of a cycle of change. One by one, things started to fall apart in my life, as if the world was helping me make space for what was to come.

One of the main issues between my business partners at that time was how vocal I should or shouldn't be in terms of my gayness. I was living my life more and more openly with Benjamin, and I argued that it was a matter of integrity that I was open about this. In the past I had found a way to compromise. ∕

On one hand, I was a public figure, speaking to companies, working extensively with charities, and involved heavily in the leadership of amateur sport. On the other hand, I was a private person who was entitled to a private life.

People in my inner circle, including my gay business partner, had discouraged me from ever coming out publicly. "Why does it matter?"

they would ask. And for a long time I agreed with them. Work and private life should remain separate. Everyone agreed that it was okay to be gay, but at the same time it should never be spoken about in a business environment.

A Jewish colleague reminded me that just because she was Jewish didn't mean that she had to share that with everybody she worked with. Fair enough, but her professional life wasn't based on sharing her experiences with people; mine was. And whether she realized it or not, every day at work she talked about her family, and didn't have to hide her preparations for holidays as they came throughout the year. I was asked to hide a large part of myself in my professional life, and although it was extremely hard, I bought into this logic for a long time.

As I began to move deeper into significant positions of leadership, though, I found myself speaking about what constitutes a good leader. "Bring your values to life. Lead by example," I would say to the audience. I would get home and ask myself, "So what kind of example am I setting, hiding who I am? What about the things I value, like honesty and respect and integrity?" Something had to give.

At that time, Toronto had many corporate fundraisers connected to AIDS or gay-related causes, and I found a compromise for my own situation by attending these events openly with Benjamin. We went to Fashion Cares at the convention center and were amazed at the designers' show and the thousands of people attending the party. I submitted items for another AIDS fundraising campaign, and even became the spokesperson for the National AIDS Walk. The more events we went to, the more integrated we became into the gay community of Toronto, and suddenly it didn't seem to matter so much that I officially came out. I *was* out.

Okay, I was out, but still not speaking about being out. That would change one October evening when I accepted an invitation to speak to a group of gay businessmen who met once a month in

Toronto. In all of the years I had been speaking, over a decade at that point, I had never spoken to a gay audience. I was nervous, not just because I had never spoken to a gay audience before, but because *I had never spoken publicly about being gay before*! This would be a big first for me.

A lot of gay activists were disappointed with me for not coming out in a bigger way earlier in my life, but I hadn't been ready. I sometimes wondered what my life would have been like had I been able to come out when I had won the Olympics. I came to understand with time that every person has his or her own process to go through, and until they have taken that journey there is no point pressuring them to be a voice, because they aren't ready. They would probably do more damage than good. I may not have been ready then, but I was now. I just hoped the audience was ready for me.

I had been expecting a gay crowd, whatever that meant, as if there would be nothing but drag queens in the audience. In front of me that night I saw men of different colors, religions, political beliefs, and incomes. They were as diverse as any group I had ever spoken to. It just happened the one thing they had in common was being gay. For some, that was where the similarities ended. I loved giving the speech, the men loved getting it, and new possibilities opened in my mind.

A few weeks later Benjamin left for Berlin. He had to go back to perform in a play, and I would join him in seven weeks, just before Christmas. We had been through so much that year, but as he left it seemed to all be coming together. My family had completely accepted us, we were becoming a part of the larger network of lesbian, gay, bisexual, and transgendered (LGBT) communities in Toronto, and we were living the way we had wanted to for such a long time.

But just as it seemed to be coming together when Benjamin left, it all came apart.

WINTER GARDEN DEBUT

The first time I went back to public speaking after my father died earlier that year, I stumbled hugely out of the gate. In front of a thousand people I blanked out live on stage, completely forgetting where I was for a moment. With lights blasting my face and a vast silent darkness in front of me, I tried to recover but couldn't completely. This was a speaker's worst night mare come true, and for a moment following this disaster I considered that it might be time to get off the speaking circuit.

Although traumatized, I had to go the next day and give another speech that had been booked months ahead. I was also very stressed still from the cancer journey our family had taken, and was feeling completely despondent in the back seat of the taxi driving into the city from the airport. I had already been debating coming out publicly, knowing that it would most likely result in a career change, but couldn't help but wonder if this blacking out was a sign that it was time. It was going take a small miracle for me to get back up on stage to speak the next day.

When I arrived at the hotel the general manager greeted me. "Mr. Tewksbury, what a pleasure to have you staying with us tonight!" I stood a little taller. "I am happy to give you the keys to the Royal Suite, the most beautiful set of rooms in town. Let me show you them."

I hadn't been in a space this grand since I was on the Site Selection Commission. It was fabulous, with a sumptuous bedroom and a deep Jacuzzi tub for four. Yummy. The room next door was the real suite, and I did run around it later. I played on the grand piano, got some champagne from the minibar, wrote my speech at the dining room table, sat in each of the four armchairs and two couches, but ultimately couldn't be kept from that tub. This intervention certainly changed my spirits. Who could stay blue drinking bubbly in bubbles?

The next day I gave an inspired speech that was met with a standing ovation. Things seemed to be all right after all.

In fact, although there had been that hard initial start back at work following Dad's death, from that moment onward things just seemed to keep getting better for me on the speaking front. My fear of having to give up corporate speaking because I was gay was replaced by a new found confidence as the year progressed. Not only had I enjoyed the chance to speak openly for the first time to a gay business group, on top of this breakthrough my speaking agents had rented a beautiful old theater in downtown Toronto later that same fall to showcase three of their speakers and I was to be one of them. Popular journalist Pamela Wallin, Canada's Barbara Walters, and author Michael Dechter were the others. Each of us was given about twenty minutes to showcase ourselves.

It was a chance for potential clients to come and hear us speak, and to mingle afterward. It was a huge marketing opportunity, and I invited everybody I knew to come and see me. Even Carol Anne promised to come, impressed to see me share a stage with Ms. Wallin. The icing on the cake was that I had landed a lucrative contract that would see me speak in twelve cities across Canada for a company the following year, and this showcase was also a chance to have this client come and see me speak live. This was going to be a huge night.

Coming off the speaking experience with the gay business group, I worked with Benjamin to ensure my twenty minutes left an impact. I had never used slides before, but I did on this occasion. We also used music to introduce me. It was intended to get the energy going because we were in such a big theater space. We arrived early and did a rehearsal and everybody thought it was great. Pamela arrived, as did the emcee, another popular female journalist. The atmosphere was wonderful because I had gotten to know both these women over the years. I was the first presenter, and as the starting time neared, the emcee and I waited together backstage.

We could hear the theater filling, and were updated frequently with time countdowns. The mood was upbeat, energetic, and exciting.

After being introduced, ABBA blasted overhead and I came bouncing onto the stage. I waved to the audience and then made my way to the podium. I gave my twenty-minute speech, as usual. People responded very favorably with a long ovation and lots of positive feedback later in the night. When I made my way to the balcony afterwards even Pamela turned to me and gave me a thumbs-up. It was a great night, a big break for us. So we thought.

A few days after the presentation I received a call from my speaking agent at the National Speakers Bureau. She told me she had some news, then told me I should sit down. Never a good sign. I was confused and nervous, having no idea what she wanted to tell me. "I just got off the phone with the consultant for the financial institution," she told me. This was the company that I was doing the twelve-city tour for in the upcoming year. A few weeks before the Winter Garden show I had been interviewed by the consultant representing the company. My agent continued, "I don't know how to put this, so I am just going to say it. This is really awkward, and this has no relation to anything we think, but your tour has been cancelled because they think you are too gay." I laughed a little, because I was so embarrassed and stressed I didn't know what else to do. I said, "You're kidding, right?" as I felt my cheeks get hot and flushed, and a sick feeling entered my stomach. She kept talking. "I have no idea where they are coming from, Mark. Maybe it was your dyed blond hair. Whatever, I tried everything I could but they have decided to go with someone else."

I hung up the phone and sat dumbfounded for a moment. I was completely numb. I took a minute and then looked over to my business partner, Jacques. "You're never going to believe what just happened. I just lost the six-figure contract because they thought I was too gay." He got on the phone to my agents to hear it for himself.

I left the office and went to get some water and some air. For so many years I had done everything possible not to be "too gay" in my working life. I had listened to everyone but myself, even compromised my own values, and look where it had gotten me. It still wasn't enough.

The irony was that I was sure the consultant himself was gay. My gaydar, which basically uses instinct to recognize one of my own, went off big time when I had met him. I had to admit that while the corporate people around me thought my presentation was enthusiastic and refreshing, an old queen in the crowd would see it as the gayest thing ever. My big blond hair, white teeth, bouncing on stage to ABBA. He was probably squirming. All of that self-loathing he still had for that part of himself was staring him in the face through me. I had no chance.

Just because I understood it didn't mean I liked it. This was discrimination of the worst kind, by one of your own. At first I was deflated. I always thought I would react more valiantly in the face of such discrimination, but it simply stunned me that people, especially another gay man, could be so small-minded and fearful.

That passed and I became upset. Then I was plain old-fashioned pissed off. I was too gay? Fuck you! Maybe I wasn't gay enough! Freedom may come with a price, but I felt like I had nothing left to lose. Bring it on!

CHAPTER ELEVEN

ENOUGH

LEARN TO LET GO

It was time to shit or get off the pot, so to speak. Losing that contract because of another gay person was a final straw of discrimination that broke my back and gave me the courage to jump into the unknown, to try something new. As unpleasant as it was, in some ways I was relieved that this was finally happening. I had been so sick of playing the guessing game. "Who knew I was gay? Who didn't? Can I talk about it here? What if I make a mistake?" Enough already. I was going to tell my whole story once and for all.

I decided to do a one-man show live on stage. Instead of corporations hiring me and my having to fit into that tight messaging box, I would sell tickets to the public and have the freedom to talk about issues that mattered to me. That was the plan. We booked a cabaret space at a famous local LGBT (Lesbian, Gay, Bisexual, and Transgender) theater, Buddies in Bad Times. We took out a small ad in the local gay paper advertising that said on December 15, 1998 at 8 p.m. I would be doing a show, "Out & About." We partnered with a local AIDS hospice organization to make the night a fundraiser. Everything was in place. Now, I just had to create the show. I had less than six weeks to do it.

At that time I was taking improvisational classes at the Second City comedy company in Toronto. Every Sunday I went for three hours of instruction, slowly learning to open myself to being in the moment onstage, free to do or say whatever came to mind. Years of exploring various philosophies had left me familiar with the concept of living in the moment, but through improvisational classes I saw this theory come to life. The best improvisational work was uninhibited, it flowed, and it had a life of its own. All you had to do was let go and keep your own ego out of the way. Instead of controlling what would happen, you needed to trust that things would unfold as they should. It may sound easy, but it was incredibly difficult to do, which was exactly how I found writing the show.

I had to overcome some major obstacles in order to come out completely. The first was myself. Writing could be a wonderful vocation when I had something to write about and the ideas flowed. When nothing came, and I knew I should be writing something because each day brought me closer to my debut date, it was hell on earth. I usually didn't write my speeches (I just did a loose outline and knew where I was going), but since this was a one-man show I decided I needed to script it formally. I sat writing for hours, and then got to the end of the day, read it back, and deleted everything because I thought it sounded so stupid, often ending the day with nothing done.

What I was writing about were many of the early stories in this book, but facing these stories from my past for the first time was overwhelming and terrifying. I had never really put my whole self out there like this before. I had assumed that creating a one-man show was going to be easy for me, like a good speech. It was nothing of the sort. Finding my voice was very hard after so many years of silence.

Part of what held me back was my fear of how people would react to me. Not for nothing was I my mother's son, and as comfortable as I was getting in my own skin, there was still a part of me that was afraid of being rejected. There was one area at the time where I came to feel very accepted, however.

For years I had been involved with various nonprofit organizations as a volunteer, and one in particular, Special Olympics, preoccupied me at that time. I first became involved when I was still swimming in Calgary and went to give medals at a Special Olympics competition. Never had I seen such raw human emotion as with these very Special Olympians. I could relate to these challenged individuals, understanding completely what it felt like to be ostracized and stigmatized by society.

I owed my ongoing national involvement with the Special Olympics organization to Mr. Brian Etherington, a successful Toronto businessman. He had suffered from polio as a child, leaving him permanently affected, and like me he knew the face of discrimination only too well. One morning in 1996, Brian invited me to a lunch at his private men's club. He was setting up a board of directors to govern the Special Olympics Canada Foundation, a new initiative aimed at securing the finances for future Special Olympians in Canada. He wanted me to be a part of the board because of my longtime involvement with the organization and my active role in sport leadership. Actually, he insisted. I joined the CEOs of some of the country's most blue-chip companies, including Coca Cola, the Royal Bank, and Toyota, as well as a few senators and other leaders, in steering this organization.

Brian had moved me deeply the preceding year when he gave the keynote address at a Special Olympics fundraising breakfast. He started the speech in his usual gracious manner, thanking the emcee and taking the spotlight away from his own accomplishments by reminding us that neither he nor the Special Olympics would be there on their own today. Then, with no warning, he went for the jugular. "By your interest individually and corporately, you are helping to level the playing field for a segment of our population that for too many years has been condemned to the room at the back of the house with the shutters drawn." I had goose bumps on my goose bumps, holding my breath for his next words. "How did people with a mental handicap come to find themselves in that darkened room? It certainly wasn't because of personal choice, or something that they did wrong. They didn't volunteer to be different … they were just led to that room by the caprice of nature itself."

He was speaking about the Special Olympians, but he was speaking about me, too. I could substitute the phrase "people with a mental handicap" and replace it with "gay people" and it had the same meaning for me. Brian continued, "I believe that each of us has within ourselves our own darkened room where we have closed a door on the full exercise of our own capacities. I rejoice in the opportunity you and I have to break some of our self-imposed chains and to allow the light into our closed-off rooms." At my table I was a wreck, not able to turn off the faucet behind my eyes.

In the weeks before I came out publicly it was my colleagues from the Special Olympics Foundation who were part of a recurring nightmare I had. Many nights in a row I imagined these powerful CEOs flying in business class together and collectively opening the paper, finding out in the back pages of the sports section a story on my coming out. As they were reacting I would wake up drenched in my own sweat, panicking at my news being out. Where was this fear coming from?

In the immediate period after my father had died, Brian had become somewhat of a father figure to me. The fear I had felt and that acceptance I had sought from Dad was temporarily transferred to Brian and his colleagues in my dreams. And I knew when I came out they might not be able to accept me, just like Dad hadn't.

Although my fear of not being accepted was enormous, my desire to live my truth was finally stronger. I was prepared to lose everything, sure that if I was completely rejected by the communities I used to participate in that something new would come my way. But it was a difficult time, with my thoughts playing tug-of-war between boom and gloom.

As I was getting ready to do my one-man show I had a strange twist of fortune: I received a call inviting me to be the guest speaker at the very event I had heard Brian speak at the year before. This was my chance to give my colleagues a small hint of what was to come, to turn my potential nightmare into a dream. I very carefully chose my words for the short breakfast speech.

When I finished, the audience stood in ovation, hundreds of people giving me positive energy, and I took it openly and gladly. I had told them that my life was about to take a new road, and thanked them for teaching me about compassion, understanding, and acceptance. I smiled to myself. That voice in my head that for so many years had haunted me by saying *if only you knew who I really am* was now replaced with the knowledge that they would very soon find out.

RUMORS AND INNUENDO

I knew a major obstacle to my coming out would be Carol Anne. She was powerful, and she had been clear that I shouldn't speak publicly about being gay. The final challenge in the weeks leading up to my one-man show was to keep what I was doing under wraps from her for as long as possible. But keeping this quiet was a major challenge. On one hand, the news was out there, in the small advertisement for my show in a local gay weekly newspaper. After all, I needed to have an audience to fill the theater for the show. But just as I had created a gay life for myself by going to events in the community, I didn't expect news of my gayness to travel beyond a small group of people. Getting ready for the one-man show, however, changed that because friends and colleagues from the mainstream press suddenly took an interest. The bridge began to build between my worlds of private community and public mainstream.

When I was creating the show and needed an outlet, I spent time with very close friends. Patty Young had been one of my closest confidantes in the world of swimming, reporting on the circuit for the *SWIM Magazine*, and we had spent hours together in different parts of the world. Now she was working for the *Globe and Mail*.

She wanted my story. One day after I shared some of my stage material with her, she paused just long enough to determine if it would be appropriate, then said it would make a great article. "No way, Patty," I said immediately. "There is too much pressure just doing this show. I don't want the media attention. Maybe once I have done it and staged it somewhere, then we can see."

At the 1996 Olympics in Atlanta I had been approached outside a venue by Steve Buffery and Christie Blatchford, two star print journalists in their own rights from Toronto. They asked me point blank, "Are you gay?" I couldn't lie to them, so I said yes I was. But then I begged them not to write the story until I was ready. They had promised to wait for me, and I had promised to tell them first. Now Patty wanted the story, because there was a bigger story of losing a speaking contract and coming out onstage, and my solution was just to say no to everyone. But then there was a twist.

Pamela Wallin had been at the Winter Garden Theatre that evening my "too gay" presentation took place, and when she spoke with Jacques and found out about what had happened, she wasn't pleased. She wanted me to do a coming-out interview on her prime time television show. She wasn't going to take no for an answer. Patty wasn't either. These two women wore me down. I had one condition. I did not want this information out publicly before the one-man show on December 15. There was already enough stress without this added media pressure. They both agreed.

On December 6th I headed down to CBC for the taping of the *Pamela Wallin* show. When I arrived at the massive building that takes up several city blocks in downtown Toronto, I took a moment to gather myself. I went to the washroom, escaped for a moment of quiet, and questioned myself to make sure everything was okay. I was clear, conscious, in the moment. I went out to the security desk, checked in, and was met by a producer to be taken to the studios.

I went through make-up and said a quick hello to Pamela, and now we were on the closed set, just Pamela and me facing each other, separated by a desk, with a couple of cameras and crew in a large, vacuous space. We were going live-to-tape, which essentially meant we wouldn't stop taping unless there was some huge screw-up. I sat in the guest chair listening to Pamela get instructions in her earpiece and then speak to the control room. A gentleman played with the microphone on my shirt and text rolled on the cameras for pacing. Then suddenly everything was in place, and Pamela looked at me and asked if I was ready. Gulp. I said yes. "Here we go. Just stand by a second." And the countdown began. In five … four … three … two … Fingers pointed to Pamela as the red light went on.

"He is an Olympic Champion. A three-time Olympic medallist. Seven-time world record holder. Member of the Canadian Sports Hall of Fame. Member of the Canadian Olympic Hall of Fame. And tonight, Mark Tewksbury talks about being gay in the world of sport for the first time."

As she said it, I felt my heart skip a beat. Every time we came back from the break Pamela would go through this intro, and each time I heard it I thought I was going to faint at any moment. I knew what I was doing, but to hear it like that coming out of Pamela Wallin's mouth freaked me out a bit. What was I doing here?

Thankfully, this thought passed very quickly because Pamela made me feel instantly comfortable. She was very sensitive, knowing this was tough for me, and she gave me the whole show so we could explore the complexity of my life for so many years. Because we were taping, we would break for just a moment when it was time for commercials, and then pick up again where we left off. It went remarkably fast, and by the end I felt really good about how the interview had gone. Now it was just the *Globe*.

I hopped a taxi and met Patty at a restaurant for the print interview. Print media was different, and could be more difficult because unlike a tape where your answers are unedited, a print journalist could take your quotes and put them into many different contexts, not always flattering. Patty and I spent a couple of hours talking, and even though we knew each other well, we kept a professional distance. I was very conscious of what I said. A photographer came, wanted to know what the story was about, as did the staff of the restaurant. The closer we got to the date, the more people started to talk.

It was only a matter of time before Carol Anne found out. Since the demise of our business venture together we had still remained in contact, just not to the same degree as before. I had been installed in so many positions with so many titles during the IOC time that we had no choice but to still work together.

At first I had been discarded to the sidelines, only getting the coldest of responses from Carol Anne, when I got any at all. There was a new athlete she had her sights on, grooming this woman to take some of the positions once earmarked for me. I didn't mind one bit. This time I was an outcast on purpose.

Over time, though, things had warmed up considerably. Carol Anne couldn't help but be impressed with names, royalty, wealth, and prestige. After she saw me speak on the same stage as Pamela Wallin at the Winter Garden Theatre, I was suddenly invited back into the fold. I had done my penance and was put back on the main bill. I spoke at an important event for the Canadian Olympic Foundation in October. I was invited out to an intimate dinner for six in November. I was on the executive committee of Toronto's bid for the 2008 Olympics.

Things appeared to be changing. But within this change too much had remained the same. Before, at least, Carol Anne and I had been partners; now she was the boss. And she didn't let me forget it. It was kind of nice to be involved again, but the way it was done left me with a bad taste in my mouth. Instead of celebrating some great posting, I felt trapped by it.

Carol Anne had stopped consulting me on things. Now she ordered. We were in the middle of a board meeting for Toronto 2008 when they were looking for someone to handle the Olympic Village file, which was huge. Without even glancing at me Carol Anne said, "Mark will take it." And that was that. It was definitely an honor, but I thought the way it was done sucked.

I knew if Carol Anne found out I was coming out, she would use all the power she now had over me to stop it, so I did whatever I could to avoid her in those last few weeks.

It wasn't easy, because one of the last public appearances I made before *my* big night was *her* big night, as CEO of the Canadian Olympic Committee. One of the kingpins behind Alliance Atlantis partnered with Carol Anne to create a fundraiser. We had a wildly successful, sold-out world premiere of the film *Shakespeare in Love*, complete with the director in attendance to speak to the VIP audience. I was the emcee.

The minute she saw me, Carol Anne made a beeline for me and told me she had heard some rumors that I was up to something. I played dumb, not opening up one iota to her prying. Hadn't her advice always been not to talk about this, I asked myself. Well, I used her own reasoning to deal with her that night. Thankfully we were both very busy in our official capacities and she couldn't delve too far into what she had heard.

As the lights went down for the movie, Carol Anne and I ran to the seats her partner, my former business partner, had saved for us in the theater. In the movie, set in Elizabethan times, there was a scene where the male actors had to dance with other male actors dressed as women. The crowd snickered. Carol Anne's partner, right at that moment, turned to me, looked me in the eye with pure glee and said, "Good luck." Carol Anne knew what was going on. And it was nice to see through her partner's acidic well wishes that some things would never change.

The Media Circus

I woke up late the morning of December 15, 1998. It was 9:10 a.m. I walked downstairs to get a drink of water and noticed the flashing light on the phone. Instinctively I picked it up and checked. The voice mailbox was full. There were messages from friends and businessmen as well as eight requests for interviews from morning shows. Oh my God!—the article.

I rushed down the next flight of stairs to open the front door and get the paper. I looked at headlines on the front page. Nothing was there, thank God. Flipped to sports, nothing on the cover. Pulled it out and flipped through the section and couldn't find anything. Hmm, why the calls? Then I saw it. On the bottom part of the front page of the paper, below the fold, which I hadn't noticed at first, glared *"A Sports Hero Declares He's Gay. Olympic-gold medal swimmer Mark Tewksbury comes out voluntarily, in a difficult and costly situation."* Oh my God! There it was. On the front page. Oh my God.

Patty would later explain to me how the editorial process works at a national newspaper. Every day the various heads of departments met to share their stories with an editorial team that chooses the headlines that make the front page. Many factors had to come together for the final decision, and on December 15, 1998, my human interest story became front-page news.

I had never actually been a news story before other than because of my swimming. And when I was the story I had always been away from home when it happened. I had no idea what it meant to be on the front page of a national paper, but I was soon to find out. I cleared the telephone of messages, made a list of ten media requests, and by the time I was through the voice mail box was full again. It didn't end. Talk shows, radio and television news, friends giving well wishes, and then more interview requests. As morning broke across the country there were new waves of requests every hour on the hour. It was crazy.

By 11 a.m. I was still in my bathrobe. The one-man show was tonight and I was supposed to have a rehearsal at 1 p.m. I decided it was time to get the day going, to stop thinking about all of this media stuff and get focused on my show. I was just getting into a bath when the doorbell rang. I ignored it, sure the person would go away. The bell rang and rang, then rang again. I got more and more pissed off, trying to relax despite this persistent ringing every thirty seconds. Furious, I finally got out of the bath, threw on my robe, marched down the stairs, and flung open the door. Stupid thing to do.

There I found a CBC reporter with a camera who wanted to do an interview. I told her no, I wasn't doing interviews until after the show, later in the week. Before I could stop her, she stepped inside my front hallway. Now she was in and she wasn't leaving without an interview. Thankfully, before I said anything I thought to call Pamela Wallin and her producers. When Pamela learned there was a CBC reporter in my house, she freaked out because she was supposed to have the exclusive first television interview. Media worked that way. It was no problem that the *Globe and Mail* was out because that was print and it could help drive viewers to the show that night. But a news clip would squash Pamela's scoop. She went into action.

I had wanted to avoid a big press thing on the day of the stage show, and here I was in my bathrobe finally escorting the interviewless reporter out of my townhouse after an hour-long stand. My 1 p.m. rehearsal was shaky, to say the least.

Around 6 p.m. I headed down to the theater. It was a beautiful night, calm and warm, and I noticed the bustling of the city on the drive down, thinking to myself, "This is it!" Because of the media coverage the show was completely packed, standing room only, with a great buzz. I had wondered exactly what I would say in the first few moments. Then as I was entering the theater that night, a truck drove by and the guys inside screamed, "Fucking fag!" and threw something. There was my opening. It was like that for the whole show. Everything fell into place—part scripted, part improv—and allowed me to share my story for one night. The show went as well as I could have hoped.

There had been a press conference scheduled for December 17th to deal with the overwhelming number of requests for interviews. Part of me wondered if we were wasting our time, since this was two days after the show. I needn't have questioned. There was an entire row of cameras and dozens of members of the press. The main question I faced was, "Why are you doing this?" Many people asked, "Who cares?"

Both the mainstream and the gay press said the same thing, but for different reasons. Some of the gay press asked intelligent questions. Their "who cares" was in the sense that I was already out. They challenged the traditional press with headlines like "The Closet Holds Few Surprises Except for Mainstream Media." Other gay rags weren't so generous, accusing me of coming out to further my career. Their "who cares" was bitchy, as in who cares, he's only an ex-athlete anyway. It was a personal decision for me to go public, and I knew people would say whatever they wanted. But it wasn't only the gay press that was divided.

The mainstream press collectively said "who cares," as in, why do you have to talk about this, yet over ninety interview requests had arrived within hours of the news hitting. The biggest shows in Canada all wanted interviews, every single one of them. I guess *someone* cared.

I had been very friendly with Valerie Pringle at *Canada AM* over the years, having first met her when she was at *Midday*. Valerie was doing my coming out interview on the morning news show. The studio was way out of the downtown core, but the show splurged for limos for all guests because we had to come in so early. As I was getting seated, Valerie was wrapping up another segment before taking her place with me. "We're giving this one a lot of time today," she said to the producer. "How long?" I asked. "About four-and-a-half minutes." Four-and-a-half minutes to capture everything. I laughed to myself. But I could see Valerie was in no laughing mood.

The second or third question out was "Why do we have to talk about this?" She was all smiles; it was the tone that was tough. I tried hard to explain it but some people just didn't get it. I wasn't there to talk about *sex*, what I did in the bedroom, because although that might have been interesting for some, that wasn't the point. I was talking about my *sexuality*, how I connected to the world, how I felt love, how I was human. It was a fundamental part of me. But I realized that in North America we still didn't talk about sexuality, really. Doing so in any form made some people feel very uncomfortable.

One talk show host later started her show by saying the infamous introductory line, "He's out of the pool and now he's out of the closet." I laughed out loud before taking phone calls live from viewers. One of the things I had most feared when I was closeted was that dreaded caller who would ask me on national TV if I were gay, but now that was behind me. I hadn't felt this good in a very long time—open, comfortable, free.

As the news of my gayness spread across the country I received an enormous amount of correspondence. The number of people who supported me was extraordinary. One of my most prized letters came hand-written from a powerful CEO. "Great to see you speak openly about yourself and the people and issues that matter in your life." There were many surprises like that for me.

Of course, not everyone liked the news, but at least for many, small-minded people, gay now had a face. I posed a problem for them because on one hand they admired what I stood for as an athlete and Olympian, and on the other hand my announcement disgusted them. I hoped to bridge that gap.

As I was heading out the door for Berlin to finally spend time with Benjamin as Christmas approached, I checked my messages for the last time. I had missed a call from Pamela Wallin, but there was her strong voice booming through the phone on the message. "Well, sweetie, it's been quite a week." She wasn't kidding. There had been a media storm, and I had been at the eye of it. Even my poor mother had cameras waiting for her when she had arrived at her job in Calgary. "You caused quite a stir. Couldn't you just have stayed in the closet?" she laughed. "I guess it is too late for that," she added. Too late indeed. I had finally crossed a line, personally, and there would be no returning from it.

For years I had been so terrified of this moment, and now it was done. It would take some time before I realized that this was only one little step. The journey of coming out, declaring who you are and what you stand for, never really stops.

CHAPTER TWELVE

OUTSPOKEN

THE SAMARANCH AVALANCHE

My first step to freedom was accepting who I was, but standing up for something I believed in quickly followed. There had been a part of me that wondered if I would be forever labeled "gay swimmer" after I came out, which would have been ironic, because those two words hadn't ever fit together in my athletic career. Both had remained polarized identities, fully a part of me but still kept completely separate. I could have never foreseen the chain of unrelated events that would unfold almost simultaneously as I came out, and with my gay part strong, suddenly there was a reason for the athlete side to stand up, too.

As an up-and-coming swimmer, I had watched the leaders of the Olympic movement from afar. I watched as, just as at every Olympics for as long as I could remember, IOC President Juan Antonio Samaranch closed the games. First on television and then eventually live as a competitor, I waited for his famous "best ever" line to indicate how a city had done in putting on the games. He struck me as extremely serious and cold. My experience with the IOC as an athlete had been that many of the members seemed to be there only for the show, in and out of the VIP box. They seemed wealthy, with most wives dripping in designer clothes and jewelry, and, most of all, they were inaccessible. It turned out I wasn't far off.

The first time I met Juan Antonio Samaranch, president of the International Olympic Committee and leader of the Olympic pack, was during the Site Selection Commission's debriefing meeting in Lausanne, Switzerland in early 1997. We were staying at the Lausanne Palace, where Mr. President had a permanent set of rooms. I was waiting for the elevator to take me down to dinner where I would dine on china embossed with gold Olympic rings. Just as it arrived I had this premonition that Mr. President would be on the elevator, but I missed my split-second chance to escape before the doors opened because he saw me. I had to get in. As I entered we greeted each other with a nod. He was with his secretary, who was always beside him with a bag of goodies when he went out in public. I was going to speak, to say something to him, but it didn't feel right to do that. There was a very royal vibe going on, like *don't talk to me, I'll talk to you*, so I kept my mouth shut. It was kind of disturbing, though. He was such a small, seemingly ordinary guy, but that diminutive physical exterior couldn't mask the power that made him seem great to so many. Mr. President prided himself on bringing a regality into the IOC. He himself had been bestowed a title, and he really seemed to take it seriously with his huge attitude. That night he thanked us with an expensive engraved watch for the hard work we had done on the Site Selection Commission. It was very nice to meet him in genuine IOC style.

The second time I met him was later that same year in the summer. We were again in Lausanne. Those of us on the Commission but who were non-IOC members were observers of the presentations of the five finalists and then of the vote for who would host the 2004 Olympic Games. Athens, Buenos Aries, Capetown, Rome, and Stockholm had been the five finalists. It was a remarkable day. Nelson Mandela spoke. Luciano Pavarotti sang. We eventually all gathered in an auditorium with satellite hook-up to different parts of the world to see the exhilaration of Athens winning contrasted with the devastation of the four cities losing. It felt a bit like leaving San Juan during the site inspections in 1996, having to keep a straight face on the highway all over again.

Immediately before the General Assembly broke for lunch, the Site Selection Commission was invited up to the front of the room to be introduced to the IOC members. As we neared the stage, I saw that Mr. President was greeting each of us with a handshake. As it was my turn, I slipped off the ring Benjamin had given me and very briefly shook his hand while looking into his solid black eyes. I didn't want him to touch anything that held sentimental value. He really gave me the creeps. His "absolute power" style of leadership made me feel absolutely disgusted. But he was the president and keeper of the international Olympic torch. Thankfully, our paths rarely crossed.

In early December, a few days before my one-man show, I heard on the radio that Mr. President seemed to be in a bit of hot water. I was on my way to Second City for my improvisational acting class on a Sunday morning when the news broke on the taxi's radio. A Swiss IOC member had let it slip that other members of the IOC had received extraordinary gifts, otherwise known as bribes, from Salt Lake City in return for votes for their candidature to host the 2002 Winter Olympics. The world media pounced, the IOC went into overdrive, and I went back into my bubble of doing my show.

About six weeks later, toward the end of January, I sat at home in Toronto as the IOC news conference was carried live from Lausanne. I was curious to see how Mr. President would handle the scandal that just didn't want to go away. The IOC Executive had called emergency meetings and this press conference would announce to the world how they were going to deal with the situation that was unfolding.

I listened with disbelief as Samaranch, in front of a packed auditorium in the Olympic Museum, told the world press that he took no personal responsibility for what had happened. The blame was instead shifted to a handful of IOC members, mostly from Africa and other underdeveloped parts of the world.

One reporter even asked explicitly if what he heard Samaranch saying was right. "For clarification, let me see if I understand this correctly. You are saying that you assume absolutely no personal responsibility whatsoever for this situation that occurred under your leadership?" Samaranch didn't disagree. What a contrast between the powerful leader I had met in the elevator and this tense, silent man who made everyone around him speak during the press conference.

There were promises of further investigations, but the higher you got up the IOC food chain, the quicker the penalties went from severe expulsions to slappings on the wrists. The bid city process would be changed, but it was a complicated system that needed real reform to become fair, not just the façade of reform. The proposed ethics committee sounded promising, until a majority of members were appointed from within the IOC. The more things changed, the more they stayed the same.

It wasn't the fact that there was a crisis that was so upsetting. All of us are human and make mistakes. I was myself a part of the problem. I took the gifts. I looked the other way when I knew we were making decisions based not on technical merit but on personal prejudice. What I found so distasteful was the way in which the leadership of the IOC dealt with the scandal. We had a chance to come clean, to fix the problems that stood behind these cracks in the armor, but nobody wanted to make that effort. Athletes of the world were being held to the highest standards possible, but the custodians of the Olympic ideals were not willing to hold themselves to anything remotely close to this same standard. Something was not right here.

There were many people around the world calling for Samaranch's resignation. Unfortunately, very few were athletes, for a number of reasons. One was that only a handful of athletes ever got close enough to the real power base of the IOC to see how it really worked. Largely, athletes preferred not to know, because to acknowledge corruption at any level would be admitting that their sport itself might be tainted. That was how I had felt as an athlete. There were rumors of steroid usage by swimmers, especially women, but I never wanted to even consider that any of my male competitors were using. How could I sacrifice what I did or compete against them with this in mind? So I had turned my head, just like most athletes chose to do through this scandal. Besides, these were the Olympics we were talking about. It was like motherhood and apple pie. No one wanted to admit that these things weren't perfection itself.

Another reason for the silence was more pragmatic. Many athletes were afraid. To speak against your sport association could directly affect your likelihood to be picked for a team, or be judged fairly, or be overlooked for funding.

Where once I had chosen to turn a blind eye, I now couldn't. I had seen too much. I knew how the system worked and had no secrets holding me back anymore. Unfortunately, I knew firsthand about the power of silence from being gay, and I couldn't endorse this IOC strategy of deflection and scapegoating by staying quiet.

I did a newspaper interview and spoke about my experience with the IOC and what the culture was like, and I asked when leadership of amateur sport would ever take some responsibility. That piece created a ripple effect around the world simply because there weren't other athletes taking a stand. Media outlets called from the U.S., Australia, England, Germany, Switzerland, and Japan. I was a bit overwhelmed and slightly scared by the international stir this interview caused, but having recently been through the process of speaking about my sexuality and seeing that everything had worked out, I made a promise to myself that I would see this thing through and stand behind my remarks no matter how hard it was.

Finally I had taken a step to live my life with some kind of integrity, and I couldn't live with myself if I wasn't forthcoming. A press conference was called to handle the requests. Little would I know how far the ripples would continue to go.

I hadn't called Carol Anne before I spoke out. I was making her very nervous, and she was glad to hear from me that evening. "You know I respect your opinions, Mark, and that you can always call me about things." *Call me first* was what she meant. We had come to agree to disagree on a growing number of issues. This night she was defending her IOC president, telling me that I had to keep in mind Samaranch's age and his cultural background. She absolutely thought that he shouldn't resign, although she admitted he must have known what was going on. She argued that, considering who we were talking about—a privileged Spanish diplomat in his late seventies who ran the IOC like his personal court—he had made some big changes. I countered that I did my best to try to forget where Mr. President came from, particularly his history with the leadership of the Franco regime. He was the head of the Olympic movement, and he had created the environment that had led to this mess in the first place. I argued that if his style or pace of change wasn't the best to make things right, then maybe he shouldn't be there anymore. It turned out that I was the one who shouldn't be there. I was the one who didn't fit.

No Regrets

On February 4, 1999, I resigned from all my posts within the Olympic movement. There had been a meeting in Lausanne at an international doping symposium, and Samaranch had done a number on the Athletes' Commission. There had been the opportunity for the Athletes' Commission members to become full-fledged IOC members in the near future, which was an excellent step forward even if athletes would be the *only* IOC members at that time who had terms. The most they could serve would be eight years. This was just long enough to know the system, but not long enough to have any real power within this complicated, sophisticated political machine. All the athletes had to do for their eight-year appointment was publicly support Samaranch, which they did.

The IOC put forward a press release positioning the IOC Athletes' Commission's *unanimous* support of Samaranch and his initiatives as being representative of all athletes around the world. I took exception. I had a complete crisis of faith in the leadership of amateur sport, from Juan Antonio right down to Carol Anne. I resigned.

I had at one time thought I could make a difference on the inside, but saw that there was little chance of that now. Knowing it could be decades before I was in a position to speak openly in this environment, I didn't want to waste my time. I had been a part of this movement for more than twenty-two years. After the initial hurt and disappointment there was a surprising freedom. I had my whole life in front of me. But that feeling didn't last long.

Keith Stein was an executive at Magna International, and was ambitious, smart, and well-connected. We met one day late in February at a local restaurant in my neighborhood in Toronto to explore doing a website together, but instead Keith couldn't stop talking about my doing something about the IOC. The allure of celebrity, power, and the Olympic world was intoxicating to him. Coming from a position of power within a maverick corporate culture, he applied the same let's go get 'em attitude to my situation, trying to get me to make change within the upper echelons of Olympic sport.

Already surrounded by money and political ambition, he couldn't stop obsessing about what I could do to drive change in the Olympic movement. He wasn't willing to accept that I was just walking away. He thought I should do something, like start an organization where people could come together and through a campaign encourage reform of the IOC.

I absolutely resisted, free at last, until he brought out the heavy artillery. "What if a group of people helped you do it?" he asked me. "Look me in the eye and tell me you could walk away if you had a chance to do something." I couldn't. The next day we had a meeting with another Magna executive, Belinda Stronach, at her mansion on the Magna compound.

The initial financial commitment was modest, but as the campaign grew, so did the level of all of our investments. I remember asking the small group of us gathered at the very beginning, "Do you realize what we are talking about here?" In the end I held out the longest, probably because I knew what the IOC was. This was not going to be fun. But I couldn't *not* do it. Belinda seemed involved for the same reason I was. If you had the opportunity to do something, why wouldn't you try? She told me one day, "I don't want to look back and think I *should have* done something and I didn't. Let's do it." I liked that about her. She didn't have to care, but she did.

And as much as I didn't want to care, I did. The courage that ultimately led me to speak publicly about my personal life was cultivated through my many years of participation in sport. Competition challenged me to live with integrity, to be an honest and fair person, which was partly why I had felt so conflicted for years about keeping my sexuality a secret. Now that same courage was needed, ironically, to speak about upholding integrity in the very sport system that had taught me these values in the first place.

The name OATH, for Olympic Athletes Together Honorably, came from Keith. We became advocates as we partnered with race-walker Ann Peel and rower Heather Clarke, and many other prominent Canadian athletes, lawyers, and activists who, together, would take on the unenviable task of reform.

If there was any chance of getting an international grassroots campaign going, we needed to move quickly. We set a goal of launching OATH at the IOC Assembly on March 16 in Lausanne, less than three weeks away. It was a very bold idea, but one that made sense. The world press was at the IOC headquarters for the news of the expulsions and reforms, so we could go on their turf in Switzerland where they would never expect us to launch an initiative against them.

An unforgettable Aunt from childhood, Dot. She was full of surprises.

Courtesy of Mark Tewksbury

Left to right: Three charming elderly ladies in my life, Jean, Grandma McDonald and Auntie Dot. I would spend a month with them every summer.

Courtesy of Mark Tewksbury

Christmas was always a big deal with our family.
From left, Mark, Mom, Colleen, Scott and Dad.

Courtesy of Mark Tewksbury

Mom, Dad and I in front of our Calgary homestead. When I was a kid,
we moved every year, but that changed with this house.

Courtesy of Mark Tewksbury

Dad could be very tough, but could also be a ton of fun.

Courtesy of Mark Tewksbury

Surprising mom at her 60th birthday! She and I are very close again.

Courtesy of Mark Tewksbury

The only coach I came out to while I was still competing,
Debbie Muir, on a holiday together in Australia.

Courtesy of Mark Tewksbury

The women around me growing up: Jeri Lyn, Debbie and Tyrell.

Courtesy of Mark Tewksbury

The only time I was straight – in the pool.

© Olivier Sanson

Prince Albert and I became fast friends upon meeting
in Monaco in 1990.

Courtesy of Mark Tewksbury

The star of the 1988 Olympics, double gold medallist
Carolyn Waldo, smiles with me before Barcelona.

Courtesy of Mark Tewksbury

My mentor into the world of international sport politics, Carol Anne
Letheren, head of the Canadian Olympic Committee, and International
Olympic Committee member.

The opulence and grandeur of an IOC meeting as experienced in a Russian hall. I am third from the bottom left. St. Petersburg was the first of eleven cities we visited as part of the IOC Site Selection Commission for the 2004 Olympic host.

Courtesy of Mark Tewksbury

There was a buzz of activity from that moment forward. We incorporated, drafted bylaws, booked travel, got a logo, and printed materials. It was fast-paced and intense but it was the only way to play against the IOC. One murmur of what we were doing and they would have used their mighty power to shut us down, undermining us and discrediting us with smear campaigns that were soon enough to come.

For the first time in recent memory the IOC was vulnerable and open to reform. We had this one chance to make a push from the outside. It wasn't going to be easy, but at least we had a chance.

The night before our launch, we went to the Olympic Museum in Lausanne where the world press had gathered for the latest IOC briefing. We positioned ourselves right outside the doors of the museum so the media ran into us as they exited the building. As the stream of press began, each of us took a deep breath and plastered them with flyers giving details of the press conference we had planned for the next day to launch our organization and make a call to action of the athletes of the world to become involved. Members of the press were startled that we were there, but were interested. This was something that had never happened before.

The turnout the next day at the press conference was big. We spoke about corruption, not just as an isolated incident in bid city issues, but as a symptom of a much larger problem that was affecting doping and judging, among other areas of the Olympic movement.

This certainly wasn't part of the IOC's plan to get the world's attention off their unfortunate problems. Athletes of the world were starting something and the IOC, particularly the Canadian members, flipped out. Dick Pound, who had earned my respect years earlier for standing out by being the only IOC Executive member brave enough to stand up to Samaranch when he maneuvered to have the retirement age for IOC members increased to 80 to serve his own political interests, led the public campaign. Unfortunately Dick's criticisms of our actions would turn out to be the most palpable of what was to come.

The intimidation, attacks, and any other means of making us go away began immediately. After dinner that evening we arrived in our rooms to find them ransacked. All of our information was taken—computer discs, film from cameras, paper printouts, all of it. Publicly the attacks in the media portrayed us as a group of disgruntled athletes. To Canadians, it was hinted that we were being sinisterly funded. By the time we proved one falsehood wrong, a new accusation appeared. Carol Anne took over behind the scenes, doing everything in her power to discredit me, and unfortunately her power was great. Other things started to happen. A right-wing paper in the United States claimed that Canadians Mark Tewksbury and Ben Johnson had been stripped of their gold medals for steroid usage. I demanded and received an eventual retraction and apology, but it was like that during this time. We were being attacked on all fronts.

It just made us more determined. We worked a global grassroots campaign to get people involved. I called many close friends, former Olympians, but got virtually no support at the time. The Olympic machine was powerful. Most people were afraid of speaking out against it in case they lost their many privileges. Rejection after rejection from people who agreed with some of what we stood for, but weren't willing to speak about it, or even put their name behind it, was hugely discouraging. "How are we ever going to get this off the ground?" Olympic speed skater Susan Auch asked me at one point. I didn't know.

But then we would get a star athlete like Gaetan Boucher or Nadia Comaneci saying, "You are doing the right thing. What can I do to help?" We would hang up from these calls and phone one another immediately, sharing the excitement. One supporter became five, which became twenty-five, which became fifty.

In the end, eighty advocates—athletes, academics, government, and interested parties from around the world—were committed to attending the OATH Symposium in New York City in June of 1999.

Senator George Mitchell was an invited luncheon speaker. An evening reception was held at the United Nations. It was world caliber. Now we would see if these diverse and disparate voices could find a common ground and ignite a movement that could change the direction that amateur sport was taking.

AN OATH TO REFORM

Athletes from all over the world had gathered in New York, and we were finishing a run in Central Park. I was behind Zola Budd, the brilliant South African distance runner who catapulted to fame at the 1984 Olympics. Here she was, as fit as ever because she now ran marathons, and we're running together! To my left was Johan Olav Koss, the legendary Norwegian speed skater and humanitarian. His presence was significant because he was recently elected to the IOC Athletes' Commission, and he had been the only member of the IOC family open enough to attend this symposium. To my right was American figure skater Peter Carruthers.

Also with our group was Franz Weber, the six-time Austrian world speed skiing champion turned businessman. Franz was a big man, strong, with huge legs. He and his young family shared time between the States and Europe. Toward the end of the run, as we walked the final few blocks, Franz approached me. "Keith told me that you came out recently in Canada as a gay man," he said. It had only been six months earlier but it already felt a lifetime away. The issue that used to drive my life for so long was now overshadowed by these bigger issues at hand. But by reflex I still waited hesitantly to hear how this big jock was going to handle the news. "That took guts, man. I am really proud to be here with you." I was proud, too, but more by the quality of people I was working with and the stand we were taking. I was open and out, but it was still new to me and I was very cautious about when and when not to speak about being gay, especially in a sport environment.

I took part in the two-and-a-half day discussion about the ideals and values that drove our collective participation in the Olympic movement. We looked at the problems of doping, of ethics, of the toll of mismanagement on athletes. The environment was open; the dissenters could dissent and then we could all find a way to common ground. We developed a collective mission and vision. It was decided that the creation of an international and independent organization was necessary to restore, preserve, and promote the Olympic ideals for present and future generations.

At the final press conference, American swimming legend from the 1976 Olympics John Naber summarized it best when he said, "We don't want to take over the running of international sport. We don't want a piece of the pie. We just want to make sure the pie tastes as good as the recipe intended it to." We left New York with an interim board of nineteen people, including some Olympic legends, representing nine countries. The road to reform had begun.

In response to the growing outside pressure, the IOC had created a commission to look at reform. Commission 2000 included many great world leaders such as Henry Kissinger, Boutros Boutros-Gali and Dick Ebersol, but it was still majorly composed of IOC members, ensuring the IOC would benefit from these reputations without giving up any real control. The window of reform was small. The IOC 2000 Commission was struck as a short-term initiative, active only until December of 1999, at which time it would submit a report that would be ratified in 2000, creating a new governance structure for the IOC. OATH had six months to organize if we were going to make any impact.

We began our campaign immediately, traveling a week later to the IOC General Session in Seoul, Korea. At the IOC hotel I had a brief meeting with a few members of the IOC Athletes' Commission. We spoke for twenty minutes, using some very heated words. They weren't impressed with the report they had received from Johan Olav Koss, the only IOC family member to take part in our symposium.

"Why would the world need something like OATH?" they asked me. We all knew the realities of the IOC, of what terms would mean for them, even of the "don't speak until asked" rule that drove IOC general sessions. Becoming IOC members meant perks, and the five-star gravy train was irresistible. These particular athletes were not willing to budge. Our meeting ended when someone arrived telling them that they had a meeting and President Samaranch was waiting for them. It was like the fear of God struck them. They bolted from that table like sprinters out of the starting blocks. I had never seen three people get up as fast in my entire life—leaving me with the bill, I might add.

OATH commissioned Dr. Angela Schneider to write a position paper on reform. She was a silver medal rower in 1984 and was now a tenured professor at the University of Western Ontario, which had an Olympic studies program. Angela led a worldwide mission to meet with leaders in sport, business, academia, and government in a very short time frame in order to have an impact.

Many members of the OATH board supplemented Angela's work by meeting with individuals around the world, lobbying for reform. I met briefly with Princess Anne at the Aquatic Hall of Fame in Winnipeg during the Pan American Games. Princess Anne was an IOC member, and I was impressed with her interest in the subject of IOC reform, as well as her response to my plea to support OATH from within. "The IOC has become a victim of its own success," she said to me. "I will look at your information."

From these various meetings came the OATH Report, a ninety-three-page comprehensive overview of what was necessary to genuinely move toward an ethical foundation for Olympic reform. The report focused on ethics and values, IOC structure and governance, doping, bid cities, and sport development, and put forward fifty specific recommendations for genuine reform. The report was completed by October, and for two months was used to lobby as many IOC 2000 commission members as possible. There were some people on the inside who were reform-minded, and this report gave them the leverage to push some of their own agendas forward.

One of the last stops on our mission was Washington DC, where we went to lobby the United States congress and senate to press the IOC to reform. The United States congress had opened hearings into the Salt Lake City scandal, and this investigation was another point of vulnerability for the IOC. The power within the IOC remained unchallenged because there was no one to whom the committee was accountable. In a whirlwind two days we met with twelve senators and congresspeople. Soon to be Attorney General John Ashcroft left a hearing to congratulate us on the work we were doing. But the response wasn't always so positive.

Our last two meetings were the most significant. The first was with Senator Stevens from Alaska, who had been instrumental in championing amateur sport bills in the U.S., and was *the* U.S. government person looked to for leadership on amateur sport issues. We were a team of seven, and after eleven presentations were getting pretty good at our dog and pony show. Senator Stevens listened attentively to us the entire time, but at the end completely sided with the IOC. He thought that the institution was dealing with the crisis, and would not support our initiative. We had been on such a high, gathering steam and goodwill over the past two days, but when we finally met someone who had real influence over the issue, we ran into a complete brick wall. Our bubble had been burst. We were disappointed and exhausted, but we still had one more meeting. perhaps the most important of all.

Senator John McCain, future presidential candidate, was chairing the IOC hearings scheduled later in the year. We all had to take a moment, refocusing for this final encounter. We entered Senator McCain's outer offices where we were greeted by his aides. The senator was very busy, we were told, and we would have about fifteen minutes. The door opened, we were ushered in, and there he was. His energy was enormous. He sat us down on a beautiful couch facing a couple of armchairs, and I began the meeting. As each person presented he nodded attentively, interrupting occasionally. At the end he simply said, "I want to hear more. What can I do to help you with this?" We left the meeting forty-five minutes later with a commitment to add a day to the scheduled senate hearings so the athletes' voices could be heard. OATH would be a part of it.

The government of the United States held hearings in the fall of 1999 looking at the corrupt behavior of the IOC in their country. Nancy Hogshead, an American gold medallist from the 1984 Olympics, cut her honeymoon short to testify on behalf of OATH. John Naber was also there as well, although on this occasion he represented the U.S. Olympians. Senator McCain even managed to get Samaranch to appear before him. Although senator after senator strongly reprimanded the IOC for its actions, there was very little they could do without a smoking gun. And that wouldn't turn up unless someone could truly infiltrate this machine of power. The real chance for change remained within, and there was very little hope of that happening because most of the IOC membership had been appointed under Samaranch's leadership. They were beholden to him for their power, and were certainly not going to do anything to jeopardize that.

I have never regretted my decision to step outside the fold of the Olympic family. During the attempted reform process I realized, though, that the only way to really change the IOC was to be a part of it. But from time to time, when extraordinary circumstances called for it, I saw it was useful to create pressure from the outside. That, essentially, was the mission of OATH.

In the end, the IOC 2000 Commission came to similar conclusions as OATH, with parts of the OATH Report even being quoted in session. Many recommendations were implemented, with just enough adoptions to have the appearance of change without ultimately changing anything. The bottom line is that the IOC, in its current structure, is above reproach. While some of the world's most respected leaders worked on the reform, after December of 1999 their work was done and they were gone, leaving the IOC to once again tend to its own business. There remains no external body to whom the members are accountable, and this lack of real accountability was where the problems started in the first place.

If you saw the announcement of London as host city for 2012 you saw past-President Samaranch sitting to the immediate right of new IOC President Jacques Rogge. Sure, things aren't exactly the same, but Samaranch is, literally, still in the picture. It will be a while before any really significant change happens. And with the change in leadership also came the closing of the window of opportunity for reform. The OATH organization remains, but in a dormant state, ready to be activated should it be needed again.

Many people around the world had given a lot to the reform movement, but this initiative was almost impossible to sustain long term, because in the end no corporations wanted to fund a global organization focused on ethics and values. Attacking the IOC and taking a stand for ethics left most companies feeling too vulnerable, not wanting the spotlight turned on their own organizations for fear of what might turn up. And this was only months before Enron and other corporate financial fiascos unfolded.

The exception was the leadership at Encana, an Alberta-based energy company, who supported us financially and summarized it perfectly when they commented, "You pricked the conscience of those who had a conscience left to prick." We had. And I had honoured the promise I made to myself that I would see this thing through to the end.

My worry of being labeled as the gay swimmer was long forgotten because I had taken an even tougher public stand for something I believed in. I was free to finally leave the world of sport after twenty-four years—at least for a little while.

CHAPTER THIRTEEN

FINDING OUT

TELEVISION WITH BORDERS

I still find it remarkable how afraid I was for so many years to live openly, especially given how things turned out.

Back in December of 1998, I had been a guest on one of Canada's most successful daytime talk shows. After my segments I arrived back-stage to find a young guy about a year or two older than I descending the stairs from the control room. "That was great," he had said to me. "Thanks," I replied, wondering who this guy was. He read my mind. "I am the executive producer of the show. My name is Jordan," he said. "I liked what you said out there about helping make things better for the next generation of kids. Take my card. Maybe after all of this excitement dies down we could talk." I put his card in my pocket for a later day.

One morning in the late summer of 2000 I got a call from Jordan asking me if he could meet me for coffee in about thirty minutes. We met, and he told me that he had inherited the role of executive producer of *Canada AM*, the hugely popular morning show that ran from 6:30 a.m. until 9 a.m. every weekday. The show would be adding a more lifestyle-oriented hour, like the *Today Show* out of New York, airing until 10 a.m. starting in September. Part of that change meant that each day of the week there was going to be featured guests, called contributors. Jordan wanted to know if I would be able to be a contributor on Mondays, as he would like to offer something motivational for people to look forward to as they started their week. "What do you think?" he asked. I was excited, nervous, and although a bit overwhelmed, I went for it. It was time to try something new.

I reported for duty in the middle of September, the same week the 2000 Olympics Games started in Sydney. I could have been at the Olympics in so many different capacities, even as a resident of the city, but it wasn't meant to be that way for me this time. Instead I was in a studio with the long-time hosts of *Canada AM*, Valerie Pringle and Dan Matheson. They were not nearly as excited as I was about the new format of the show. I couldn't say I blamed them. They saw their two-and-a-half–hour, live, on-camera shift go to three-and-a-half hours, and they weren't thrilled about the added burden.

As I was brought onto the set for my first segment, I was really nervous. It was the first day of the new, extended format of the broadcast, and while it may have looked calm at home on the television set, behind the scenes things were crazy. I was on edge. It was one thing to be the guest on a show, but to be the "expert" was another thing entirely. I found out the good old-fashioned way how live television worked. I fucked up. I had assumed that creating content for my segments each week would come very easily, because I was used to speaking on stage for over an hour at a time. I was wrong.

The second week on the show Dan and I did a seven-minute segment together. It was about three minutes into it when I realized I had nothing left to say. Dan could see that I was like a deer in the headlights, too stunned to even blink. We were live on air for four more minutes. Each second felt like an eternity. Dan was incredibly gracious, saving me by thinking of stories himself. When the camera went off he smiled at me and said knowingly, "Not as easy as it looks, hey?" For someone who thought he could speak, this wasn't easy at all.

I made many mistakes. I didn't wait for formalities with former Canadian Prime Minister Kim Campbell before jumping into a discussion about girl power. Dan slapped my wrists for lack of protocol, although I still remember the former prime minister giggling with me and saying, "Mark for IOC president," as we broke for commercial. Valerie thought what I was doing every Monday was "cheesy," I think until she slowly started to enjoy the segments. Besides, we both loved Yahtzee, which strangely connected us.

With time I found my way and slowly got used to the routine. Sunday nights became early to bed, and for a while I felt like I was swimming again. A car picked me up in the early hours of the morning and brought me to the studios. I went straight to makeup, which for a studio show had to be plastered on because of the hot, bright lights. It was hectic and stressful but always interesting.

Live television, especially a show as monstrous as *Canada AM*, was exciting because you never knew exactly what was going to happen. That included what was going to come out of the hosts' mouths. Dan was easier to read than Valerie. When he was uncomfortable his arms would be crossed, his voice would go up slightly and there would be a little scrunch in his face. Valerie was much more complicated, which I greatly appreciated. Watching the show from home she seemed all smiles and borderline bubbly at times through that small screen, but behind that exterior was a razor sharp mind that used that perky façade as a powerful weapon to lay traps with her questions. With her you could never let down your guard.

On a Monday in June 2001 we were shown a news clip about an uproar that had occurred in Calgary because another former conservative prime minister, Joe Clarke, had marched in the gay pride parade. Valerie lobbed me a bomb disguised as a concerned question. "Why this reaction from *that* part of the country, Mark? You are from Calgary (and gay); maybe you could provide some insight?" She was all smiles. I summoned all of my communication skills so as not to offend either the gay community or Albertans in my response. But this opened a door for me. It was the first time in over a year that I could speak openly about this issue. When the opportunity arose to finally speak, I certainly didn't shy away.

It was a very empowering experience. Poor Dan was so uncomfortable when I started talking about being gay that he almost squirmed in his chair. The news clip that had sparked this discussion had shown a man of color, a visible minority, leading the charge against gays. "I don't understand why minorities continue to discriminate against other minorities," I said. "If we all worked together we might actually make some social progress." I ended my little monologue by saying the best reaction to being gay had come from my friend's mother, who said it didn't matter who her son loved; it was that he *could* love that was important. There was actually a moment of silence amongst my *Canada AM* colleagues when I finished speaking, another first. Dan finally broke the moment by hitting the table and singing, "All you need is love." Love, and apparently a little push.

Working with Dan and Valerie showed me that if you wanted to make it in television you couldn't be like anyone else. You had to be yourself and be able to express your point of view. There was no room for counterfeits or replicas—you'd get torn to shreds. But eventually I would also learn that within the universe of television, everything, even individuality and self-expression, had its limits.

SUMMER GARDEN DEBUT

I first met my friend Alexander Chapman on New Year's Eve 2000. Alexander grew up in Guyana, raised by his grandmother until the age of eleven, at which time he was sent to live with his father in a town in southeastern Quebec. At school Alex and his brother were the only non-white kids in a sea of two thousand students. Thin and tall with big brown eyes and long, long eyelashes, Alex buried himself in books to endure the discrimination that came with being a visible minority in a white sea. Day after day at school, a gang of tough girls decided that they were going to get him. They relentlessly went after Alex, making fun of his looks and doing everything possible to make his life hell. But they had greatly underestimated this feminine-looking young black man.

One day in public speaking class, the teacher asked the students, "Who's going to go first?" Those tough girls started chanting his name, "Alex! Alex! Alex!" He *had* to go first. Instead of cowering from his tormentors, Alex marched to the front of the room, where he faced the class head on. He could choose anything he wanted to speak about, so he gave a scathing speech about what discrimination felt like. He told the class how rude, insensitive, and inhumane it was to torment somebody. The girls who had bullied him shrunk in their seats. Alex got an A from the teacher and won the respect of his classmates.

As a friend I admired this strength, boldness, and humanity. Alex was the person everyone came to when they had a problem. One night shortly after I met him he had reached a hard low: his boyfriend was becoming violent. When I arrived at Alex's apartment I didn't recognize it. Where once there had been walls of art and mirrors, now there was shattered glass. I went to spend time with him every day after this, supporting him through this rough time. Little would I know that ultimately the one to benefit would be me.

During most of the fall when I was beginning my television career at *Canada AM*, Benjamin was over in Berlin continuing his career as an actor. We had been together for more than three years but were constantly challenged with finding a place we could live, work, and thrive together. Benjamin had studied at a German theater school, but Toronto wasn't a hotbed of German productions. In Germany I faced the same problems Benjamin did in Canada. We explored every option possible looking for a solution.

The best route seemed to be having Benjamin immigrate to Canada, but the complications were endless. Benjamin was Swiss, not

German, so moving to Canada would mean he would have to permanently give up his visa to live and work in Berlin, closing that door forever. Strike one. Immigrating to Canada as a same-sex couple would be difficult but potentially possible, although it came with a huge cost. Regardless of whether or not we stayed together, if I sponsored Benjamin to immigrate I would be financially responsible for him for years. Strike two. Living in cities where we couldn't participate fully eventually took its toll on both of us. Being completely dependent on each other for survival was romantic at first, but slowly eroded our own feelings of self-confidence and respect. Strike three.

I was in Montreal filming *How It's Made* for the Discovery Channel when I called Benjamin. For months we had been wrestling with finding a solution, and on this day I saw clearly what the answer was. "Benjamin, we have been back and forth on this for so long. We just can't seem to make that final commitment because the stakes are too high. I think we have to let go."

He didn't want to hear what I was saying at first. I didn't want to be saying it either. But finally we had to agree that maybe love wasn't enough to make this work. It would take many more calls until the reality of the situation sank in for both of us. He had opened me to so many things, we had been through so much together, but we both saw that our own livelihood as individuals meant letting go of this couple. I returned home to Toronto, the townhouse taking on an emptiness that was unbearable. Benjamin would never be coming back again, and suddenly the space was overwhelmingly large for just me. I was clear in what we were doing, but it didn't take away any of the sadness or loss that I was feeling.

Where I had once picked up Alex, it was now Alex who picked me up. We were inseparable. For me it was the beginning of an important time in my life where I learned to take really good care of myself. Alex was a good teacher. I learned to cook, to garden, to bake, to open up, to appreciate being alone. He reconnected me with the value of friendship, just hanging out with someone and spending time. We shared our life stories with each other, including the struggles of youth and coming out, which was rare. Strangely, the pain that many gay people go through in adolescence never gets spoken about, even with other gays, as the trauma from that time is too painful for many people to relive. We flock to larger urban centers for a new start, often without addressing the circumstances that forced us to move in the first place.

My favorite ritual was the "unbirthday parties" we would have for each other. When you needed to have an excuse to get together with friends to lend some moral support, instead of waiting for a formal occasion we would hold an "unbirthday party." It would be late on a rainy Tuesday afternoon and Alex and another friend would come over to my townhouse, roast lamb with vegetables, cook shrimps with curry, and make ginger beer and black cake with nuts and rum. More friends would join us later and we would watch movies or television or play music, drink wine, or smoke a joint and just hang out.

Alex helped me reconnect to community, but more importantly he showed me how to connect to myself. I felt like I was part of an extended family, and we were there for each other in good times and bad. Little would I know just how much I would need this support with what came next.

INTOLERABLE

I was driving a rental car to an airport at 7 a.m. on a stark, cold, February morning in 2001 when a news bulletin came on the radio. Carol Anne Letheren, head of the Canadian Olympic Committee, had been giving a speech the night before and had collapsed in front of the audience. She had suffered an aneurysm of the brain and had been rushed to the hospital.

I gripped the wheel with both hands, completely unnerved by the announcement. I thought of the time we spent together with the

IOC. Back then, I had done the math and calculated that it would be decades before Carol Anne would be eighty and have to step down from her influential position. She had had such a life force that I would never have imagined that she might not live to be an old woman. By the time I got to my home in Toronto I learned that she had died. She was fifty-eight years old.

I had seen Carol Anne only twice in the years since I had left the Olympic movement. The first had been at the 1999 Pan American Games in Winnipeg. I had been there with OATH, and one night after attending various sport events had gone for dinner in a nice French restaurant downtown. I was there with another OATH person, who said to me, "Whatever you do, don't turn around. You are not going to believe who is at a table on the other side of the room." "Who is it?" I asked. "It's Carol Anne," he said. I froze.

I had wondered when this moment would come. Here it was. Both my heart and my mind started racing. I think she saw me, too, but neither of us knew exactly what to do. I was plotting what to do when Sheila Copps, former deputy prime minister of Canada, arrived. She stopped by the table to say hello. She was meeting Carol Anne for dinner, so she knew what was going on. She had a big smile on her face as she neared my table. "Hello Mark," she said. She looked toward Carol Anne's table and said to me, "This should be interesting. Have you said hello to Carol Anne yet?" I said I hadn't. She pulled me over with her. I was impressed with how diplomatic Carol Anne could be. I knew that she had been on a personal mission to destroy my reputation, but she put on her best poker face with me in front of Sheila, making pleasantries and meeting my eyes before we both looked away. I went back to the table, paid the bill, and left. I had lost my appetite.

The second time I ran into Carol Anne had been over a year later, just as she was about to leave for the Sydney Olympics and as I was starting on *Canada AM*. I lived on a busy, popular street in Toronto that was in the same neighborhood as Carol Anne's, and one Saturday morning around 9 a.m. I turned the corner to head toward the subway and there she was. It was one of those moments. If we could have pretended not to see each other we would have, but it was impossible not to because there was nobody between us. We were far apart, but there was no avoiding each other because we had already made eye contact. I took a big breath and started walking toward her.

Our encounter was surprisingly upbeat this time. The IOC reform process had ended months earlier, and the intense strain of our relationship had passed as well. The first minutes were awkward, but then Carol Anne spoke of heading over to the Olympics shortly, and the tension lifted. "We should meet for lunch one of these days when I get back," she said. "Absolutely," I responded. We both knew it would never happen. I thought of that empty lunch date as I heard of her death.

The day before the funeral I went to view her body with Megan Fowler, my good friend who worked for the Canadian Olympic Committee and who had covered for me at the games in Atlanta. Carol Anne's memorial would be held the next day and there was a grand room at the funeral home where we could go and pay our last respects. As I entered the enormous space I could see her coffin covered with the Olympic flag about twenty-five meters away. Pictures of her were spread throughout the room, along with beautiful bouquets of flowers, flags, and other Olympic memorabilia.

Her partner was standing near the coffin. We had had some rough times together, so I was relieved when he put out his arms and started to walk toward me. He met me halfway. I found myself standing in the middle of the room, sobbing in his arms as he talked quietly in my ear. "Carol Anne loved you so much," he said to me. "I know she did," I said back. And I did. But I also knew that it would have been impossible for us to have ever been close again. Too much had happened. Yes, there was love, but as with Benjamin, the love between us wasn't enough to overcome the obstacles that ultimately kept us apart. But I was grateful that I had come to pay my respects. Carol Anne had had a huge influence in my life, and I needed to say goodbye privately.

She was buried on February 7, 2001, my thirty-third birthday. Her service was held in an auditorium packed with close to a thousand people. Federal and provincial cabinet ministers were there. The mayor joined business leaders from across the country in saying their goodbyes. Dick Pound represented the IOC Executive, posthumously honoring Carol Anne with the Olympic Order for her contributions to the Olympic movement. It was all moving, at least until former business partner Toller Cranston took the podium.

Toller started by sharing some personal stories about the happy times that he had spent with Carol Anne recently at his compound in Mexico, but then it took a turn. He spoke about the greatest disappointment in Carol Anne's life being those who had betrayed her by trying to tear down the IOC. I completely flushed and sank in my seat, feeling under personal attack in that moment. My friends Megan and Peter each gave me a hand and squeezed, looking horrified for me.

But the worst was still to come. Perhaps it was because she was adopted that Carol Anne loved the underdog. Following Toller was Rubin "Hurricane" Carter, who gave the last tribute of the day. Rubin had been sent to jail for twenty years for a crime he didn't commit and had survived going to hell and back, which made him extremely colorful. Carol Anne had become friends with him when he adopted Toronto as his new home. He was usually a great speaker, but as he passed the hour and ten mark of his inspirational tribute, many of the dignitaries started to leave because they had planes to catch. It was as if Rubin had forgotten where he was or what he was doing, almost speaking in tongues while we sat there wondering if this service was ever going to end. As the memorial slowly descended from inspirational to uncomfortable, I couldn't help but think what a perfect ending this was to Carol Anne's complicated, double-edged life.

ANYTHING BUT FAB

A week later, on February 13, 2001, I was running out the door to catch a plane. The phone rang. I thought of ignoring it, but my curiosity got the better of me. It was a reporter from the Canadian Press who had wanted to check something with me. He had just received a news release from a local gay publication in Toronto called *Fab*, and was calling to verify the headline before going to print. Immediately something didn't feel right.

A week earlier, the morning of Carol Anne's funeral, I had been in the offices of *Fab* doing an interview. Something about seeing her body the night before had completely thrown me, and I had been outspoken to a fault during this interview session. I had seen death, and my own mortality was staring me in the face. I shared an intimate story with the editor about being at a gay pride event in Toronto and trying a variety of drugs and having a really bad experience. Since this was a local gay publication I was completely candid about my own experimentation with recreational drugs. I hadn't thought for a minute that this story would go any farther than that. Big mistake.

As the Canadian Press reporter read the headline to me I dropped my bag, surprised I didn't fall to the ground as well. "Tewksbury Addicted to Ecstasy," he read. Gulp. Gulp. He asked me if this was true. I replied, "No, it wasn't. My drug of choice was much softer." He asked if I meant cocaine. I laughed, because although I knew this wasn't funny, what else could I do as this began to unfold. "No," I replied, "I mean pot." He laughed as well, but told me that he was going to have to run the story the next day. I left for the airport with a sick feeling in my stomach.

The original interview had been conducted by then editor of *Fab* John Kennedy. This article was supposed to be the beginning of a longer-term relationship, but it turned out to be the beginning of the end. Although *Fab* was a local gay paper, they sent a media release to the mainstream news outlets with highlights of stories that would be featured in their upcoming issue. The interview that John had written, which in itself was not a bad article, was sent to a copy editor who took the story completely out of context and focused on the words "addiction" and "ecstasy," and put them together to make a catchy headline. Nobody fact-checked, verifying the misinformation. And with that my fate was sealed.

I spent the night on the phone. One of my first calls was to my mom. I warned her what was coming and she just said, "Oh, honey, I'll be fine. It is your life. I just hope you'll be all right." How far we had come over the years. Calling Jordan from *Canada AM* was not as pleasant. As I told him about the article and the impending news blitz that might occur the next day, he moaned. We had just finished shooting a spa trip in honor of Valentine's Day that would be airing later in the week, and this was the last thing he needed. He told me not to panic yet, because there was a chance that nothing would come of this. He would call me back after checking with the newsroom at CTV to see if anything had come across the wires. Something had. He called his boss who called his boss, the head of CTV News. We braced ourselves.

I woke up in my king-sized bed at the majestic Chateau Frontenac in the heart of Quebec City on Valentine's Day, my heart filled not with love but dread. I opened my door to get the paper that was awaiting me on the floor, and I could see my picture in front of every room as I looked up and down the hallway. In the upper part of the front page of the *Globe and Mail*, where they featured banners highlighting articles that were inside the paper, was a picture of me taken immediately after winning the Olympics accompanied by the headline, *Olympian's Drug Confession*. Oh God. I flipped to the sport section, and in the biggest print I had ever seen read *Tewksbury Used Marijuana*. I turned on the television and read my name on the banner that went across the screen. The voice mailbox of my cell phone was already full, but before I could give this any more attention I had to turn my focus to the speech I would be giving in less than an hour.

As luck would have it, both the *Globe and Mail* and CTV, the station I worked for on *Canada AM*, were owned by BCE, the company I was speaking to that morning. I would have done anything to stay in bed with the sheets pulled over my head, given how I was feeling, but there would be none of that. I would have to face the fire. I altered my speech, confronted this thing head on, highlighting standing behind your actions even when you make mistakes. The audience was gracious, but no matter how you looked at this, it wasn't a great day.

Going back to work at CTV was even less fun. I had been brought onto *Canada AM* as a lifestyle expert. I had to hop from being interviewed about this on the first part of the show, then change hats to make my regular contribution on the same program. The news department didn't appreciate that their lifestyle boy was making the news, especially for smoking pot.

I was handed over to the public relations department to coach me on how to deal with the upcoming interview. They would pose a question to me and I would answer it as honestly as I could, at which point I would be told that no matter what I did, I shouldn't answer like that. "But that's the truth," I told them. "This is television, Mark. You have to tell the television truth." Which meant that I shouldn't really say anything at all.

The interview with Dan on Monday came and went. He dealt with the issue but didn't try to end my career in the process. But from that day forward something had changed. The hierarchy at CTV suddenly saw me as a controversial figure, and I saw that in the land of television you were encouraged to be unique, as long as that version of yourself wasn't flawed. It seemed that there was very little room for difference after all in that small screen world.

The funny thing was that, beyond the blue suits, nobody cared about this damn story. People on the subway with me sure didn't. After seeing me come out, then fight for reform of the IOC, then become a regular on the morning show, people couldn't have cared less about something as trivial as smoking pot. In fact, either people didn't pay enough attention to it to remember, or they thought it was cool. A few people said, "Hey, I saw that story on you. I wondered why they didn't have any real news to report." To strangers this made me human, real, flawed, which is why I thought it made sense to tackle the truth on television, not tell the television truth.

In the end it was one of the best things that ever happened to me. From that moment forward people connected with me in a different way. But the strain that had developed over sharing degrees of truth would continue to challenge me, eventually forcing my life to change in ways I had never imagined possible, especially as a formerly closeted former athlete.

CHAPTER FOURTEEN

VALUED

Dr. Tewksbury

As a kid I had watched my parents become involved with my swimming career as volunteers, and it made an impact. I have been volunteering for social change movements for many years since. This work played an important role in helping me find my own voice and stand up for things I believe in.

Volunteerism has come in many shapes and forms. My involvement with the IOC was as a volunteer, although a five star lifestyle with a healthy daily honorarium made giving up time especially easy, even if it didn't always attract the most selfless people. The opposite was true of the people involved with the Children's Miracle Network, the organization that looks after fundraising for sick children. These were sick kids and you had better not screw around. Thankfully, these people didn't. I helped them raise as much money as I could for a number of years.

One night at a dinner in Florida I found myself at the same table as Marie Osmond, one of the founders of the Children's Miracle Network's annual telethon. I hadn't expected that, as a Mormon, she would have so much vavoom, but her outfit really showcased her highlights. She positively beamed just a few seats away. As we went around the table before dinner doing introductions and it became my

turn, she screamed, "Oh my God, you look like my brother Donny."
"I know," I replied, blushing. "I've been told that before."

Sitting with Marie was one of the few times in my life when
celebrity struck me. I had been about eight years old, living in the
basement bedroom in Calgary that had terrified me, when I watched
the *Donny & Marie Show* on television every Friday night. It was filled
with singing and skits, with a gay sensibility, and I loved it. I had
big teeth and feathered hair and I sang a bit back then, and people
often told me that I looked like Donny Osmond. In a strange way
Donny Osmond was probably my first "drag" performance, imitat-
ing his looks and moves. It was even stranger to hear the resemblance
coming out of Marie's mouth twenty years later.

The magic of volunteering was that you get more back than you
could ever give. And then sometimes you get even more.

Two honors would come to me at this time, within a year of each
other, that helped me endure some of the battles I had chosen. Working with OATH, I had been beaten up pretty badly by the relentless,
well-financed IOC public relations machine. Little things had started
to get to me, like whenever I attended Olympic events my win in
1992 had been conveniently edited out of the montage of memorable
moments. But in the midst of this, in June of 2000, the International
Swimming Hall of Fame inducted me into their ranks at a ceremony
in Fort Lauderdale. The induction sent me an important message:
that regardless of being gay or outspoken, my athletic accomplishments stood on their own merit. It meant a lot to me.

The other honor came as a huge surprise. The professor in charge
of the gay archives at the University of Western Ontario, along with
Dr. Angela Schneider, was nominating me for an Honorary Doctorate of Laws from his university. They told me straight up that my
application might not be accepted right away but would stay under
consideration for five years. This was a test (Angela, the gay professor and I), and all involved expected that we would be waiting a long

time, given that Western was a very conservative institution. Surprisingly, my nomination was accepted within three months. In June of 2001, I became one of the University of Western Ontario's youngest recipients of a doctorate, my honorary degree noting my athletic excellence, ethical leadership, and active humanitarianism. To top it off, I had received an invitation to address the graduating class.

Although the gay archives professor hadn't asked, I knew that he would be disappointed if I didn't mention being gay in my speech. Although out, my speaking life had remained mostly segregated; business audiences didn't really want to know too much about the gay experience as opposed to the Olympic ones. But this was different. I was being honored for my work, which included my work as a gay person in the gay community. I had to address it.

Half an hour before I had to report to the academic ready room where all the professors donned their colored robes, each color representing various faculties and levels of education, I took a break outside. The pomp and circumstance of academia was just as intimidating as being at my first Olympics. It was a warm sunny day and I was pacing trying to figure out exactly what I was going to say in my speech. Time was running out, but finally it hit me.

As the award ceremony commenced, I was very nervous. Dr. Schneider had read a moving citation, and I found it hard to stand up to formally become Dr. Tewksbury. Then I had to speak. My knees were wobbly as I made my way to the podium. I spoke about lessons I had learned from some of the great people I have met in my life, and about the road of possibility that lay ahead for the graduates, especially if they were open to taking it. I finished my allotted twenty minutes by saying that if someone had told me ten years ago that I would stand up against the IOC, I would have told them no way. But it was the right thing for me to do in that moment, so I did it. Then I said if someone had told me that I would speak publicly about a very private part of my life, being gay, I would have said no way. But again it was the right thing for me to do, and I did it. The gay archives professor beamed.

It had been a huge day for me in a way that I hadn't considered before it had happened. Through this honor my worlds of gay, sport, and ethics had finally come together in one place as I was being recognized for all three. Little did I realize that this was just a baby step. The real collision was on its way full speed ahead.

MONTREAL CALLING

I often visited my friend Peter Schleicher in the early 2000s, staying in the spare bedroom of his apartment in downtown Montreal when I invaded for a weekend of fun. The city came alive for six or seven months every year before it had to hibernate again for the long, cold winter. For many summer weekends in a row, I traveled to Montreal, slowly falling for this incredible city.

Montreal kept calling me. I started to work on a television show on the Discovery Channel, *How It's Made*, which was shot entirely there. And while I was in the city working, I went out and experienced its world-renowned nightlife.

Montreal had an energy that I hadn't known before. The streets of downtown were filled with people, bustling with an exciting vibe. I had always enjoyed going to Europe, and this city gave me the same sensation, but with a North American sensibility. The city's only demand on its people was that they participate, which they did. Festival after festival invaded the city every summer, leaving the citizens of Montreal culturally rich, and summer drivers permanently frustrated. People were out everywhere, and there was a spirit of individual style, live and let live, that allowed many kinds of diversity to flourish.

It was in Montreal that for the first time in my life I didn't have to think about being gay. Here I just felt like a Montrealer, unique but with the same freedom to be different as everybody else. Although I loved being there, at that moment I couldn't imagine taking the next step of moving there. But the seed had been planted.

In the fall of 2000 I received a message at my office that Jean Chrétien had called. I figured it wasn't the prime minister of Canada, but rather the vice president of Tourism Montreal. I called and arranged to meet the "other Jean Chrétien," as he called himself, when he was in Toronto later that month. Little would I know that this meeting would mark the beginning of the next chapter of my life.

It started simply. Jean helped me understand that Tourism Montreal greatly valued the gay and lesbian community and had been working very hard with all of its members in the hospitality industry on a long-term strategy to support this niche market the best way possible. Because I directly profited from that strategy, I told him in person how much I loved coming to his city for all of the reasons he was telling me about. He asked if I would be interested in traveling with him for a few presentations on behalf of Montreal. I thought it would be great. And with that it began.

In the spring of 2001, I received *the* call. The city of Montreal was supporting a bid for the Gay Games in 2006 and Jean asked me if I would consider being a part of the bid committee. There were very few openly gay Olympic champions in the world, and even fewer with IOC experience, so he thought I would bring a lot to the team. But he left the decision entirely up to me.

I really had thought that I was out of sport forever. I had worked so hard to try to break free from that world, wanting to distance myself from sport probably because I didn't feel that I could ever truly be myself there. Here was sport coming back to me, but this time it was gay. The irony wasn't wasted on me. I told Jean I would think about it, because I really wasn't ready at that moment to make any commitment to another volunteer sport organization. But there was something else.

Given how open I was about my life, I still wasn't one hundred percent sure I wanted to do this. I had only heard about these games once before and had no real concept of what they were. Like many people, my first question was, why do gay people need their own games? On one hand I knew, because I had experienced the homophobia that still permeated amateur sport; the deeply buried, unconscious remnants of my own internal homophobia were probably one reason why I was so hesitant to get involved in the first place.

After doing some research I found out that the games were started in 1982 in San Francisco by a former decathlete, Tom Waddell. Legend had it that he was at the closing ceremonies of the 1968 Olympic Games in Mexico City when he had a eureka moment and wanted to create this experience for gays and lesbians who had been suppressed in sport. He shared his dream and mobilized a community, and the first Gay Games brought about fifteen hundred athletes together in San Francisco. The games had grown enormously over six incarnations, with the Gay Games in Amsterdam attracting more than fourteen thousand participants.

Montreal had a business plan for 2006 with a huge goal: nineteen thousand athletes and five thousand cultural participants. That year's games would mark the first time in twelve years that the games would be held in North America. The Montreal bid committee had support from all three levels of government. Now they wanted mine.

My decision didn't come easily or quickly. It wasn't that I didn't believe in the project—I did. I just hadn't ever brought the gay and sport worlds together in my own life. In fact, I had done everything possible to keep them separate. For all of the integrating that had taken place in my life to find a level of comfort in my being gay, I still ran from the world of sport. Deeply ingrained in my thinking was the idea that the minute I put on a swimsuit I had to act a certain way, straight, in order to fit in. Being openly gay in a sport environment— bringing gay and sport together—was something so new for me, so different, that I feared to even go there. But I did. And a couple of things surprised me.

The first time I went to a gay swimming competition I met three former teammates and learned that at least three other guys I had swum with in my career were gay, too. None of us had ever reached out and spoken to each other about it. The years of suffering and the burden could have been shared by seven of us, but none of us had any idea at the time how to raise the issue, or dared to take that risk for fear of the consequences if we were wrong.

The other thing I couldn't get over was that all of these competitors I saw before me were gay. There were hundreds and hundreds of swimmers at this competition. It was inspiring, but it took me some time to adjust to the fact that you didn't have to hide who you were in this environment. This experience tipped the scales for me. I agreed to meet to talk about being active in Montreal's bid.

The leadership shared their vision of the project with me. They clearly knew what they were doing. There was a level of expertise that reminded me of my time working on Toronto's 2008 Olympic bid. They asked me if I would like to become a part of the bidding committee. I said yes. They asked if I would present the bid on behalf of the team in Johannesburg because of my English language skills. I said yes again.

I was in. I just didn't realize what exactly I was in for. Then again, none of us did.

THE JOHANNESBURG DECISION

Whether Montreal would host Gay Games VII or not would be decided in Johannesburg, South Africa, in October 2001. The months leading up to that saw me in Montreal many, many times perfecting our bid and presentation. Winning the candidature would bring a huge benefit to our local LGBT sport community, as well as a huge economic return to the city and country, and no stone was left unturned to ensure we had done everything possible to win. But regardless of how much our bid had going for it, it was still an uphill battle.

Montreal was bidding against three American cities, Atlanta, Chicago, and Los Angeles, and the group that would ultimately decide the winner, the Federation of Gay Games (FGG), was more than seventy percent American. The FGG was a nonprofit, volunteer organization with a post office box on Castro Street in San Francisco. They owned the Gay Games brand and event, and it would be before them that we would make our final pitch in the fall.

My first introduction to this group came during the site visit that summer. Having been through the site selection process with the IOC, I found it interesting that there were four site inspectors from the FGG, but instead of each of them visiting all four cities to get a complete picture of all of the bids, the four broke into teams of two and saw two cities each. Roberto Mantaci, a swimmer and mathematics professor from Paris, joined Derek Lietcy, a cyclist and one of the original members of the San Francisco Arts and Athletics Association, in Montreal to check the facilities.

The Federation, although owning an event that had grown exponentially over the years to a gathering of Olympic proportions, had been plagued by money problems. The last four host committees had faced deficits, placing the FGG in a less than desirable financial situation. There was no staff to support the volunteers, resources were already stretched, and another financial difficulty would be disastrous. A lot was riding on the games in 2006.

I had no idea yet of the inner workings of the Federation. Over three days we took Roberto and Derek on tours of the sites, to numerous media interviews, and to receptions held in their honor, and now we were winding down, trying to get a sense of where Montreal stood. From time to time it became apparent that Derek and Roberto had very different ideas of what cities should be considering in their candidacies. "Difference of age?" I asked Roberto, looking to make light of the situation. "More like a difference of mindset," he responded very seriously. I had thought it was Derek, the older and more liberal minded of the two, whom we had needed to impress. It would only be in Johannesburg where I would learn that it was the much younger and seemingly conservative Roberto who was politically active, and who would eventually make our lives in Montreal so difficult.

Our team arrived en masse in Johannesburg for the annual meeting of the FGG. We were about twenty people in total from Montreal, and we joined the other bid cities for the orientation session at the beginning of the week. Derek was there, as well as a woman from the gay and lesbian figure skating group. They spent an hour telling us the rules of the federation meetings, so that we were clear on process before the actual proceedings started. All of us from the bid cities were given observer status, and it was strongly suggested that all bid committees just sit back and watch since most of us didn't have any history with the FGG. I had déjà vu, as if I was attending an IOC meeting all over again, but this time without the money or expertise, just the attitude.

Over the next seven days I observed the Federation as I had been instructed to. I was struck by how charming and attentive they could be as individuals, but how rigidly rule-bound and obsessively procedure-oriented they were as an organization. The word "federation" had to me implied some kind of knowledgeable, authoritative, well-organized group that was responsible for leading international LGBT sport. Instead, it seemed we found an organization with a handful of individual members who ran the show but directly represented no one, with a transient secondary level of federation members representing member organizations, many of whom seemed to know as little about the Federation regulations and procedures as I did.

I watched as the individual members in their blue blazers took new members under their wing, making suggestions to them as to how to vote and act, much like Carol Anne had done with me in the early IOC days. I found it ironic that the Gay Games had been started because our community didn't feel comfortable playing in the traditional sport world, but at the same time the leadership of gay sport behaved in a similar fashion to the IOC.

Granted, there were also some differences. Where IOC members would be in jeopardy of having heart attacks because of their age, FGG members were prone to hissy fits due to their temperaments. There were many times when the bid city representatives at the back of the room were left looking at each other in disbelief at the outbursts we witnessed during the general sessions.

The FGG's passion was obvious, but was it enough? I would later tell many of the FGG leaders how much I admired the effort it must have taken to survive all of these years. Still, I had the feeling I was among a well-intentioned group of people who lacked the financial and human resources and perhaps the basic sport knowledge necessary to really make things work. Going to committee meetings was like reinventing the wheel, trying to create systems that would serve LGBT sport when most of those systems had already been developed in the traditional sport world and simply needed to be adapted to take into consideration some of the LGBT community's specific needs. I had become involved with this project largely because it was my hope that one day the homophobia that I had endured in the world of sport, as Tom Waddell had, would be a thing of the past. For me this was about building bridges, evolution, making *all* spaces safe for *all* athletes. In Johannesburg it seemed we were witnessing the opposite, a lack of integrating proven concepts and best practices from the sports world. That was why the possibility of Montreal's involvement excited me so much, because it didn't matter if you were gay or straight, the entire community was behind this project.

The final part of the bid process involved two steps. For the first step, each bidding city presented to the general assembly of the FGG, followed by a forty-five-minute question period. Competing cities were allowed to sit in on each other's presentations, which was difficult, especially because Montreal had drawn the first presentation spot. The second step happened the following day, when each city sent two representatives to the front of the room and collectively endured another two-hour question period from the general assembly.

My honorary co-president, Lucie Duguay, and I formally presented Montreal's candidacy. We had many things going for us, including videos from the mayor of Montreal, the premier of Quebec, and the prime minister of Canada, a first for the FGG assembly. On top of their moral support, each level of government had also collectively guaranteed $3 million to the project should we win.

After hearing all four bids and putting us through a question and answer session from hell, the FGG went into a long "in camera" session where they voted on who would host the 2006 Gay Games. When we were finally called back into the room and they announced that Montreal was the winner, all hell broke loose—in a good way. It would take a while for hell to break loose in a bad way.

Two significant things happened in Johannesburg beyond winning the candidacy. First, in our presentation we had used a check to represent the nearly one million dollars in license fees that our successful games in Montreal would pay the FGG. I actually held it up as a prop, which some people from other bid cities who were observers took as demonstrating our trying to buy the games. This wasn't at all what was intended, but perception was reality and for some we had crossed a line.

We would later learn that the votes had gone 31 for Montreal, 13 for Atlanta, 11 for Chicago and 1 for LA. We had won by a significant majority, but if you added up the votes from the three other bids, it was 31–25. This tight margin gave room for an unfortunate anti-Montreal sentiment to be born, and that tide kept gaining momentum long after we had all left Johannesburg.

The second thing worth noting was that there was a leadership change within the FGG. Roberto Mantaci, our site inspector in Montreal, had run and won as the male co-president of the organization.

Kathleen Webster, a martial artist and lawyer who lived in Philadelphia and whose girlfriend was also part of the inner circle of the FGG, had won the female co-presidency.

Unfortunately their vision of delivering future games would be very different from ours. Unlike the IOC, when a city won the Gay Games they didn't sign a contract on the spot but instead began the negotiating process of the final licensing agreement. Montreal had left the Federation meeting in South Africa with a victory, but without a signed contract. This small detail would not be so small in the end.

GET REAL

Every once in a while, someone will come along in my life and stir things up. They speak to me so frankly, with no sugar coating, and like it or not the truth comes out. Barbara Coloroso was such a person. I met her for the first time when I reported to work on *Canada AM*. Barbara had been a nun and had spent a year in silence as part of her training. Since that time I don't think she ever stopped talking. I appreciated her a lot because she was so real, extremely opinionated, and unafraid to speak her mind. Upon meeting her it came as no surprise that she was a very well-respected authority on parenting, and that her no-nonsense style and frank advice made her a best selling author on children's issues. Which didn't mean she wasn't full of surprises.

Barbara had the ability to shock even me with some of the things she said. One day when we were talking about relationships she said that her mother superior might have had it right when she said that perhaps the most evolved human beings are bisexual. Leave it to Barbara to throw that one out live on morning television.

One very late summer day in 2001, Barbara convinced me to go kayaking with her. It was not something I would usually do, but how could I say no to this passionate, white-haired former nun? At the marina she started a conversation with me that I was finding irritating. She had watched me for a year doing television and had some hard questions for me. Barbara quizzed me about my segments. "I think you have something really important to say, Mark," she started. "I am just not sure if you know what it is. You need to simplify your messaging." I was stunned, but upon reflection realized that she was right. I kept trying to explain to her what the essence of my message was, but it seemed to only become more cumbersome and diluted in the process. She told me not to worry about finding the answer. "Let it come," she advised wisely. It eventually would. But it all started with a push from Barbara. She asked me to get real, which came at a time when I needed to apply the same exercise to all parts of my life.

I had thought that I was living an open life, but the reality was that gay wasn't something that was ever discussed in a business environment. Now I was part of the Gay Games, and every time someone asked what I was doing, the word *gay* suddenly popped up. It wasn't always easy. Many times I would see people, especially businessmen, get that blank look in their face when I simply said the word. Our flowing, easy, interesting conversation came to a complete halt. But experiencing this time and again helped me realize that you never knew when you might be called upon to declare who you are, or what you stand for.

On the other side of the building where I worked on the *Canada AM* set was the sport network TSN. Over the years I was a favorite guest of a show, *Off the Record*. Although sport oriented, this show was more about issues than sport itself. Each show pitted four guests against each other in a politically incorrect style, and host Michael Lansberg loved controversy, hence the open invitation extended to me by the producers.

My particular show included Gene Simmons, the lead singer of the rock band KISS. In the latter part of 2001, Gene was making the media rounds promoting his tell-all book. The big news was that he had slept with 4,500 women. During the taping of the show, Gene was typically outspoken, but it wasn't what he was speaking about that was so distasteful.

He was sitting directly across from me in an armchair, and to his left was Thea Andrews, a female sportscaster who happened to be drop-dead beautiful. Every time Gene stated to speak he would make some innuendo about adding Thea to his long list of conquests. I could see that she was extremely uncomfortable in this situation. I couldn't help myself; I made an intervention on her behalf.

When Gene made his next innuendo I interrupted and said, "Can't you see that she's not interested, Gene? Give it a rest. Besides, look straight ahead. I want to be number 4,501!" His mouth literally fell open, completely silencing him for the first time during the show. The studio erupted in laughter as Michael and the other guests fell out of their chairs. Thea was safe from that moment onward.

Change was in the air for me. I became bolder, clearer, with Montreal 2006 pulling me with such a force that things in my life either fell away or solidified. There was not a lot of room for anything in between. The segments on *Canada AM* had been part of a larger business venture that included a juice bar, which only lasted a year. My ignorance of how tight profit margins were in the juice business cost me a small fortune. It also saw the end of my five-year business relationship with Jacques. I had received an honorary doctorate from Western, but I liked to think of the juice bar experience as my very expensive PhD in business.

I wanted to move to Montreal to get active on a regular basis with the preparations for the games in 2006, but Jordan, my executive producer, wanted me to stay in Toronto for at least three more months. *Canada AM* was starting a *Change Your Life* series that would run for eight weeks. I had never been comfortable as a "life expert" telling people how to live, but Jordan was insistent. He wanted me to lead this series. It was probably a huge opportunity, but I just couldn't do it at that time. I was being pulled in a different direction.

I hadn't realized when I came out that it was truly only a beginning step. When I finally brought the worlds of gay and sport together, it brought back some horrific memories of discrimination, fear, and abuse for me. That was probably partly why these worlds had remained so separate for years. These were some very difficult issues to deal with, and I was finally in a place in my life where I felt I could put my demons to rest. But to do so would take a little private time, which I wanted to give myself.

I was changing my life, like they wanted the viewers to do on the TV show. But television didn't want me to actually do it, just to talk about *other* people doing it. One Sunday night before going to do the show the next morning I called my close friend Debbie and jokingly said, "How can I tell people how to live their lives when I feel like mine is falling apart?" In typical Debbie fashion, she dared me to go and say that very thing live on air the next day. So I did.

Valerie and Dan had left the show earlier in the year to be replaced by hosts Lisa LaFlamme and Rod Black. I was sitting with Lisa when she introduced the *Change Your Life* series that would soon be coming to the show. Then she gave the floor to me. On live TV I said, "That's right, Lisa, we will be doing an eight-week series, and I have decided to do my own 'change your life' project before we start. I have decided to finally look at that part of myself that has been driven by self-hate and loathing for so many years." She looked at me with wide eyes, then into the camera in shock, not knowing what to say but quickly recovering and breaking for a commercial. As soon as the camera went off she grabbed my knee and told me that she had hoped that I was getting some help. I was. Debbie's dare had worked.

Jordan was deeply concerned about my segment, saying it was too dark for viewers of the show. He argued that the audience didn't want to see their television personalities' weaknesses, that the viewers at home needed me to be strong for them. I countered that I thought viewers would like to see something real and would come along on this journey with me.

The next week I was asked to come into the studio before 6 a.m. so that I could tape my segments before the live show started, avoiding any surprises for CTV. I met with Jordan after the show that week and told him I was moving to Montreal. He let me make the move, agreeing that the roads the show and I were each embarking upon were too different at that time to reconcile. The following Monday I was given a beautiful bouquet of flowers and a book and pen, along with a montage of highlights from the eighty weeks I had been on the show. This would be my last episode before signing off of *Canada AM* for good. It was said that the truth shall set you free. It had.

CHAPTER FIFTEEN

WAKE-UP

Kentucky Fried Mark

Moving to Montreal was more challenging than I had anticipated. Not only was I moving to a new city, but it came with a new language, a new culture, and a new sense of community. For the first few weeks I was overwhelmed, not knowing where to start. At least I had a great friend two floors down.

My friend Peter Schleicher, who had supported me through Carol Anne's funeral, also helped get me settled into a 29th floor apartment of La Cité. I lived in a high-rise above an underground city that included a major grocery store, gym, post office, flower store, video store, dry cleaner, organic food store, dollar store, pharmacy, numerous restaurants, bank, movie theatre—every amenity I needed. It was a soft place to land in the middle of winter, a great place to get my bearings while settling into a new life.

One morning, before going down to join Peter for coffee at his apartment on the 27th floor, I checked my emails only to find this incredible invitation to come and be a guest at the upcoming 2002 Kentucky Derby in May. Why was I being invited to the Kentucky Derby? It turned out that along with the actual horse race there was an entire festival that took place, and the leadership of the festival included a discreet gay man. Every year one gay person was invited among the many other celebrity visitors so that the local gay community could secretly have one of their own to cheer during the festivities. This year they were having an athletic theme due to the recent Olympics in Salt Lake City, and I was their gay celebrity choice.

Over the years I had received some very interesting invitations. I had given a guest sermon at the Metropolitan Community Church of Toronto. I had talked at the Salzburg Festival in Austria. I had spoken to twenty-five thousand people on the steps of the Sydney Opera House at the launch of Mardi Gras. But this invitation was right up there. I was offered two first-class flight tickets, hotel accommodations, and passes to the entire program over four straight days, climaxing with two seats on Millionaire's Row for the running of the Derby. With the spare ticket I asked Peter if he wanted to go. He was thrilled to be asked. Two months later, on May 2, 2002, we were off to the races.

A steamboat race would mark the beginning of the celebrations. The next four days were surreal. Southern culture met horse culture met Hollywood culture. Peter and I joined a pack of celebrities that included the gay police officer from *Six Feet Under*, the mom from *That '70s Show*, and Kim, one of the popular *Survivors* in that day.

We traveled from event to event, one crazy adventure outdoing the next. I took part in the Pegasus Parade. My name and "Olympian" were on the side of the car. I was in the car alone wearing my medals and I could see people in the stands reading my sign, looking at me and then wondering who I was. I made a swimming motion with my arms and suddenly it was as if everybody remembered me. Of course they didn't—why would they know me?—but no one wanted to be left out, so once one person cheered, everyone did. At one point I was stopped in front of people who had already cheered, and the crowd started chanting U-S-A to me. One large man yelled, "Thanks for what you did for our country, man." I didn't have the heart to let them know that, actually, these medals belonged to Canada and, to make matters worse, I had beaten an American swimmer to get the gold.

One night we went to the Barnstable-Brown Party, essentially an over-hyped house party in a mansion that was the hottest ticket in town. Thousands of people lined the street around the Barnstable-Brown house, hoping to catch a glimpse of someone famous. They weren't disappointed. Bo Derek was chatting with Alice Cooper. *That '70s Show* mom, Debra Jo Rupp, hugged co-worker Ashton Kutcher. And I was accosted by a misguided police officer. I was leading our celebrity pack through the party when this burly police woman looked at me hard, couldn't figure out who I was but saw the celebrities behind me, and literally shoved me out of the way so that they could pass. "Uh, actually, I'm with them," I said to her as I noticed her "To Serve and Protect" badge. Apparently that was to serve and protect famous people only. I let them lead and Peter and I followed.

But right when I thought maybe I had had it with this intense celebrity culture, something funny happened that made up for the less appealing moments and brought me back down to earth. Of all the celebrities at this lavish house party, the one my gay host from the festival most wanted to meet was Prince Albert of Monaco. I laughed when he told me, because Prince Albert was the only celebrity that I knew at this damn party. "Prince Albert is here?" I asked. "Come on, show me, and I'll introduce you." Prince Albert was as shocked to see me as my host was that we knew each other. As they made small talk for a moment I grabbed a program of the "celebrities" attending the party, and found my name listed as U.S. Olympic Gold Medallist. I was becoming assimilated quicker than with the IOC. At this rate, by the day of the Derby they would have an American passport for me!

During the actual running of the Derby I drank mint juleps and made two-dollar bets on Millionaire's Row. Angelica Huston gave me another rare star-struck moment of my life. Earlier I had had a nasty encounter with a woman who played the lead on *Sabrina, the Teenage Witch* on television. I was in the buffet line, waiting with everyone else for my turn at the jumbo shrimps, when this woman ignored all of us and headed straight for them. "Excuse me, this is called a line," I said strongly to her. She gave me a look that showed she could act like Sabrina, the teenage bitch, but I couldn't have cared less. All of the celebrities and socialites holding their plates gave me a one-handed clap for having the guts to say something, including Ms. Huston. I took the opportunity to have my picture quickly taken with her.

Many times I wondered if I had made the right decision leaving my role on television for a new life in Montreal. I guess I was supposed to go to the Kentucky Derby to get my answer. Celebrity and fame looked interesting from the outside in, but inside out it could be unreal, plastic, and other than bringing attention to worthy causes, quite worthless. Montreal was the city in Canada in which I was least recognized. I would cherish this; it allowed me to stay real. At the Derby I went to see a short movie on the history of the winning horses. The excellence and heart displayed by these champions was the one thing that moved me most amongst all the fakeness. Vicki Gabereau, the much-loved Canadian television talk show host, had given me some advice the year prior when I was wrestling with what to do with my career. She had told me, "Go where the work is." I realized that I had gone where the work was *and* where my heart was. I was passionate about the work I was doing. One without the other didn't make sense to me anymore.

HALLOWEEN DRAG, CHRISTMAS DOLL

The first thing I had done when I had returned to Toronto from Johannesburg in October of 2001 was visit my friend Alex. It was Halloween time and he had something to spring on me. Two of our friends wanted to do drag that year but were only going to do it if I would do it, too. "They will do it only if I will?" I repeated. Alex answered, "Yes." "Then we had better call them to tell them we're on," I replied.

On Halloween night the three of us had our makeup done by one of Alex's housemates, a full-blown drag mama. He did all of us in exactly the same way, transforming our faces completely by whiting out our eyebrows and painting on a brand new face. We wore matching rhinestone jackets, skirts, and cowboy hats, each one of us in silver, blue, or black, as well as matching wigs in varying lengths. We looked like the Mandrell sisters—from hell.

After two hours of preparation we hit the town. The shortest of us was six foot four when all done up with hair and boots. We caused a commotion as people saw one, then two, then three of us tall beauties looking exactly like triplets. We ended the night at a cocktail lounge partying with Jason Priestley. Ben Mulroney, Seamus O'Regan, and Thea Andrews, all colleagues from CTV were hanging out. It took Ben a full ten minutes of conversation before realizing it was me.

Drag had stayed in the closet for all of those years since *The Rocky Horror Picture Show*, and it was safe to say it would stay there permanently. By the end of the night my feet were killing me, my eyes felt stuck together from the false eyelashes, and my makeup was surely running all over my face. Every guy should be forced to go out in drag at least once in his life to see just how the other half lives.

This was a time in my life when I resolved all of the secret desires and fantasies that I had had in my life. And it wasn't just drag that came out of the closet. Eventually Barbie did, too. Slut Barbie had made the move with me to Montreal, and she was in her usual straddling position on the faucet in the bathroom. By this time, though, the lingerie outfit she had been wearing was downright nasty, the black slowly fading to a purplish, gray color. To be honest, I didn't really even notice her anymore. She had become nothing more than a fixture in the bathroom not unlike that extra bottle of conditioner that sat in the corner of the bathtub for years.

On Christmas morning as I went to open my stocking, I noticed that there were all kinds of boxes waiting for me. My curiosity piqued,

I opened the first to find thirty pairs of Barbie shoes. The next had outfits, another purses and bags, and finally one more with jewelry. I thought it was a bad joke, but my boyfriend had found all of these things at one of those bazaars that pop up around Christmas, and this was my gift from him.

I have to be honest—at first I thought this present was ridiculous. I was a man now, and men don't play with Barbie. But for the heck of it we changed Slut Barbie into a nice outfit, and it completely transformed her. I became fascinated, unable to believe how good she looked, and somehow Barbie's transformation was mirroring my own.

On one hand it seemed crazy, a thirty-four-year-old man playing with Barbie, but that was the way it was. I stopped judging. Besides, it was incredible to see how many of my friends actually enjoyed changing her clothes and dressing her up, too. Even Debbie couldn't resist her charm. "This is surprisingly creative and fun," she told me as she searched for the right pair of shoes. Exactly.

As silly as it seemed, Barbie played a major role in our lives at that time. My boyfriend had studied as a fashion designer, winning a full scholarship to study in Paris, but hadn't pursued his dream. Barbie inspired him to start making clothes again, at first for her, then for real people. Eventually he started his own fashion business.

By the following Christmas, Barbie was taped shut in her box in the storage closet in the basement. Whatever I had needed to get out of my system was gone. Neither Barbie nor my relationship with that boyfriend survived until the next year, but I learned from this experience that not everything is intended to last forever. Regardless of the length of time together, we were all better off for allowing ourselves to have had the experience.

TWO BECOME ONE

Part of getting ready for Montreal's event in 2006 meant seeing the delivery of the games before us in Sydney in 2002. I stayed a few days with an old friend, Alan, who happened to become roommates with my other dear friend, Noel, whom I affectionately called Nola. During the games Nola wasn't feeling well, having problems with his throat and stomach. When I moved in the week after the event for a few days' holiday and catching up, he went to the doctor for some tests, and I was the only one home when he arrived back. He walked through the door and instantly started doing laundry. The dryer was blocking Nola's face from me. "Hey Nola, how was your ..." I noticed that he was crying. "I have cancer," he said. Oh God, here we go again.

Nola was my dad's age when he had been diagnosed, and although they had lived very different lives, I knew that it would take a miracle for him to beat this thing. Still, I had to remain hopeful, and after the first big breakdown, Nola decided being positive was the only way to be. But that was part of the problem. Nola made us all believe that he was always all right, when really he had been hurting for some time. He had left going to the doctor for an examination and tests until the pain was absolutely unbearable, and by then it was too late.

I promised Alan I would be part of the support team in any way I could. Alan would take the role my sister had taken, acting as chief caregiver and decipherer of information. I would help financially, ensuring that Nola lived as comfortably as possible.

Before I left Australia I spent a Saturday with just Nola. We did all of his favorite things, like buying new music and going for coffee and dessert. We did everything to pretend that this was just another Saturday together, not acknowledging how dreadful the circumstances really were. Neither of us knew at the time that it would be our last day together.

I called often from Canada, at first talking to Nola but then, as he got too sick to speak on the phone, getting all of the updates from Alan. It was a lot to take on, but at least Alan had some support from Nola's mom and dad as well. Nola, his parent's only child, still went home two or three nights a week to stay with them, and his father, now into his eighties, was there to drive Nola to the hospital or wherever he needed to go. Alan watched Nola get weaker and weaker, to the point where they had crossed the street in front of their apartment and Nola hadn't had the strength to lift his foot high enough to clear the curb, and their one attempt at a normal outing got canceled.

Nola had always been diligent in keeping his two lives separate, his home life with his parents on one side and his gay life with the rest of us on the other. One day when Nola was looking at what the future would hold he realized that he wouldn't be able to keep these two lives going anymore because he was too ill. He would need twenty-four-hour-a-day help. Within ten days of that realization Nola was gone, letting go quickly when the hard reality hit him.

I had already booked my airline ticket and was leaving in a day or two to see him when Alan called to tell me that Nola had died that morning. Like my father, he had been fifty-five years old and had lost his battle to this wretched disease within six months of diagnosis.

I had at least had the chance to speak to Nola on the phone before he passed away, having an impulse to call him the day before. His mother answered from the hospital room, and held the phone to his mouth so I could hear him say something that sounded barely human, but understood that he was trying to tell me he loved me.

Instead of traveling to see Nola, I went to say my goodbyes in person at his memorial service. Most of the arrangements for the funeral fell on Alan's shoulders. I went to be a support system for him, to spend time with Nola's parents, and to help Alan pack things up and get moved into a new apartment.

Nola had vigilantly kept his two worlds separate during his life, but finally in death they came crashing together. Nobody spoke blatantly about gay out of respect for his parents, but when I did part of the eulogy I couldn't stop myself from calling him Nola rather than Noel out of habit after all of these years. It was pretty obvious with a backyard full of well-groomed men that something was up. Although his parents belonged to the furthest right-wing political party in Australia, they needed every one of us to help ease the burden of their loss.

In the end I saw that Nola's mom had wanted this coming together of Nola/Noel's double lives to happen for years. Sadly, in Nola's death, the path had been cleared.

I went and visited Nola's parents almost every day while I was in Australia. His dad would come and collect me just as he had done for Nola for all the years I had known him. I went with them to their local rugby union club where we had lunch and played the poker machines. Years earlier, Nola had been my bridge to embracing gay, beginning the process of my not being ashamed of who I was. Now it was my turn to do the same for him, but through his parents, reflecting back to them the incredible person Nola had been to me, helping them embrace the many different parts of this seemingly simple, but very complicated, person they knew as their son.

THE REAL DEAL

The signs that Montreal's relationship with the Federation of Gay Games would be difficult began almost immediately. In Vancouver for the FGG's annual meeting in 2002, we had a run-in with one of the co-presidents about the discriminatory language we felt was being used against the "drag queens and dykes on bikes" of our own community by the FGG in their vision paper. This intervention was not appreciated, at all.

At that meeting Montreal had to make a formal presentation to the general assembly about our progress to date, which was already significant. I was excited about making the presentation, but was surprised to be met with nothing but cynicism and criticism from the Federation hierarchy. It was like the story of the boy who cried wolf. Finally, a city had a big vision of what this event could be *and* had the means to carry it out, but the Federation had heard this song and dance too many times before to believe it. We were caught in a very difficult place, paying the price for the mistakes of others in the past on one hand, but having a different reality that no one seemed to want to acknowledge on the other.

At the end of my formal update the floor was opened for questions. An FGG member from Seattle started. "Mark, it is great that you are there, but what happens if you leave or get hit by a bus or something. Does anybody else on the Montreal team speak English?" My francophone co-president answered in perfect English, which was met with a standing ovation of solidarity from the multilingual Europeans. But it was exactly this kind of condescending, insensitive, unilateral worldview that made dealing with some of these people so difficult.

The mood in the room was so distasteful that the partner of the founder of the movement had to stand up and make an intervention on Montreal's behalf, telling the group that they should at least give us a chance and share some of our excitement. I felt like I was back in junior high school.

Instead of celebrating a team of experts that had an enormous amount of experience in sport and events, the FGG leadership seemed threatened. We wanted to work together, but it was clear to me that for them this was not about partnership; this was more about domination and control. The problem was, we were too strong to be pinned down. From their perspective we had no history with the Federation and no right to input. As far as we could see, they were obsessed with the value of the Gay Games brand, but we were the ones responsible, at least for the next four years, to represent that brand in the market.

Ironically Montreal was in a place to build awareness, grow LGBT sport, and create a real market value for that treasured brand, solving a lot of the problems that the FGG had faced in the past. Together all of our dreams could have come true. But they just weren't willing to trust us.

By the time we got to Sydney for Gay Games VI, things were getting out of control. Montreal was very well organized, and we had created a brochure that we would be giving to all of the thousands of participants in Sydney. It was an ideal opportunity for outreach. But since we still didn't have a signed contract with the FGG and they disagreed with some of the content of the brochure, which they hadn't approved, they made us destroy the brochures instead of distributing them—all of them. Yet another sign of things to come.

With the Sydney organizers facing millions of dollars in deficit despite remarkable games and Montreal leaving with a still unsigned contract, the FGG threatened not to give us the ceremonial flag at the closing party. Although they did eventually hand us the flag, I had the feeling that no matter what we did we would be in the wrong. We were damned if we did and damned if we didn't, and I couldn't help but wonder if the common denominator of the past four failures by host cities might have been the Federation itself.

If things had been out of control before Sydney, they got downright nasty after that. Facing another Gay Games with a deficit, the Federation decided that in order for the Games to come to Montreal, we would have to change our plans entirely. We had won the right to host Gay Games VII based on a bid of twenty-four thousand participants and a $22 million budget. The Federation now wanted us to cut that by more than half, with ten thousand participants and a $10 million budget as a starting point. They wanted us to fire staff and use volunteers until more funding came in. But this created a catch-22 for us, because we were over a year and a half into the delivery of the project already. We had hired a professional staff to deliver the games and *specifically* find more funds, which was starting to happen. We felt that without a staff to put time into the project, no new money would come and we would fall short as the other games had in the past. The argument went round and round. It was looking more and more difficult for us to come to some sort of agreement.

We had heard over and over the problems the Federation had had with past cities, and one by one we addressed them. We had female leadership. We had strong financial partners. We had outreach to LGBT sport teams. We had sport expertise. We tried to meet in the middle at sixteen thousand participants. Still, this wasn't enough.

After yet another try at negotiating, we still couldn't come to an agreement. It was heartbreaking that the leadership of the FGG seemed only to be able to look at the mistakes of the past without recognizing the differences that we had going for us today in Montreal. I still believed we would work together; that it was just a matter of time before our respective negotiating teams came to an agreement.

It was in San Francisco in August of 2003 that I realized just how desperate the situation was. We were at an international gay swimming championship promoting Montreal 2006. The president of the international gay swimming organization was a straight woman, and we hung out at the pool all morning making small talk. She was always as nice as could be to me, but something wasn't adding up.

Although Montreal 2006 had been sponsors of this meet, we were not being treated particularly well. I learned that I had been denied the chance to speak to the athletes at the closing banquet, something I had done in the past, but didn't know why. That changed the next day when one of Mrs. President's colleagues accosted me in the gift shop, threatening me to make sure Montreal signed the licensing agreement or the FGG would pull the games. Then, with a nasty smirk on his face, he added, "What a shame you won't be able to speak to the swimmers at the end of the meet, Mark. Guess you should have signed the contract." So there was the real deal. We were being sabotaged by the inner circle of the federation.

Call me naïve, but I just hadn't expected it to be this way among fellow gay sport people. I thought that given how much challenge we had all been through, the last thing we needed was to do this to each other. I'd come to this event volunteering my time to genuinely do everything I could to make a difference for the better for the LGBT sport community, and this was how I was greeted by people in positions of leadership. It hurt me deeply, and I ended up having the strangest reaction. At lunch an hour later I was so disappointed about the situation that I spontaneously burst into tears.

One night to escape all of the politics and nastiness, I went out to dinner with swimmers from across the U.S. who were there to compete. Before eating we went around the room and introduced ourselves. When it was my turn I had said, "I am Mark Tewksbury, co-president of the next Gay Games in Montreal 2006." One of the other guests said, "Montreal isn't hosting the games; they're going to Chicago." I almost fell off my chair. It turned out the Chicago buzz became one that wouldn't go away over the next couple of days at the pool. I asked the swimmer his name, but he realized that he had said something he shouldn't and wouldn't give it to me. But I did know he was from Salt Lake City, the same club as Mrs. President. What a coincidence!

The morning after the meet ended I ran into Mrs. President in the lobby of our hotel. Out of respect, I had waited until the end of the competition to ask her about what I had heard, but now that our paths had crossed, I had to ask. "I need to talk to you. Please come with me for a moment," I said to her.

I could feel the mood change instantly as we walked toward a quiet corner, her face betraying her true character as the air around us thickened. This was not going to be fun. "I was at a dinner the other night and a swimmer from Salt Lake City told the group that Montreal wouldn't be hosting the Gay Games. Do you have any idea where he might have gotten this information?" She freaked out. "Who was it?" she snapped. Immediately came the denial. "I have no idea what you are talking about."

When I pressed her more she caved and eventually told me that the executive of the FGG had told her to shut Montreal down at this competition because we weren't officially the hosts of the Gay Games until we had an agreement.

"So this is how it was going to be," I thought to myself. She had lied to me, then denied knowing, then admitted to a truth that put the blame on others. Worse still, she had done it all while being sugary sweet to my face, and then turning around and backstabbing me in the next moment. Unfortunately, her attitude was a perfect example of the inner circle of FGG members. They played brutally hard. If they couldn't control you then they would do everything in their power to destroy you.

As Mrs. President left San Francisco, she put a completely different spin on what had happened between us and almost immediately started a hateful personal smear campaign against me. She would jump up and tell people what a horrible person I was every chance she could get. It was just like the good old days, enduring attacks on my character by the IOC. At least I finally knew exactly what we were dealing with.

CHAPTER SIXTEEN

GROWING PAINS

THE SHOWDOWN IN CHICAGO

Many people ask me if I still swim. After a twelve-year break I am finally back in the water swimming occasionally. For many years I did other things to stay in shape, like running. In 2003 I ran the New York City Marathon, the first of two marathons for me that fall. The other didn't involving running, but rather trying to come to a deal with the Federation.

Things kept going from bad to worse. By Labor Day our relationship had completely come off the rails. As part of our outreach to the local Montreal community to help build awareness of the upcoming Gay Games we had planned a weekend of activities. We started Thursday night with a fundraising dinner that brought together the local LGBT, sport, business, media, and political communities of Montreal. We had hoped to sell four hundred tickets but had to stop when we surpassed the five hundred mark. The dinner also brought in more than $50,000 to put toward our outreach program to bring athletes from underdeveloped parts of the world to Montreal for the Games. The rest of the weekend the focus turned to a remarkable two-day demonstration of LGBT sport on the street. The weekend was a huge hit, but unfortunately I had to miss most of it.

The Federation leadership knew this weekend was planned, and on Thursday morning before our gala dinner we received a letter informing us that we no longer had the right to associate our weekend with the Gay Games name. The letter shook us to the core, confirming the suspicions we had that this group seemed determined to do everything possible to work against us. This was getting to be a complete nightmare.

Earlier that spring I had become co-president of Montreal 2006, putting me in a unique position. I hadn't been part of the negotiating team yet, so I was untainted from the process. The Federation had had a team of three people negotiating, who then reported to a larger Montreal Liaison Task Force, who in turn reported back to the general membership of the FGG.

In a desperate attempt to salvage any chance of saving the games, I spent the entire weekend on the phone personally calling *every single one* of the forty-plus Federation members to try to find a solution to the mess we were in. "Both sides have failed in the negotiating process, reaching an impasse." I would start. "It is time for those of us who haven't been a part of this to step in." I felt sick about the situation we were in, leading a multi-million-dollar project but watching this relationship slowly unravel and fall apart. I pleaded with the FGG members for anything that could break the deadlock, suggesting new negotiating teams, mediation, arbitration—whatever it would take.

Almost unanimously the Federation members refused to speak at length to me, deferring to their three-person leadership team in charge of negotiations. Some FGG members were furious at me for calling, which to this day I still can't figure out, given that the situation was extremely grave for both parties.

Those who did talk to me enlightened me to a couple of things. Either they didn't have a clue what was happening, because they were part of that secondary group of members that were kept in the dark, or they were part of the inner group that controlled the organization that had a long list of reasons of why we weren't to be trusted in Montreal. They thought we were just an excuse for a big party. The lasting argument was that we were just a front for tourism. The reality was that cities bid for big sport events *because of* and *for mutual benefits* with tourism. Not to do so would have been irresponsible as it gave our project unprecedented financial security that previous games had not had. The FGG was our partner, but since the negotiating team didn't seem to understand the concept of partnership, no matter how hard we tried to convince them, it fell on deaf ears. The other argument was that we didn't know sport. That I found unbelievable considering I was an Olympic Champion co-president with extensive IOC experience, our CEO had a degree in sport management, her assistant had led the local LGBT sport team, and our sports department was filled with gay and lesbian people who had worked for years within the Quebec sport federations. How much more sport knowledgeable could we be?

It became clear to me that we were dealing with an organization that had been deeply wounded and had no trust anymore. Nothing we could say would change that. As we proved all of their points wrong over time, the leadership of the FGG still found other reasons not to support us. Although arriving there differently and on a much smaller scale, it seemed to me that a sense of entitlement had tainted this organization just as it had the IOC. The hundreds of volunteer hours the leadership had put into trying to make their event and organization work over the years made them feel as if they were the only ones who had the right to participate in a leadership capacity.

What was so frustrating was that the negotiation team never fully represented what was happening to the larger membership of the FGG and never allowed Montreal to speak with them directly so that at least both sides could be heard. They were the gatekeepers and anything we did to circumvent that was just met with more hostility.

It all came down to a final negotiating session in Chicago at the November 2003 FGG Annual Meeting. A few weeks earlier, one of the negotiators had sent a distinguished business leader in Montreal who had once been a member of parliament a legal letter questioning his honorable title, and threatening to pursue his actions to the full extent of the law. The business leader's crime? Sending an email to the full FGG membership whose addresses he had found listed on the FGG website. And this negotiator was whom the FGG chose to sit across the table from us.

Negotiating is not fun, even at the best of times. Admittedly it took two sides to get into this mess, and from our end we changed the negotiating team to remove the personalities that together with the FGG team became explosive. We had requested that the FGG do the same but were refused, and in the end it was the same three people sitting at the 11th hour bargaining table who had brought this thing to an impasse in the first place.

Financial control was one of the rough points. It was something we couldn't give away. The FGG had no legal responsibility if something happened, but the board members in Montreal certainly did. Because we were the entity legally responsible should their be a deficit, and because we received government funding, the financial decisions had to stay in Montreal. Period. This would be one of the major deal-breakers. The FGG made some concessions that day, but on this financial matter they were not willing to compromise the issue of control.

Negotiations got worse and worse. Name-calling broke out. Tempers flared. When at 1:00 a.m. a last-ditch effort to salvage things saw a contract return to us with the same language, our lawyer met with theirs to say we couldn't accept it. Montreal "walked away," as the FGG put it. Perhaps it was more appropriate to say that after two years and more than sixteen solid hours of negotiation, the two sides couldn't come to a deal.

The absolute last chance to salvage the situation came at the actual FGG Annual Meeting two days later. The negotiating team would put a recommendation forward. Finally, it would be the whole assembly that would have to decide our fate.

It turned out that Mrs. President from swimming was given the honor of chairing the meeting. At the opening session, an observer asked whether the day's sessions would be open to all or held in secret. Mrs. President reprimanded him just for asking the question. "You know the three monkeys: monkey see, monkey hear, monkey speak?" Mrs. President shrieked, placing her hand over her mouth for effect, "You are the monkeys that *don't* speak." The room erupted, insulted and outraged. Talk about a banana republic. I knew this situation wasn't funny, but I couldn't help but think if we were all monkeys, did that mean that no deal for Montreal 2006 would be called a banana split?

The FGG closed the doors and met privately all day long. Only the small team of FGG negotiators presented their side of the story. Members from Europe and Canada requested that Montreal speak to the assembly, and Montreal was finally told that we could come into the room and face the general assembly, but would only be allowed to answer their pre-prepared questions. "Am I not allowed to make a statement to the members to explain what happened?" I asked the vice-president of the FGG, who was acting as the go-between. "I am afraid not," he replied. "Can I say anything at all other than answers to the questions?" "No."

Standing in the hallway for hours on end, waiting to get news, and being treated so harshly made me feel more like I was in Moscow at the politburo than a hotel in the United States of America. Everyone had limits, and I had reached mine. I had never felt so humiliated, controlled, manipulated. And this was from members of the LGBT sport leadership. In my wildest dreams I had never imagined that the worst treatment I would ever experience would come from my own. But the ugly reality was staring me in the face, like the gay corporate client who had canceled my contract years earlier.

I was given thirty minutes to answer the questions, but only took twelve. I could have elaborated more, made some eloquent pleas for one more chance, but I didn't have it in me anymore. I was exhausted, insulted, and after people actually snickered at me when I spoke, disgusted.

I left the room making one key point: Version 13 of the six-hundred-page contract, the one *already signed* by Montreal, was still on the table if they wanted to accept it. I also clearly stated that Version 13.5, the one the FGG negotiating team was trying to force on us, would *not* be acceptable for Montreal because of the financial control issues. Version 13 gave them the controls they were looking for but left the financial oversight with us, and we thought it was more than fair. We left the room so they could discuss it.

That's when things got interesting. It would only be months later at another LGBT sport meeting that it was confirmed that the independent lawyer the FGG had hired to lead the negotiation process had stood up in front of the general assembly and stated plainly that there was nothing in Version 13 that the FGG couldn't live with. He had given the green light to partner with Montreal. One executive member had reacted quickly, "I am really surprised to hear you say that at this time." The motions that were put forward to the FGG general membership reflected that surprise, never including a chance to vote on Version 13. Instead they gave Montreal 2006 a final ultimatum to accept their Version 13.5 or else, although I had clearly stated we could never accept it. The whole split and ensuing battle could have been avoided.

THE 1ST WORLD OUTGAMES

I arrived back in Montreal to face all of our major partners in the project at a meeting in City Hall. There were representatives from each level of government, from the media, and from the corporations that were already signed on as sponsors sitting around a huge table, wanting to understand the situation. We had been very clear with the FGG before Chicago that we were past the point of no return with our project.

Two years into the delivery of games, half the house had already been built, and while we had desperately hoped they would be Gay Games, there would be games in Montreal in 2006 regardless. Ironically, while the Federation didn't trust us, every single one of our major financial partners, the ones who were putting money in the project, did. We, and they, all agreed to continue to honor the project, including time and financial commitments, through to the delivery of games in 2006.

On the Federation side, the murmurs of Chicago hosting the Gay Games hadn't just been in my imagination. The games indeed were heading to the windy city. In the spirit of friendship we had grown so accustomed to in our negotiations, Chicago's dates were set for two weeks before Montreal's in July of 2006. This decision was made by the FGG despite some of their own members pleading to put the games back a year so that athletes would not have to choose between two events.

There was, understandably, an uproar from the athletes of the world. They didn't want this split to happen, and felt that both sides had failed them. I felt stuck between a rock and a hard place. It would be impossible to explain the nuances of what had gone wrong, or even to understand how different our worldviews of delivering games were. It was as if we were both standing in the same room at 78 degrees Fahrenheit, but one group would swear it was hot, while the other thought it was cold. After endless tries, we couldn't find a way to reconcile this difference.

Very few LGBT athletes had firsthand experience of how the Federation operated, and most didn't care about the business and political side of the movement. All they knew was that they had life-changing experiences at the games, and by the time the press conference took place announcing yet another deficit, most of the athletes were already on their way home. Few saw the devastation that was left within the local LGBT community.

A positive outcome of the split was that more participants than ever before started to investigate the significance of how this event should be delivered, and the effect that the business side might have on the future of the games themselves. Participants started to realize that without change there might not be a future. How many deficits could the global LGBT sport community endure?

People around the world who had experienced the FGG, particularly those who had hosted games in the past, overwhelmingly sent letters of support. We were not alone in our disillusionment of how things had been run. The problems hadn't started in Montreal. After enough sport leaders spoke up, it became clear that we had to at least bring some of these people together to discuss the future of the LGBT sport movement. There was a crisis and something had to change. A think tank to bring together these people was planned for January 2004 in Montreal, the first step toward a new future for LGBT sport worldwide.

On the coldest day of the year, more than twenty leaders from the U.S., Canada, Australia, and Europe came together in Montreal. Two FGG executive members also showed up uninvited, but we politely asked them to leave. It was nothing personal, but people didn't want them there. The environment of FGG meetings was stifling, with people feeling they were unable to speak openly, and in order to truly discuss the future a different climate was necessary. I felt very strongly about creating something beyond Montreal, legacy being a key element of traditional sport. This meeting would determine what might be the future beyond 2006.

Rachel Corbett, an open lesbian who had worked most of her career in the traditional sport world as an organizational development and governance expert, was brought in to lead the sessions. Rachel knew very little of the FGG or of Montreal, and was perfect for the role. The collective sport experience in the room was impressive, with representatives attending from seven FGG member organizations, three national Olympic committees, and five national sport governing bodies.

At first there was enormous skepticism about this meeting. People expected to be dubiously led by Montreal into some kind of self-serving decision. But that changed quickly.

Rachel simply had us look at the best sport practices in the world, studying models from the IOC, the FGG, other multi-sport games organizations, and the Canada Games movement. Instead of reinventing the wheel, we tried to find what would work best in these various models for LGBT sport. People said they had never discussed some of these issues in their years and years of attending FGG meetings.

By the end of the first day, major progress had been made. People started to see the possibilities of what we could collectively create by working together instead of feeling controlled, bullied, and intimidated. It was the spirit of the meeting that was new. Cynics spoke their minds. There were no rules for who could or couldn't speak, or when. Halfway through the first day a participant from Europe suggested that we should rearrange the furniture in the room so we could interact more directly, so we did. We discussed issues and process, but didn't make process an issue. People who disagreed with a point were allowed to say so openly. If they saw that the majority was going against them, they felt comfortable supporting the majority. Magic slowly started to happen when even the most hardened critics started to get excited about the future, building on the successes already out there to create a winning global formula.

On Sunday morning the hard question was asked: "Do you believe that the Federation can be reformed?" One by one the Federation members in attendance stood on their own accord and said that no, given their experience with that organization, there was no chance of reform. The FGG had a singular focus of delivering games, with no intention of broadening that mandate to include long-term, direct organizational support to develop and grow sport leagues, clubs, and tournaments in between games.

This group of leaders decided that if there was going to be a sustainable future for LGBT sport, they wanted to shape it so that it could reach its full potential. This wasn't about a brand or games. This was about creating a vibrant LGBT sport movement that *included* a major international quadrennial games, but that had a mandate to continue growing sport and service to members in the years between games, among other things.

Finally, there would be an organization that would share best practices, meet the evolving needs of LGBT athletes and teams, and partner with broader LGBT and traditional organizations that shared this vision. As brutal and hard as the split had been, the experience with this new group of leaders from around the world was uplifting and inspiring. We saw, as we came together from all parts of the world, what the potential could be if we shared our knowledge and experience with each other, and trusted each other. At the end of the working sessions we gave each other a tearful standing ovation.

Eight weeks later, GLISA, the Gay and Lesbian International Sport Association, was launched. A vision, a mission, key areas of activity, and governance principles that would ensure a democratic future for this organization was presented publicly for the first time. The interim board included representation from Europe, Canada, the U.S., and Australia. The mandate was to build LGBT sport worldwide, and to partner with Montreal to deliver a new global quadrennial event with sport, culture, and human rights in 2006, the 1st World Outgames.

It would take some time to learn to trust a partnership again, given all that we had been through in the past two years. And it certainly wasn't a free ride. At the beginning of the think tank there had been one particularly cynical participant, Catherine Meade, a tough-ass lawyer from Toronto who had been to many Gay Games. She had arrived ready to crucify Montreal for the split. Two months later at the launch, she became the first female co-president of GLISA. A new future was born.

OLYMPIC PEER POWER

Life has always been give and take with me. I have seen time do incredible things, sometimes the seemingly impossible, but all unfolding on its own accord. I thought I had left the Olympic movement forever in 1999 when I had stepped down from all of my IOC posts, but in 2004 all of that changed.

It had been years since Carol Anne's death, I was again on fairly good terms with Dick Pound, the Canadian IOC Executive member, and even our athlete representative and I had kissed and made up since our confrontation in the hotel in Seoul. There was only so much time in the day, and my dance card was full with my deep commitment to LGBT sport. But in the year leading up to the Athens games, invitations poured in from the Olympic movement and I couldn't say no. It was time to go back to my roots.

In the spring I was invited to speak at Lake Louise to the top Canadian winter Olympic athletes in preparation for Torino 2006. Some of the legends of the past were hosting this weekend. I was the final speaker on Sunday, sharing my experiences leading up to Barcelona. I remembered one of the most powerful things I had heard years earlier had come from Olympic skiing legend Nancy Greene, because she shared her humanity with us. She had fears, flaws, and quirks, but she still managed to become the best. After hearing her I had hope for myself.

I shared the same kind of speech with these Olympians on that day. I laid it on the line with them, sharing the practical things I did to get myself as ready as I could be. It would be almost a year later when I would read an article in the newspaper that said, "Wherever you are, Mark Tewksbury, Thomas Grandi says thank you. Thank you for coming to the Olympic Excellence series with other Olympic legends." I gave and I got back. I was truly overjoyed to watch through the media as Thomas won not one but two world cup titles that season. It was my first step back to the Olympic movement.

On June 20, 2004, the Athens Olympic flame came to Montreal. The city asked me to be one of the citizens to carry it. I was number eighteen in the first group of twenty runners, and we were all herded onto a bus to drop each runner at the next exchange point. The enthusiasm was contagious whether we were young or old, English or French, Olympian or citizen, and we couldn't help but clapping and cheering for the next runner. The flame had this surprising effect on all of us. When it actually came to be my turn I was so nervous, praying the thing would light, which it did, and then holding it out in front of me for the kilometer that was mine. Whether I wanted it or not that year, the Olympic spirit was reignited within me.

About four days before the opening ceremonies of the Olympics in Athens in 2004, I received a call in Montreal from the Canadian Team. They were already onsite at the Olympics. One of the staff from the Canadian Olympic Committee in Ottawa had a request. "Before the athletes' reception in two days we want to have a former Olympian speak to the team for the last time before they go and compete. We would be honored if you would be the one to address them." The honor was all mine.

I have been speaking for a long time, but there is no group that is as special to me as my athletic peers. They understand completely what I am talking about, and in a very short amount of time a lot can be conveyed. Getting ready to speak to our Athens Olympians, though, I had never been so nervous before a speech. I had five minutes to address them. I simply said, "You are here now. This is it. Stop thinking about it, dreaming about it, and now just live it." I shared my story of twelve years earlier, when I asked myself, "Why not me?" before the final of the 100-meter backstroke when thinking about who would win the race that night. Later during the games, I ran into parents of the Canadian athletes and they told me how their kids had reacted to my story. It was the second step back.

Finally, I spoke to some of the same athletes later in the year at a weekend that was preparing them for retirement. There I spoke about being gay, depressed, not sharing that with anybody at the time, and continuing a horrible double life. I was completely open with my peers, bringing my gayness directly into the Olympic family, but in a way they could relate to. After my speech, the head of the Olympic committee asked me to have lunch with him, looking for ways to work together. I had left the Olympic movement because I never felt like I could truly be myself in this world. That was over now. I had come back home, and now home was ready for me.

THE PINK TRIANGLE

On the last night of the Canadian Olympic Swimming Trials for Athens, more than thirty former Olympians representing forty years of Olympic swimming history gathered. The night was memorable for a number of reasons. My former roommate from the World Cup circuit, Marcel, was there with his beautiful wife, Mikala. I hadn't seen them in ten years, long before I had come out. In all the time I shared a room with Marcel we had never discussed my homosexuality. I had a few minutes with Mikala privately as Marcel was wrapping up another conversation and I asked her how they were with my being gay. Coming out never ended. Mikala looked at me surprised and said, "Mark, didn't Marcel ever tell you? I was raised for a few years by a gay couple in Amsterdam when I was a child. I have had a deep fondness for gay people my whole life." It was my turn to look surprised. It was more and more remarkable to me to find out how close I was to people who could have supported me through all of those years of swimming if I had only been able to speak about it. But then again, I still saw how hard it would have been had I chosen the wrong person to come out to. Homophobia was still alive and kicking, even in 2004.

After the competition that night I joined some friends for a night on the town. At a nightclub I found myself in the middle of a group of women, dancing and laughing and having a great time as my straight friends watched me. As we left they joked that every straight guy needed to have a gay friend to attract the women. We headed back to an apartment for a nightcap.

I was telling the guys about my role in Montreal 2006 when one of them got very serious and said, "I don't get it, Mark. It is one thing to come out, but why would you want to put yourself out there like that, becoming a poster boy for this gay sport movement? Lots of people, kids, look up to you, not just gay people." His question had a bit of an edge to it, and I felt momentarily challenged. He didn't mean to put me on the defensive; he just really couldn't understand why I was doing what I was doing.

Before I answered, another friend told us of something that had happened at the pool that night. A guy in the stands had said it was tough to get young men, in particular, to start in swimming clubs. "It doesn't help when your last Olympic Champion's a fag," this guy had said. "Who would want to be associated with that?"

It hurt me as my friend said the words, even though I had come so far in my life. No matter how strong I became, the ugly words of discrimination always struck a blow. But at least now I was doing something about it.

Over the years I had worked really hard to establish goodwill through speaking and volunteering, and now I wanted to use those positive feelings people had toward me to challenge them to look at gay people differently, especially gay sport people. For me it was hard to believe that there were still no openly gay football, baseball, basketball, hockey, or soccer players playing on professional teams. Being an openly gay athlete led me to the human rights movement. Coming from Alberta, I hadn't thought about gay rights as human rights, but of course that was what we were all seeking. I just wanted to be treated equally, not discriminated against because of whom I loved, but allowed to participate fully in the different communities I lived and worked in. It was that simple and I have never regretted taking a stand for these basic human liberties. '

Later that summer I traveled to Munich, Germany to be a part of the EuroGames. This was a successful continental version of what our 1st World Outgames would be on a global scale, and there were more than five thousand accredited participants.

I got off the plane and gave a presentation on the history of gay and lesbian rights in Canada, sponsored by the Canadian government, at a renowned cultural institution in Munich called Amerika Haus. The next day I was on stage hosting the opening ceremony live in front of twelve thousand people in the stands. It was exhilarating, exciting, and empowering. But right when I thought the gay community had come so far, I would be reminded of just how far we still needed to go.

After the competitions were over, I traveled to Dachau, the Nazi concentration camp that was located just outside the city limits of Munich. I knew that it was going to be a hard trip, but wanted to take the opportunity to face the atrocities of the past in person, to get a better understanding of how something like this could have ever happened.

The only small trace of identification the Nazis gave the prisoners were triangles representing their race, nationality, or culture. Jewish people from Germany were given one color of triangle, Czechs another, homeless people another, and so on. At the very end of the tour we were shown a memorial statue. It was magnificent, with stained glass triangles of different shapes and sizes held together with steel to represent the thousands of people who had been murdered here. The tour guide gave us a test. He said, "There are three colors *not* represented here. Can anyone tell me what they are?" Someone shouted out brown, which was right. The brown triangle had represented the homeless people, and they weren't represented on the statue because there hadn't been an organized lobby for those people. Someone else said black, and that too was correct, because the black triangles were given to criminals, and they didn't feel that criminals should be honored. Finally we realized that there weren't any pink triangles, the color given to gay people. "Why is that?" the guide asked us. "Because it was alright to kill gay people," I answered slowly with utter disgust. "Their lives weren't worth remembering either." I felt empty as I said it but the words just came out. "Remember that this was mounted in the 1960s," the guide said. The energy drained from my body and I felt like I was going to be sick. I was overcome by an intense mixture of hurt, outrage, and frustration. My swimming friend had asked me why I did what I did. I wished he could have been there to realize for himself.

CHAPTER SEVENTEEN

FULL CIRCLE

ATHENS ROCKED

I was out one day when someone asked if I would be going to the Olympics in Athens, and I happily replied no. With all of the media reports, I was certain that the heat and lack of preparedness of the Athens Organizing Committee would result in the most disastrous games ever. I would be wrong on all accounts.

When I got home there was a message from an executive producer from CBC, the Canadian Olympic network. CBC was looking for a way to add an edge to their coverage. Would I be interested in joining the prime time team for the first week of the games? I would be an in-studio analyst, giving my perspective and insight into the swimming events that had taken place that day.

It was an offer that literally came out of left field. I had been to the Olympics many ways, but never with the media. After a day of thinking about it, I gladly accepted. It would mark my Olympic journey coming full circle, returning to the city that I had seen in 1996 with the IOC as part of the site selection.

The Olympics in Athens were an incredible experience. In spite of the criticisms that the organizing committee had endured, the world overwhelmingly agreed that they had pulled off delivering the games in the finest of form. It was a perfect integration of antiquity and modernism that left all of us in awe. The opening ceremony alone made us all stop and take notice. It was interesting and full of surprises, just like the games themselves.

My schedule during the games was completely wacky. Brian Williams's prime time coverage aired live from the broadcast center on Canadian time, which meant I worked the 1 a.m. until 6 a.m. shift. My segments were usually on around 4 a.m., and I got back to the hotel a couple of hours later. I ate breakfast as my dinner, then slept until the early afternoon when I got up and had lunch as my breakfast and started all over again. Each night I arrived at the swimming venue a couple of hours before the finals started, getting a debriefing of what had happened during the day. I watched the finals, figured out the three or four stories that would be my focus, then called them in to the senior producer. Swimming ended around 9:30 p.m., which gave me a break for a few hours before heading back to the broadcast center to get ready for my nightly spots.

I hadn't known what to expect before heading over, but I certainly wasn't thinking that the Canadian team would do as poorly as they did. Swimming was always an important sport, because it was one of the first out of the gate and set the tone for the rest of the Canadian team.

After the first two nights things weren't looking good, but I did my best to try to buy some time for the athletes before we became too critical of their performances. By the third night it was becoming disastrous, and I spent the rest of the week trying my best to put the team's performances in perspective for viewers at home in the most fair but frank way possible. Unfortunately, there was no way to sugar-coat what was happening. The head coach was coming under huge fire, and because he had been one of my favorite coaches when I had swum years before, it was not fun having to criticize him. Thankfully my Athens experience wasn't all like this.

My only regret in sport was not swimming an extra half-year, especially to say goodbye to my buddies from the World Cup circuit. It turned out that most of them were in Athens in one form or another, and we became reacquainted. Most told me they suspected I was gay when we had been swimming together. *Why didn't anybody tell me?* Bruno, my buddy from France, almost fell over, not because I was gay but because I could speak in French with him. I even ran into a group of Australian swimmers and there, standing right in front of me, was my "mate" Matt*, the swimmer that I had mistakenly gone to kiss decades earlier. As we made eye contact there was no awkwardness this time. I smiled at him and simply said, "We shared a moment years ago." He just smiled back. For me, Athens turned out to be full of surprises.

One day in the press center I heard that a Dutch athlete, Johan Kenkhuis, had written an open letter to the press declaring that he was gay. I was fascinated by this story and wanted to meet this guy but likely wouldn't. Although I had a good accreditation, I was only given access to the media zones at the venues, which meant I could never get close to the athletes unless they came to the interview room after winning a medal. Three nights later I got lucky, as Johan was part of a silver medal winning relay. It looked like I would get to talk to him after all.

As the team arrived, this strapping handsome man with a shaved head fielded questions from the press before heading into the corridor for a scrum. I was like a twelve-year-old girl, my palms sweaty and my stomach doing flips as I watched from the sidelines for a chance to break in and have a moment alone with him. Although my source was good, I couldn't be sure that it was one hundred percent accurate because I hadn't actually seen the article, so I was rather nervous about approaching Johan. This was his big moment, winning an Olympic medal, and I didn't know how to approach this very personal story with all of the other media around.

I waited and waited, and finally the press person for the Dutch team came to me and asked who I would like to talk to. I told her

Johan, and as she pulled the swimmers away, she motioned for me to walk with them for a moment. I had taken one of my business cards and scribbled on the back, "Johan, I am also an out athlete, winning the Olympics in 1992. Please give me a call," and left my number. I would have just a very brief moment with him, so I wanted to get to the point but at the same time wanted to respect him. Had someone done this to me after I had won a medal, I would have dropped dead on the spot. Sure, it was twelve years ago, but I wanted to be really careful.

We had about ninety seconds together. I started, "Johan, I mean you total respect, and I am not sure if this is relevant to you, but I want you to know that I was a gay Olympian years ago. I have heard that you are also an out athlete, and wanted you to know you aren't alone." His eyes bugged out. I thought I had made a huge mistake. Then he responded, "News travels fast. Yes, I am gay. But I have to go." I handed him my card, and was left in the media zone buzzing from our brief encounter.

We met the night before I was leaving for home. We spent a couple of hours talking, sharing our experiences in sport. It turned out that his boyfriend had been in the stands with Johan's parents and family. Johan's father bought tickets for him like everybody else in the family, and he had stayed with them during the games. Johan was completely open to his teammates and his best swimming friend turned out to be a lesbian.

I told him about what we were doing in Montreal and with GLISA, and urged him to share his story. "But there is nothing to share," he said. "It is completely normal." There was a moment of pause. "But Johan, that *is* the story," I told him. How incredible that twelve years after I retired I saw someone living the dream that I wished had been possible when I was a swimmer. Less than a generation later and the impossible became possible in at least one place in the world. There was hope after all.

THE BOOMERANG CURVEBALL

When December 15th comes around, I often find myself transported for a moment to that crazy day when I did my one-man show in Toronto. The date always passed without much fanfare, at least until 2004. On that day, I was visiting a friend in New Jersey and was checking my emails. There was nothing extraordinary, until I opened the email from my speaking agent. The short note from one of the staff simply said that she was forwarding me a very personal email. That was the understatement of the year.

I started to read:

Mark,

It's been quite some time between writing you this letter and telling myself that I would write this letter. Sorry that time has passed. Mark, I'll tell you the whole story, which will also give you some idea about how long ago this started.

I was sitting at the kitchen table one morning reading the Calgary Herald with my wife. She asked if I had read this article about you. I mentioned that I had not yet. She broke it down for me; you were out of the closet. Although that came as no surprise (at that time), some of the other things mentioned in the article made me feel awful and deeply regretful and so I told myself that I would write this to you.

I knew what was coming before I read the next sentence.

In the article you mentioned that you were run out of your junior high, and had to switch schools because someone had broken into your locker and written "fag" and "homo" all over your books. Well Mark, that was me, Chris Marcil. That was Donny Little and Matthew Brown and Bob Harvey and Jim Stone.

All those years I had always wondered what had happened. Now it was finally there in writing, in front of me. My friends from that time, including the quarterback who I had coveted, had broken into the locker. I kept reading, barely breathing.

Here's what really happened.

You were not yet at school that day. The guys were all waiting to get into either music or industrial ed. Someone just casually pulled at a lock on a locker and it opened. It was your locker. Hey, whose locker is it? Oh, it's Mark's ... Ha ha ha, let's trash his locker, and we did. Never, NEVER did we actually think that you were a homosexual. Those words were simply (how horrible does this sound) the words kids used. I can GUARANTEE you that if I wasn't there at that moment, and it was my locker that happened to open, the exact same thing would have happened. Everyone called everyone a fag. In fun, in jest. "Hey gimme back my pen, you homo!" In fact, at that time, most of us barely even knew that homo was short for homosexual.

When your locker was trashed at St. Cyril, it was not gay bashing and it certainly wasn't a hate crime. It was just some guys being jerks, giving one of their buds a hard time. It's a good thing you're one tough mother ... because tragedy over such an adolescent thing would have been too much to comprehend. I can't fathom what you must have been going through back then.

I'm rambling, Mark, and not making much sense. I know that in your life, and in the people that you have touched and helped, and come in contact with,

*there's a message in here somewhere. I hope that you
find it and use it.*

You're doing a hell of a job.

For what it's worth, I'm terribly sorry.

I finished reading the email overcome with emotion. How different my life might have been had I known this perspective that day. It was beyond my ability to even consider that these guys were jealous of me back then; that they saw me as the jock; that they didn't really mean any harm; that it was just a stupid prank. That stupid prank almost killed me.

It had turned out to be a cruel precursor of much uglier things still to come. The worst thing you could call someone at that time was a fag or homo—it just turned out *I was one*. Funny, Chris never thought of boys calling each other homos or fags as being a hate crime, much like I hadn't thought of gay rights as human rights. Somehow, many of us were shown very young that gay was one of the things it was okay to collectively ridicule and despise. If I was to believe there was no hate in those words, then there was certainly no humanity, either. They were just mean-spirited, ugly words, even more hurtful if you happened to actually be gay. The negative power of a single word could leave you filled with a deep feeling of shame inside.

But somehow my life had worked out. This incident sent me on the path that brought me to the height of Olympic sport, to being an advocate for human rights, to becoming who I am today. But I couldn't help but wonder after re-reading the email a third time, *what if it had never happened?*

HOME SWEET HOMO

In the winter of 2005 my mother was preparing something special for me. It was my thirty-seventh birthday, one of those middle years, but

I was in Calgary for a speech so she had arranged for everyone to get together for a night of celebration in my honor. This was extra special because I was going to see my brother, Scott, for the first time since the International Swimming Hall of Fame induction in 2000.

Scott was in the restaurant business, and he was never able to get away for the traditional holidays. We had planned for an entire year to give Mom her ultimate Christmas gift and all come home together. Three weeks before, Scott had called, upset but also embarrassed because he wasn't going to be able to make it after all. "But Scott, you booked this for a year." "I know, but tell that to my boss." It wasn't his fault, but to make it up to Mom, Scott came to Calgary with Melanie the same time I was there to celebrate my birthday.

I went back to Calgary as often as possible. My sister, Colleen, had two kids now, Megan and Matthew, and somehow they changed everything. Where once I had dreaded going back, reliving the horrors of my own childhood, I now could lose myself in theirs. Colleen had always wanted to be a mother, and she did it really well. Her daughter Megan was a lot of fun to be with, in particular. She had a big trunk of dress-up clothes and loved to play. So did I. But she had an insight that was brutal. I had taken a friend I was dating home for a visit once, and the first thing this four-year-old had asked me when I saw her the next time was, "Where's your buddy?" Nobody had said it so perfectly.

Going back to Calgary had become easier because I now had my own home in Montreal. I had found an 1885 cottagehouse in downtown Montreal and moved around the same time we went solo with our Outgames project. I was so stressed when I came home that I never did anything to the place. It was left with no window treatments, no comfortable spaces, and as winter loomed it was becoming increasingly depressing inside the house, forget about outside. I had inherited a Barbie pink bedroom (don't ask) and a turquoise blue hallway, and they were slowly driving me crazy. My good friend Alex, who had taught me to cook and garden and live, gave me the ultimate gift—turning a house into a home. The same weekend the sport leaders from around the world descended upon Montreal to create GLISA, Alex descended upon my house to create a new décor. The sport leaders left after three days, Alex stayed fourteen months, give or take. The renovation from hell had begun.

It started in the bedroom. I found a small budget to paint and do something with the bed. But in looking for a bed we found a 1920s art deco dining room table with built-in extensions and six chairs. It was inexpensive and we snatched it up, and before you knew it we had begun a process that would ultimately see every one of the nine rooms of the house redone. Slowly, piece by piece, meter of fabric by meter of fabric, we returned this beautiful turn-of-the-century home back to its original glamour.

I now had a new set of problems: it was hard for me to ever leave. I discovered the beauty of settling down, finally, into my own home. That year, Alex had said something significant to me. "This house represents a new period in your life, Mark. You always gave so much away. Remember, charity begins at home." And now with Alex I had created a home for myself. Actually, that year I realized I had more than one.

Sitting at my mom's dining room table for my thirty-seventh birthday feast I felt completely at home, perhaps more so than ever before in my life. I hadn't seen my brother for so long, not for any particular reason, but because life just happened that way. I had picked him and Melanie up at the airport, and I was completely smitten with them both the minute they arrived. We talked and talked and talked, staying at the kitchen table drinking home-made wine until 4 a.m. Voices carried and we had kept Mom up, but somehow the glow that she had the next day knowing her two sons were home and reconnecting told me she could deal with it. Home for Scott was Phoenix, but after two straight nights of partying and catching up, we all agreed that we would come back more often to Calgary now, for our niece and nephew. If we didn't make the effort then it wasn't going to happen, and the kids were well worth it.

Megan sat beside me at my birthday dinner, all dressed up in a new outfit that her Auntie Melanie had brought her. In the kitchen earlier, after I had made my trademark high-pitched shriek, my niece Megan had called me Auntie Mark. We all cracked up laughing. Megan certainly was an insightful little girl.

When we did a toast before dinner, Megan really got into it and hit my glass with all of her force, spilling milk all over her new dress. Contrary to popular sayings, she did cry over spilled milk, big crocodile tears in fact. She was terrified that she had ruined her new dress-up outfit.

As Mom took Megan downstairs to help with the laundry it struck me that things had come full circle. My mom was now Grandma, Megan was now me playing dress-up, I was like Auntie Dot, the difference being that I was able to be open about my sexuality and life as part of the next generation and evolution of our family. Taboo topics were opened, spoken about, and then finally integrated because the things that had once been issues simply weren't issues anymore. That was how things changed in the end.

Part of what had brought me to Calgary that winter was an invitation to speak at a college that was launching a "positive space campaign" that created safe places for LGBT students on campus. Unfortunately, before I went to speak there were threats of protest, posters were torn down, and security had to be assigned. I was sadly reminded why it was still important to speak publicly about these issues. But thankfully Calgary has become more progressive over the years, and the protestors were in the minority. The speech went off without a hitch.

The *Calgary Herald* came to hear the presentation and to interview me for a story, and my mom called me a few weeks later to share it. As she told me about it over the phone, she said, "I'm really proud of you, Mark. I know it isn't easy doing what you do. I just say go for it." "Thanks Mom," I responded. I didn't know what else to say. My mom had never said anything like that before. I felt wonderful, realizing I had never loved my family as much or felt closer to them as I did at this time in my life. The incredible part was that they had been there all along; we just had to learn how to be comfortable with each other, which now, given all that we had been through together, we finally were. I could feel the love rise from deep within me, inside out.

INDEX